JUSTICES AND PRESIDENTS

JUSTICES AND PRESIDENTS

A
Political History
of
Appointments to the Supreme Court

Henry J. Abraham

New York
Oxford University Press
1974

TO MY FAMILY:
Mil, Phil, and Pete

Preface

This work has its genesis in a series of graduate seminars in constitutional law and the judicial process that I conducted at the University of Pennsylvania in the mid- and late 1950s. The subject matter had always fascinated me, and while I lay aside writing this book in favor of other publications during the ensuing years, the project was never dormant. I gathered a host of data, developing a separate file for each of the one hundred individuals that have served on the highest court of the land, until the end of the Warren Court era in 1969 determined me to write what had been gestating for almost two decades.

What I had initially conceived as a fairly straightforward analysis of Presidential motivations in the appointment of the several Chief Justices and Associate Justices of the Supreme Court of the United States, gradually evolved into a far more ambitious undertaking as the book took shape. Backed by the advice and counsel of sundry colleagues, it seemed almost artificial merely to cite reasons for an individual's selection without concurrently evaluating his subsequent performance on the bench. Thus, the book addresses itself also to the nominee's work on the Court, both in terms of Presidential expectations and in those of my own perception of his performance. Quite naturally the book expanded further by comprising what, in effect, is a "mini-history" of the Court itself—and an attempt briefly to encapsulate and categorize the Presidential performance as well as that of his nominees.

Inexorably, aspects of the book are subjective: judgment of performance inevitably involves value orientation. Yet I have endeavored to be objective and scholarly in my analyses and evaluations. Temptations to be "cute" are omnipresent; but they serve little purpose in what, after all, is a historical-political account of the reasons why Justices were appointed and how they lived up to their nominators' expectations. What follows, then, represents serious judgment based on carefully gathered and pondered evidence. Admittedly, perhaps many of the explanations and evaluations will prove to be at once controversial and less than astonishing or thrilling. Yet they are based on more than two decades of teaching and research in the field and on lasting interest as well as fascination with an unique aspect of our system of government.

My research was conducted in the traditional mold of going to the most reliable sources available. That meant both primary and secondary written data; but it also meant personal interviews with a great many individuals in and out of government, including a number of Justices of the Supreme Court, who were truly helpful. Some of the gathered information developed diametrically opposite assertions or evidence (for example, the real reasons for Mr. Justice Goldberg's decision to relinquish his post on the Court) necessitating the kind of judgment Mr. Justice Frankfurter was fond of styling as "inescapable." Accordingly, the book contains numerous such judgments; but they are judgments based on carefully weighed conclusions. As the Bibliographical Note indicates, the sources of my information were indeed broad and numerous, yet—given the unavailability of the papers of many among the Justices—new or different revelations may well lie in the future. In the meanwhile I hope that my account will shed at least some light on a subject that continues to prove to be at once intriguing and challenging.

No work of this kind could have been written without the deeply appreciated aid and comfort of my colleagues in the disciplines of government and politics, history, and law. So many have been of so much help that it would be presumptuous to attempt to list them all. But I should like to acknowledge specifically, and with particular gratitude, the unfailingly wise counsel and support extended to me through the years of gestation by Professors Robert J. Harris, David Fellman, Wallace Mendelson, Alpheus Thomas Mason, and William M. Beaney. They were always there—be it for a quick quaere or as a sounding board, or as a critic. For invaluable aid in the formative stages of the project I am lastingly indebted to my former student and subsequent colleague, René Peritz, without whose tireless efforts it would never have gotten under way and without whose dedication it would never have come to fruition.

Acknowledged with genuine affection are the research assistants who do the legwork and the typists who produce the manuscript. The research assistants were Peter B. Harkins, Rocco D'Amico, Robert G. Badal, Paul Lutzker, Judith F. Lang, Gilbert E. Geldon, Steven S. Fadem, Norman H. Levine, Mark A. Aronchick, Frank C. Lindgren, Andrew B. Cohn, Perri Beth Madow, Susan J. Dlott, Michael E. Marino, James J. Magee, Michael K. Duffey, John W. Epperson, and Eston E. Melton. Those who so faithfully did the typing were, above all, Rosemary Cicchetti, and Theresa L. Brunson, Marie M. Cross, Bonnie L. Foster, Edna C. Mitchell, Cora L. Pitts, and Lena G. Garrison.

There remains a special thank you to two mainstays at the Oxford University Press: to my superb editor, James C. Amon, whose expertise, encouragement, and insight were essential; and to Joyce Berry, whose sensitivity, literateness, and intelligence atoned for her omnipotent red pencil. I could not have written the book without their dedication.

More than in any other of my writings to date I hasten to post the obvious caveat: that all errors are my own responsibility.

H. J. A.

Keswick, Virginia
January 1974

Contents

1

Prefatory Remarks:
The Nixon Era

For three and a half years, from June 1968 until December 1971, the attention of the American public was drawn to the highest court of the land more closely than at any time since the epic "Court-packing" battle between Franklin D. Roosevelt and the United States Senate in 1937. On June 26, 1968, President Lyndon B. Johnson announced Mr. Chief Justice Earl Warren's intention to resign from the seat he had occupied since 1953 and the nomination of Associate Justice Abe Fortas as his successor. It was a historic event, the start of a fascinating epoch of political maneuvering that would not be resolved until December 10, 1971, when William H. Rehnquist was confirmed as an Associate Justice of the Supreme Court by the less than overwhelming margin of 68:26. When the Senate, after more than three months of partisan and often acrimonious debate, had defeated a motion to vote on the Fortas nomination in the fall of 1968, Fortas requested the President to withdraw his name from further consideration. In turn the Chief Justice withdrew his resignation, commenting: "[S]ince they wouldn't confirm Abe they will have me." And so they did for another full term of Court until late May 1969, when Earl Warren stepped down and was replaced by Warren Earl Burger, Chief Judge of the U.S. Court of Appeals for the District

3

of Columbia. Burger's investiture was President Richard M. Nixon's first of four successful nominations—but the four came from a total of eight attempts.

Judge Burger, sixty-one years old at the time of his appointment and of impeccable Republican credentials, was the prototype of the kind of individual Presidential candidate Nixon had promised the country he would nominate to the bench upon his election: one whose work on the Court would "strengthen the peace forces as against the criminal forces of the land"; one who would have an appreciation of the basic tenets of "law and order," being "thoroughly experienced and versed in the criminal laws of the country"; one who would see himself as a "caretaker" of the Constitution and not as a "super-legislator with a free hand to impose . . . social and political view-points upon the American people"; one who was a "strict constructionist" of the basic document; and one who had had broad experience as an appeals judge on a lower judicial level. Burger's confirmation by a vote of 74:3 was both speedy and decisive. The President was jubilant: not only had *his* kind of candidate overcome the hurdle of Senate confirmation with all but *pro forma* ease, but he had a second vacancy to fill.

Earlier, in May of 1969, Mr. Justice Fortas, under intense public and private attack as a result of revelations concerning his relationship with convicted financier Louis Wolfson, had resigned from the Court—the first Supreme Court jurist to do so under that type of pressure. Fortas had broken no law and he fervidly protested his innocence, but his highly questionable judgment and the integrity and prestige of the Court had clearly mandated his move. The not-inconsiderable number of Warren Court haters in the Senate were delighted, and the President—again publicly citing his criteria for Supreme Court nominees—accepted Attorney General John N. Mitchell's suggestion of Chief Judge Clement F. Haynsworth, Jr., of the U.S. Court of Appeals for the Fourth Circuit. Haynsworth was a native of South Carolina and a Harvard Law School alumnus. To his basic specifications Mr. Nixon had added the desire of choosing a Southern jurist of conservative judicial bent. Of course the Court already had at least one Southern strict constructionist, indeed a constitutional literalist of the first magnitude, in the person of the distinguished Mr. Justice Hugo Lafayette Black of Alabama, but that was not exactly what the President had in mind. Judge Haynsworth, a relatively able jurist meriting a "B-minus" in the minds of most Court-watchers, fit all of the President's specifications to date and, perhaps even more significantly, those of such influential Southern Senators as Strom Thurmond (R.-S.C.), James O. Eastland (D.-Miss.), and John L. McClellan (D.-Ark.).

Indeed, most of the Senate seemed disposed to confirm Judge Haynsworth for the Fortas vacancy. But to the President's anger, frustration, and embarrassment, the hearings of the Senate Committee on the Judiciary provided clear evidence of the nominee's patent insensitivity to financial and conflict-of-interest improprieties. Apparently, as with Fortas, no actual legal infractions had taken place—but how could the Senate confirm Haynsworth when it had played such an activist role in causing Fortas's resignation? It could not, and among those who vocally opposed the South Carolinian and voted against his confirmation were such anti-Fortas, strict-constructionist leaders as Senators Robert Griffin (R.-Mich.) and Jack Miller (R.-Iowa). Down went the Haynsworth nomination by a vote of 55:45 on November 21, 1969—largely for the reasons indicated, although the candidate had also drawn considerable fire from labor and minority groups for allegedly anti-civil libertarian and anti-civil rights stands. A livid President Nixon, however, chose to lay the blame for his nominee's defeat upon "anti-Southern, anti-conservative, and anti-constructionist" prejudice, and he vowed to select another "worthy and distinguished protagonist" of Southern, conservative, and strict-constructionist persuasion.

To the dismay of those Senators who had counseled confirmation of Judge Haynsworth lest a successor-nominee be even less worthy of the high post, the President—again on the recommendation of his Attorney General—quickly countered by nominating Judge G. Harrold Carswell of Florida, a little-known and little-distinguished ex-judge with six months of experience on the U.S.

Court of Appeals for the Fifth Circuit. "He is almost too good to be true," Mr. Mitchell was reported to have said. The appointment was an act of vengeance—one intended to teach the Senate a lesson and to downgrade the Court. The Senate, intimidated by the President and the Attorney General, was disposed to confirm him. But suspicious reporters and researchers soon cast serious doubt on that "almost too good to be true" rating of the nominee. Immediately damaging was the discovery of a statement Carswell made to a meeting of the American Legion on August 2, 1948, while running for a seat on the Georgia legislature. "I yield to no man as a fellow candidate or as a fellow citizen in the firm, vigorous belief in the principles of White Supremacy, and I shall always be so governed." To be sure, the nominee, pointing to his youth and inexperience (he was twenty-eight at the time), now disavowed that statement and any racism as well. But an examination of his record on the bench cast further doubt on his objectivity in racial matters: while serving as U.S. Attorney in Florida, Carswell had been involved in the transfer of a public, municipally owned Tallahassee golf course, built with $35,000 of federal funds, to the status of a private club. The transfer was obviously designed to circumvent a contemporary Supreme Court decision proscribing segregation in municipal recreation facilities.

Still, the Administration appeared to have the votes for Senate confirmation given the vivid memories of the Haynsworth battle, the intensive wooing of doubtful Senators by the White House and the Justice Department, and the natural predisposition to give the President his choice, all things being equal. But things were far from equal, for as the Carswell opponents continued their attack it became apparent that—quite apart from the controversy surrounding his civil rights record—the candidate was patently inferior, simply on the basis of fundamental juridical and legal qualifications. If Judge Haynsworth had merited a "B-minus," Judge Carswell scarcely merited a "D" on the scale of relevant ability. Senator Roman Hruska (R.-Neb.), the President's floor manager of the nomination, made a pathetic fumbling attempt to convert the candidate's mediocrity into an asset: "Even if he is mediocre there are a lot of mediocre judges and people and lawyers. They are entitled to a little representation, aren't they, and a little chance? We can't have all Brandeises, Cardozos, and Frankfurters, and stuff like that there." Hruska's remarkable assertion was seconded by Carswell-supporter Senator Russell Long (D.-La.), who observed: "Does it not seem to the Senator that we have had enough of those upside down, corkscrew thinkers? Would it not appear that it might be well to take a B student or a C student who was able to think straight, compared to one of those A students who are capable of the kind of thinking that winds up getting us a 100-percent increase in crime in this country?"

This line of argument failed to convince the doubtful Senators. Instead they became increasingly aware of the lack of ability of the nominee—who, among other debilitating features, held the dubious record of having been reversed by appellate courts more than any of the other then sitting federal jurists except eight! Yale Law School Dean Louis H. Pollak styled the Carswell nomination as one of "more slender credentials than any Supreme Court nominee put forth in this century"; perhaps even more tellingly, the distinguished William Van Alstyne, Professor of Law at Duke University, opposed the nomination. Van Alstyne, an ardent and vocal backer of the Haynsworth nomination, now testified: "There is, in candor, nothing in the quality of the nominee's work to warrant any expectation whatever, that he could serve with distinction on the Supreme Court of the United States." When the final vote on confirmation came on April 9, 1970—three months after the nomination—the President's choice went down by a vote of 51:45. Among the "noes" were such significant Republican votes as those of Margaret Chase Smith of Maine, Winston L. Prouty of Vermont, Marlow W. Cook of Kentucky, and Richard S. Schweiker of Pennsylvania.

It was indeed a bitter defeat for the President. Not only had he seen two nominees rejected within less than five months, but his carefully divised "Southern strategy" had suffered a serious blow. His reaction was swift and vitriolic. Conveniently ignoring the basic issues for his candidates' defeat, he blamed it instead on sectional prejudice, abject politics, and philosophical negations, and told the country:

> I have reluctantly concluded that—with the Senate as presently constituted—I cannot successfully nominate to the Supreme Court any federal appellate judge from the South who believes as I do in the strict construction of the Constitution. . . . Judges Carswell and Haynsworth have endured with admirable dignity vicious assaults on their intelligence, their honesty, and their character. . . . When all the hypocrisy is stripped away, the real issue was their philosophy of strict construction of the Constitution—a philosophy that I share.

Quite to the contrary, several distinguished federal jurists in the South were eminently qualified to serve, jurists who indeed shared the President's philosophy of government and politics, and whom the Senate assuredly would have confirmed. It could not, in good conscience—given the Fortas precedent, the public concern, and the nature and role of the Supreme Court—have confirmed Haynsworth and Carswell, especially not Carswell. The latter, in an ironic footnote, was soon to be defeated by his constituents in the Florida Senatorial primary, during which he was photographed with a lettered sign around his neck, "Heah Come de Judge." It is an intriguing thought that had Haynsworth been nominated *after* Carswell he might well have been confirmed.

President Nixon followed up his blast against the rejections with the petulant suggestion in a publicized letter to Senator William B. Saxbe (R.-Ohio), that the Senate had denied him the right to see his choices appointed. That right, he insisted, had been accorded all previous presidents—a patently false statement: since 1789, 26 of the 136 nominees formally sent to the Senate for confirmation have been rejected—close to one out of five candidates (one out of three in the nineteenth century). Moreover, the President's collateral suggestion to Saxbe and the nation, that Senatorial advice and consent to nominations (expressly provided for in Article II, Section 2, Clause 2 of the Constitution) is merely a *pro forma* requirement, is utterly incorrect with regard to nominations to the judiciary and the Supreme Court. Mr. Nixon, who was fully familiar with the contrary judgment of practically all students of constitutional law and history, as well as with Hamilton's equally contrary assertions in *The Federalist Papers* (#76 and #77), must have known how wrong he was. His anger and frustrations were understandable, but his historical misstatement was a distinct disservice to country, Constitution, and Court.

Announcing that the Senate would never confirm a Southern strict constructionist, President Nixon now turned to a Northerner, Harry A. Blackmun, sixty-one, of Minnesota, judge of the U.S. Court of Appeals for the Eighth Circuit. An old and close friend and ideological ally of Mr. Chief Justice Burger, Blackmun had served for eleven years on the federal bench. His nomination was as anticlimactic as it was non-controversial. To the relief of the Senate he appeared to have impeccable credentials and, although he did not rank with the country's most distinguished jurists, he was quickly confirmed on June 22, 1970, by a vote of 94:0.

It was too late for Blackmun to participate in the remaining decisions of the 1969–70 term of Court, which had functioned with but eight Justices since May 1969, but at last the Fortas seat had been filled. There would be no further vacancies for fifteen months, but when they came President Nixon would find himself in another and multiple imbroglio.

In September 1971 terminal illness compelled the resignations of Justices Hugo Lafayette Black and John Marshall Harlan, the two most influential figures then on the highest bench. Both were veritable giants of the law, often on different jurisprudential tracks but imbued with dedication, intelligence, and judicial excellence. Their places would be incredibly hard to fill, and the President would have to search long and diligently for worthy successors. Yet he did neither. Instead he resorted to the "trial balloon" method and had names leaked to the press.

Thus in early October it became apparent that his first choice was Republican Representative Richard H. Poff of Virginia. Although Poff had less than two years' experience in legal practice, he was an able and fair member of the House Committee on the

Judiciary and apparently filled the President's "Southern seat" prescriptions. But newsmen were quick to uncover civil-rights skeletons in the Poff closet, and while the Senate might have confirmed him, given his over-all ability and his popularity among his colleagues, it would not have done so without a battle. Poff asked the President to withdraw his name from consideration in order to save his family and himself from an embarrassing, damaging experience. (In 1972 he resigned from Congress to become a Justice of the Supreme Court of Appeals of Virginia, the highest tribunal of that state.)

The President now decided to send for appraisal a list of six potential nominees to the Committee on the Judiciary of the American Bar Association, the influential group that had endorsed the Haynsworth and Carswell candidacies. The list, which was widely publicized in the media, was singularly marginal in terms of distinction and stature. It was headed by California State Court of Appeals Judge Mildred Lillie (the first woman to be considered for nomination) and Arkansas municipal-bond lawyer Herschel H. Friday, a good friend of Attorney General and Mrs. John N. Mitchell and recommended by Mr. Chief Justice Burger and Mr. Justice Blackmun. The other four potential nominees were Sylvia Bacon, a judge on the Superior Court of the District of Columbia (seven months of bench experience) and part-author of the "no knock" search and "preventive detention" provisions of the District of Columbia crime bill; Senator Robert C. Byrd (D.-W.Va.), long-time opponent of civil rights legislation and ex-member of the Ku Klux Klan who, although a graduate of law school, had never practiced law; and two recent Nixon appointees to the U.S. Court of Appeals for the Fifth Circuit, Charles Clark of Mississippi and Paul H. Roney of Florida, with a combined total of three years of judicial experience. It is not surprising that the President's selections were widely criticized as manifesting a "relentless pursuit of mediocrity." The American Bar Association, in an uncharacteristically frank statement, urged the President to "add some people with stature," and its Committee on the Judiciary quickly ranked the Administration's two top choices, Mrs. Lillie and Mr. Friday, "unqualified" and "not opposed," respectively. When the Committee's action became public—it and the Department of Justice accused each other of leaking the data to the media—the President angrily withdrew the list of "The Six," and the Attorney General announced that he would no longer submit Supreme Court nominees (as contrasted with lower federal judicial candidates) to the Committee for rating purposes. The Committee, in turn, announced that it would not be prevented from issuing evaluative post-nomination commentaries.

In a dramatic television broadcast President Nixon subsequently revealed to the country his "formal" nominees, whom he had evidently held in reserve. Possibly, as a number of commentators had charged, he did not really expect support of his initial slate and assuredly not of the first two—although the Administration indignantly and conceivably quite truthfully denied any such assumption. The two new selectees were of infinitely higher calibre than "The Six." This was especially true of the person the President identified first, Lewis F. Powell, Jr., of Richmond, Virginia. Powell was a past-President of the American Bar Association, a distinguished member of the legal profession in the Harlan mold with recorded views on criminal justice and governmental "paternalism" akin to those of the President. Here then was the President's "Southern strict constructionist"! And not only was his designation received enthusiastically but it was confirmed rapidly by a vote of 89:1, the sole negative vote being cast by Senator Fred R. Harris (D.-Okla.). It was thus crystal clear that the Senate would not refuse to confirm a qualified nominee from the South.

For the second vacancy Mr. Nixon nominated a far more controversial figure: the relatively youthful (forty-seven) William H. Rehnquist of Arizona, an U.S. Assistant Attorney General. Rehnquist was a brilliant ideological conservative who had been one of Senator Barry Goldwater's chief aides in the latter's unsuccessful 1964 campaign for the Presidency. Rehnquist's career had been chiefly political, but his legal credentials were considerable, including a stint as a law clerk on the Supreme Court to Mr. Justice Robert H. Jackson—one of the truly coveted posts for a young attorney. A fine lawyer with a quick, lucid mind, he stood considerably to the right of both Powell and perhaps the President himself. It was thus not surprising that his nomination would engender opposition from a number of segments in and out of the Senate—including the American Civil Liberties Union which, for the first time in its fifty-two-year history, formally fought a nominee for public office. Rehnquist came under strong attack, especially for his championship of such "law and order" issues as preventive detention, limited immunity against compulsory self-incrimination, "no knock" police entries, and wire tapping and eavesdropping; for his hawkish defense posture and advocacy of broad-gauged Presidential war powers; and for his tough stance against street demonstrators. But these were, after all, ideological commitments shared by a great many members of the body politic—quite conceivably by a plurality. Thus, although his confirmation was delayed for a number of weeks it came with a margin of forty-two votes in December 1971.

The country seemed to breathe a sigh of relief at being spared another Haynsworth-Carswell episode, which almost certainly would have resulted had the President persisted in selecting nominees from "The Six." Had it not been for the many wounds sustained by the governmental and confidence process, and had the preceding two years not been so potentially damaging to the prestige and posture of the Supreme Court, one might have regarded these struggles as a salutary educational experience for America's citizenry. They had certainly served to alert the public to both the substance and the procedure of the power struggle that periodically brushes the system of separation of powers and its attendant checks and balances.

What follows is an attempt to explain the process of staffing the Supreme Court; to give a historical overview of Presidential motivations in the process; and to analyze the results of Presidential expectations.

2
How They Get There:
Court Staffing

The question of the principles that govern the selection of the men and women who sit on our judicial tribunals is both a moral and a political one of the greatest magnitude. Their tasks and functions are awe-inspiring indeed, but it is as human beings and as participants in the political as well as the legal and governmental process that jurists render their decisions. Their position in the governmental framework must assure them of independence, dignity, and security of tenure.

The two basic methods of selecting jurists under our system are appointment and election, although today a system combining the two is becoming increasingly prevalent. Yet the process of selection is assuredly more complex than that suggested by W. Curtis Bok's fictional Judge Ulan in *Backbone of the Herring*, who quips: "A judge is a member of the bar who once knew a Governor." [1]

Most of the roughly 12,000 judges on our state and local courts are still elected, although the gubernatorial appointive method, often with legislative or bar advice and consent, is being resorted to increasingly—generally a development to be welcomed. On the other hand, the number of states adopting versions of the California and Missouri plans is growing. Under the California Plan (which at present applies only to some of that state's courts), the governor nominates one individual per vacancy to a commission on qualifications composed of the Chief Justice of the State Supreme Court, the presiding judge of the District Court of Appeals, and the Attorney General of the state. If the commission approves of the Governor's choice he or she is declared appointed for one year only. At year's end the appointee stands for popular election on a non-partisan, non-contested ballot for a full term (usually twelve years) with the voters answering only one question: "Shall ————— be elected to office for the term prescribed by law?" The answer has usually been "yes," and there is no limit on the number of terms to which a successful candidate may aspire. In the infrequent case of a "no," the Governor nominates another individual under the same procedure.

The Missouri Plan, which is used to staff a majority of Missouri's courts, follows the same principle but utilizes a somewhat different method: nonpartisan nominating boards or commissions take the initial step in the nominating process. They usually consist of the Chief Justice of the State Supreme Court as Chairman, and, representing the state's appellate districts, three lawyers elected by the state bar and three laymen appointed by the Governor (one from each district). Unsalaried and serving for staggered six-year terms of office, the commission members nominate three candidates for every vacant judgeship to the Governor, who is obliged to choose one of the three to serve for one year, as under the California Plan. After this probationary period the appointee faces the electorate, again running solo on a nonpartisan basis (although party allegiance is known). The question on the ballot reads simply: "Shall Judge ————— of the ————— Court be retained in office? Yes. No. (Scratch one.)" The electorate's response has not only been generally affirmative: of 179 judicial elections conducted under the plan between 1940 and 1970, it rejected only one—Judge Marion Walter of the Missouri Circuit Court, who had been prominently identified with the Pendergast political machine. Even so, he received 46 per cent affirmative votes.[2]

Widely hailed as the most viable and most commendable systems of judicial selection on the state level, the California and Missouri plans—in particular the Missouri Plan—combine the democratic notion of accountability to the electorate with an intelligent method of selecting presumably qualified individuals for judicial office. The requirement of facing the voters contains an inherent incentive toward judiciousness, and since a candidate must run on an established record rather than against opponents allied with a political party, the judges are shielded from the crasser aspects of the political process. The political parties in the approximately sixteen states using similar or varying plans [3] have respected the philosophy of the plans, and by and large have made little effort to influence elections under them. The plans have also been defended by the judges, who find themselves generally free from worries about forthcoming political campaigns. The prediction that awareness of establishing a good record on the bench might lead to popular or political judgments has generally proved incorrect—which is not to say that the judges serving under the plan are not aware of their elective aspects.

Yet most political observers are inclined to believe that, given our constitutional system of government with its separation of powers and the attendant checks and balances, the appointive method is the most desirable—provided it is buttressed by lengthy tenure, or, preferably, as long as the appointee exhibits "good behavior" (which as the Constitution describes it for federal judges means, in effect, for life or until retirement). The term of office of the appointing authority, be it a Governor or the President, is usually briefer than that of a judge—and the appointing authority is certainly not beyond that accountability for which there is no substitute in a representative democracy. In the final analysis our judicial system constitutes a blend of "neutral competence and representativeness." [4]

The main concern of this book is the federal judiciary. All of its approximately 535 active members and its 125 senior or semi-retired members were and are subject to the appointive method as spelled out in the judicial article (Article III) of the Constitution and in the article dealing with executive power (Article II, Section

2). Thus the President is responsible for nominating candidates, and their confirmation depends upon a simple majority vote in the Senate. The Chief Executive inevitably shares this heavy responsibility with a number of different participants in the governmental cum political process. This is not true of the selection of Supreme Court nominees, who are very much the President's own choice. Of course, he consults with the Attorney General, with friendly political leaders from the nominee's home state and, if they are *personae gratae* to the President, with sitting members of the Court—especially the Chief Justice.

But the selection process for the numerous lower federal court posts involves many more people. Among them are influential members of the executive branch and political leaders of the President's party from the candidate's home state—especially members of Congress, but also state chairmen and chairwomen, national committee members, Governors, and concerned Mayors; members of the federal and sometimes high state judiciary; members of the Senate Committee on the Judiciary; members of the American Bar Association's Standing Committee on Federal Judiciary; and outstanding or interested lawyers and persons in private life. The ultimate recommendation, however, comes from the Attorney General who, in effect, makes the choice. This was true of Attorneys General Francis Biddle (F. D. Roosevelt), Tom C. Clark (Truman), Robert F. Kennedy (J. F. Kennedy), and John N. Mitchell (Nixon).

The founders of the Constitution struggled at length over the selection of the federal judiciary. Under the Randolph Plan of Union, selection as well as confirmation by the "National legislature" was proposed; an inevitable counter-suggestion would have vested that power in the "chief magistrate" alone. Representatives from the small states were unhappy with the notion of exclusive executive appointment, fearing favoritism toward the large states, which they suspected might "gratify" the President to a greater extent. Madison recommended appointment by the Senate alone but after second thoughts disassociated himself from this proposal. Ultimately, Ben Franklin's efforts and a spirit of compromise between large and small interests resulted in the adoption of a system modeled after one then being used in Massachusetts. It is still used today, and on balance it has proved to be workable professionally as well as politically.

Although many forces influence the judicial selection process, the developing politics of federal judicial selection emphasize three major factors or considerations in staffing the national judiciary: (1) the need to take into account the wishes and the influence of public and private leaders with interests in a nomination; (2) the mountingly influential role of the American Bar Association's Standing Committee on Federal Judiciary (established 1945–46), which has assumed a controversial, yet professional, evaluative posture in the nomination process and which has demonstrated considerable clout in that process since the mid-1950s; and (3) the advisory role played by sitting members of the bench, especially members of the Supreme Court, who would appear to be taking an increasingly influential part behind the scenes. Rare is the appointment in which these three factors do not now play a significant role.

The first-mentioned is the one most apparent to the general public. As a practical matter it is almost impossible for the Chief Executive to select and see confirmed a candidate for the federal bench without the approval of the political leaders of the candidate's own party. Approval by the home-state Senators of the nominee's political party is especially important, although under certain circumstances an influential home-state senator of the opposite party—for example, a Dirksen in the Johnson Administration or a Johnson in the Eisenhower Administration, may well be able to swing some weight, too. The President might succeed in seeing his choice confirmed (absent outright Senatorial hostility), for the highest bench, which has always been regarded as the President's personal appointment preserve, but practically no such allowance is made for designees on the lower rungs of the judiciary. Should the President nonetheless persist in submitting a name that is not at least marginally acceptable to the candidate's home-state Senators, almost certainly the latter will invoke "Senatorial courtesy," which means certain death to the candidacy. Senatorial courtesy is based on the assumption that the Senate will jointly condemn an affront to one of its members by defeating the measure before it —provided, however, that the aggrieved member offers a reasonably cogent explanation. When the defeat of a judicial nominee is at stake, the condemnation customarily issued is that the nominee or the way he has been chosen is "personally obnoxious."

Numerous instances of the application of Senatorial courtesy are on record, with the practice at least partially accounting for rejection of several nominations to the Supreme Court. It appears to have been the sole factor in Grover Cleveland's unsuccessful nominations of William B. Hornblower (1893) and Wheeler H. Peckham (1894), both of New York, whom the Senate successively rejected by votes of 24:30 and 32:41, respectively. In each instance David B. Hill, Democratic Senator from New York, invoked Senatorial courtesy; Cleveland had snubbed Hill in his quest for a replacement for the seat vacated by Mr. Justice Samuel Blatchford of New York. Cleveland then had his revenge when he refused to name a third New Yorker to the vacancy—instead he turned to the Democratic Majority Leader in the Senate, Edward D. White of Louisiana. Senatorial courtesy had also figured prominently in the defeat of Reuben H. Walworth of New York, a Tyler (Whig) nominee, in 1844 (21:26) and, although somewhat less so, in that of George W. Woodward of Pennsylvania, a Polk (Democrat) nominee, in 1845 (20:29). Both Senators from New York, Democrats Silas Wright and Nathan G. Tallmadge, had opposed Walworth, and "Independent" Senator Simon Cameron had declared his fellow Pennsylvanian "personally objectionable."

Even so reasonable and eminently fair a public figure as Senator Paul H. Douglas (D.- Ill.) successfully invoked the spirit, if not the letter, of Senatorial courtesy in his 1951 battle to block Harry Truman's nominations of Illinois State judges Joseph P. Drucker and Cornelius J. Harrington to two newly created Judgeships in the Northern District for Illinois of the U.S. District Court. Douglas objected to both men chiefly on qualification but also on other grounds. As the Senator explained to his colleagues:

. . . Great as the knowledge of a President may be, he cannot, in the nature of things, in the vast majority of instances, know the qualifications of the lawyers and local judges within a given state as well as the Senators from that state. However excellent his general knowledge, the President does not have the detailed knowledge of the qualifications, background, and record of judges in a particular State. . . . I must reluctantly raise my objection to the appointment of these candidates because of the manner and method of their selection, and because the result would, in my judgment, be antagonistic to the cause of good government and the maintenance of a strong, independent judiciary.[5]

Backed by an overwhelming referendum in support of his position (and his own candidates) by the Illinois bar, he thus appealed to the courtesy of the Senate; its Judiciary Committee supported him unanimously, and the Senate itself sustained his position without even a roll call. Douglas had won his fight, but he had failed to convince the President to send up *his* two nominees, whose names he had "cleared" with Democratic party leaders and members of the Illinois bar six months earlier and forwarded to Attorney General J. Howard McGrath. The result was stalemate and a compromise candidate for one of the three existing vacancies—with Illinois being the loser by the presence of two continuing vacancies. Thus it is clear that the Senate's power is a veto power—an awesome weapon, to be sure, but a negative one. True, some Senators of the President's own political party are possessed of such influence and power that often they will insist not only on the right of prior consultation and approval of the Presidential choice, but also on the right to choose lower federal judicial candidates. Yet it takes two to dance that particular political tango—and other interested parties are inevitably waiting to cut in. Still, the President courts defeat of his selection if he designedly antagonizes or deliberately fails to consult the fellow party Senators concerned. Senatorial courtesy may well no longer be used as crassly and as indiscriminately as it once was, but it remains one of the three key considerations in the judicial nominating process.

A second factor—one that has gained recognition only in recent years—is the incontrovertible evidence of the influence of sitting members of the judiciary. It has been apparent for some time that incumbents in district courts and in courts of appeals have been consulted about their possible future colleagues. Studies of biographical and autobiographical data, which have become increasingly available during the past two or three decades, make it clear that Presidents do sporadically consult with Supreme Court Justices—most frequently with the Chief Justice—for advice on future appointments. The initiative usually lies with the Chief Executive; yet it may also emanate from the Justices, as a mid-nineteenth-century event illustrates: in 1853 Associate Justices John Catron and Benjamin R. Curtis not only personally urged President Pierce to nominate John A. Campbell but accompanied their plea with supportive letters from all of the remaining sitting Justices (regardless of political or sectional persuasion). Other Justices who lobbied prominently and successfully with Presidents in the last century include Robert C. Grier (for William Strong, 1870); Noah H. Swayne (for Joseph P. Bradley, also 1870); Morrison R. Waite (for William B. Woods, 1880); Samuel F. Miller (for David J. Brewer, 1889); and Henry B. Brown (for Howell E. Jackson, 1893). The Presidents involved were, respectively, Ulysses S. Grant (twice), Rutherford B. Hayes, Grover Cleveland, and Benjamin Harrison.

The champion influencer to date has unquestionably been William Howard Taft, the only person to have served both as President (1901–13) and as Chief Justice of the United States (1921–30). Taft actually coveted the latter post more than the Presidency, but he was not about to relinquish his place as a leader of America's bar simply because of his elevation to the highest court. He had, after all, appointed six of its members while he was President, two of whom were still serving when he reached the Court. And Mr. Chief Justice Edward D. White, whom Taft ultimately succeeded, had been elevated by him to that post in 1910. Taft, on leaving the Presidency in 1913, began to establish a long record of rendering both solicited and unsolicited advice on judicial candidates, literally bombarding the Executive

Branch with suggestions, and he assuredly did not stop when President Harding nominated him as Chief Justice in 1921.

Indeed, it is no exaggeration to maintain that Taft, rather than Harding, was basically responsible for selecting—or at the very least approving—three of the four individuals whom Harding sent to the Supreme Court before his death in 1923: George Sutherland (1922), Pierce Butler (1922), and William Howard Taft! Taft merely acquiesced in the President's choice of the fourth, Edward T. Sanford. Taft's lobbying activities in his own behalf were perhaps matched only by his efforts on behalf of Pierce Butler—a classic illustration of Taft's influence over Harding, who seemed almost to fear him at times. Harding's Attorney General, Harry M. Daugherty, a Taft ally and no mean special-interest lobbyist himself, thus told Taft's brother, Henry, that the President "would not approve of anybody for appointment who was not approved by [the Chief Justice]." [6] And among those whom Taft successfully blocked as not having "sound views" or being of "our kind" was the great Judge Learned Hand of New York, whom Harding wanted to appoint to the Supreme Court in 1922. Taft himself had appointed Judge Hand to the U.S. District Court in 1909 (and would back his promotion by President Coolidge to the U.S. Court of Appeals for the Second Circuit in 1924). Another Taft victim was Benjamin N. Cardozo, who might "herd," or so Taft feared, with Justices Holmes and Brandeis. Cardozo did become a Supreme Court Justice—but not until after Taft's death in 1932. On the other hand, despite Herculean (and nasty) efforts Taft failed to block President Wilson's contentious appointment of Louis Dembitz Brandeis in 1916.

While Taft's power to influence the selection of jurists has been unmatched, other Justices have also been influential, notable among them three Chiefs: Hughes, Stone, and Warren. Thus Charles Evans Hughes successfully urged F.D.R. to promote Associate Justice Harlan F. Stone to Chief Justice when he stepped down in 1941. And President Truman asked Hughes (then retired) to come to the White House to talk with him about a successor to Stone when the latter died in 1946. When Oliver Wendell Holmes stepped down in 1931, President Hoover consulted him on the candidacy of Stone's fellow New Yorker, Judge Benjamin N. Cardozo. Hoover, a reluctant dragon indeed on the Cardozo nomination, also asked Justice Stone for additional names, "just in case." Judge Learned Hand and Woodrow Wilson's Secretary of War, Newton D. Baker, were Stone's alternate choices. But Stone was convinced of Cardozo's superior qualifications and, suspecting the President's motives, sent him a string of memoranda and editorials extolling Cardozo in preference to the other two. He also tried hard to allay Hoover's political reservations concerning another "Brandeis co-religionist" on the Court. In fact, Stone went so far as to offer to resign from the Court in order to make room for Cardozo. But Hoover yielded. F.D.R. consulted with Stone before selecting Professor Felix Frankfurter and Truman did likewise before he named Senator Harold H. Burton (R.-Ohio). Mr. Chief Justice Earl Warren was an influential participant in President Kennedy's decision to nominate Secretary of Labor Arthur J. Goldberg to succeed Mr. Justice Frankfurter on the bench—a choice evidently discussed with and fully approved by Frankfurter as well. Warren was also heavily involved in President Johnson's unsuccessful selection of Abe Fortas to succeed him in 1968—although L.B.J. was so completely committed to his long-time friend and confidant that any adverse reaction from the outgoing Chief would hardly have deterred him.

A third major factor to influence the process of judicial selection is the enormously influential role played by the Standing Committee on Federal Judiciary of the American Bar Association (A.B.A.). Established during President Truman's initial incumbency in 1945–46 as the Special Committee on Federal Judiciary, its role in the selection of jurists was more or less formalized at the end of the Truman Administration through the determined efforts of Deputy Attorney General Ross B. Malone. The Committee has been utilized in varying degree by all Presidents since then, and its work represents a significant attempt to complement, if not replace, the "political" aspects of judicial selection with "professional" input; that is, input from the organized bar. The attempt has been crowned with considerable success. An obvious measure was Deputy Attorney General Richard H. Kleindienst's announcement to the A.B.A. convention in August 1969 that the Nixon Administration had "accorded" the Association's Federal Judiciary Committee absolute veto power over all federal candidates to the bench (Supreme Court excepted) whom it considered unqualified. The Administration even offered the same concession with respect to local judgeships in Washington, D.C., if the A.B.A. wanted it. The Kleindienst disclosure marked the high point of the A.B.A.'s effort formally to influence the selection of federal judges. It also signified an extraordinary delegation of executive constitutional power to a private agency. Such a delegation of executive responsibility might well be questioned by students of judicial process. Consultation with legal or other professional groups is a valid function, but the responsibility for choosing the candidates for judicial office is clearly delegated to the President in Articles II and III of the Constitution. That responsibility should not be thus diluted.

The American Bar Association represents less than half of the nation's lawyers, and a relatively narrow segment of the "legal establishment" has traditionally dominated its Judiciary Committee, although an effort to become more representative seems to be under way. To date, however, almost all of the Committee's members have been successful lawyers, partners in large, big-city firms, veterans of local bar-association politics. They tend to be older men. This is not to say that the Committee is inevitably conservative, for it has had prominent members with liberal tendencies, such as Bernard G. Segal, President of the A.B.A. in 1969–70. Nor is it to say that the Committee suffers from components dominated by seasoned, cautious, prestigious professional members—not at all. But it does re-raise a crucial question: should a limited, private-interest group be accorded power of such magnitude that, in the words of Mr. Kleindienst, "the White House will never submit a nomination when the A.B.A.'s federal judiciary committee has issued a not qualified rating." [7] There was something perversely refreshing in President Truman's bemused delight in frequently ignoring the A.B.A.'s "unqualified" label; in President Kennedy's lectures to the A.B.A. on the responsibility of governance; and in President Johnson's early "wheeling-dealings," although he was badly burned by his pushing, under intense pressure from the Kennedy family, of the candidacy of Francis X. Morrissey, justly rated "unqualified" by the A.B.A., for a position on the United States District Court for Massachusetts.

The "unqualified" label becomes particularly contentious when viewed against certain of the criteria used by the A.B.A. Committee in applying it. Thus, although the Committee will approve the suggested promotion of a judge up to the age of sixty-eight if he is already sitting, it will rate "unqualified" anyone not sitting who has reached sixty-four. Those who have had no trial experience are also rated "unqualified"; in fact, the Committee usually insists on fifteen years of experience "in the rough and tumble of legal practice." Consequently, President Kennedy's selection of Sarah T. Hughes for the U.S. District Court of Texas in 1961 was disapproved by the A.B.A. Committee because she was over sixty-four; but the Senate confirmed her nonetheless. Ironically, she administered the oath of office to Vice-President Lyndon B. Johnson aboard the Presidential plane after President Kennedy's assassination. James R. Browning, the Clerk of the Supreme Court, another Kennedy nomination to the lower federal bench, was also rated "not qualified" because he had had no trial experience. He too was confirmed. But even before the Nixon Administration's determination to regard the A.B.A.'s rating as binding, an overwhelming number of "not qualified" rankings by the Committee carried either with the President or with the Senate.

The Morrissey case had been the turning point. In September 1965 Johnson publicized his nomination of Boston Municipal Court Judge Francis X. Morrissey for a vacancy on the U.S. District Court in Massachusetts. It is highly doubtful that the President would normally have selected or approved him, but Morrissey, an old and loyal friend of the Kennedy family, had apparently been assured a Federal Judgeship by private commitment from

President Kennedy to his father not long before the assassination; and Johnson felt obliged to uphold what he regarded as a matter of honor. The A.B.A. Committee promptly rated Morrissey "not qualified" after hearings and investigations had loosed a cascade of adverse information: Morrissey's law degree was from an unaccredited Georgia "diploma mill"; he had failed several courses in that institution; he had failed the Georgia state bar examination twice and had barely navigated it on the third try; he was a candidate for the Massachusetts legislature during the period he was allegedly establishing domicile in Georgia. In addition Charles E. Wyzanski, Jr., Chief Judge of the Court to which Morrissey was being nominated, charged that the candidate had neither familiarity with the law nor the ability to learn it, and that he was generally incompetent. The press had a field day in lambasting the nomination, with the *Washington Post* calling it "nauseous" on its front page.[8] Yet the Association of the Bar of the Commonwealth of Massachusetts endorsed the Morrissey candidacy; the Senate Judiciary Committee, with seven members not voting, recommended confirmation by a 6:3 vote; and Senator Edward Kennedy continued to champion it vigorously until late October. At that point he recognized the inevitable and, in a dramatic, emotion-choked statement delivered on the floor of the Senate, asked his colleagues to return the nomination to the Judiciary Committee for further study. But Judge Morrissey decided that he would not continue what had become an embarrassing and degrading quest although the F.B.I. had apparently backed his veracity on several disputed points. Two weeks after the Senate had sent his nomination back to committee, Morrissey asked President Johnson to withdraw his nomination, and the latter complied, praising Morrissey for his courage. But President Johnson never again nominated a candidate who had not been sanctioned by the A.B.A. Committee, and from 1966 to 1968 he sent 128 nominations to the Senate. Johnson's over-all record ultimately compared favorably with that of his two fellow non-lawyer predecessors, John F. Kennedy and Dwight D. Eisenhower.

The drama of the Morrissey episode fully demonstrated the

power and influence the A.B.A.'s Standing Committee on Federal Judiciary had accumulated. "Not qualified" is the lowest rating assigned by the Committee, which uses three other rankings when it passes judgment on potential nominees to the lower federal judiciary: "qualified" (Q), "well qualified" (WQ), and "exceptionally well qualified" (EWQ)—with the latter used very sparingly. These ratings are subject to change annually, but they seem to have become standard for lower courts. A different evaluative method, to be described below, is utilized for Supreme Court nominees. The Committee consists of twelve members, one from each of the eleven federal judicial circuits and a chairman. They are chosen by the President of the A.B.A. because of their standing in the bar, their credibility with the bar's leadership, their knowledge of "what is required," their commitment to hard work, and because they are presumably free from political entanglement. Members may not hold public office at the time of appointment, which is for three years, and they receive no compensation except out-of-pocket expenses. If a member belongs to a law firm, it is expected that the firm will free him or her without penalty, since the tasks of membership require a considerable expenditure of time and effort.

The Committee sensibly assumes that it must consult with the Executive Branch of the government before a public announcement is made concerning a judicial nominee. Although this procedure does not prevent leaks, it does minimize them, assuming full cooperation between the government and the Committee. Thus, when the Attorney General submits a nominee or a list of nominees to the Committee, its work commences *in camera*. Investigating a candidate normally takes from six to eight weeks. The first step is to submit a detailed questionnaire, often running from fifteen to twenty pages and covering some thirty points of inquiry. One of the questions asks the candidate's judgment and evaluation of the ten "most significant" cases at law the candidate has handled. A candidate is usually interviewed at length by a committee member, one from the candidate's judicial circuit if possible. Through interviews with lay and professional individuals—

including all of the pertinent federal judges in the candidate's area, top state judges, local law school deans, lawyers, and certain non-lawyers the Committee member becomes familiar enough with the candidate's qualifications and character to render, presumably, a useful appraisal of his ability. The information thus gathered is then passed on in an informal report to the Committee Chairman, who subsequently submits a complete report to the Committee and to the Attorney General; the latter must decide if he wishes the A.B.A. to render a formal report. If he requests one it is circulated for a formal vote to all members of the Committee with each acting independently and by mail. The F.B.I. at the request of the Justice Department then makes a painstaking investigation, the results of which are submitted to the Attorney General, who makes the ultimate recommendation to the President. If the President approves of the candidate the nomination and the complete dossier are sent to the Senate Judiciary Committee for its action.

As already indicated, the role of the A.B.A. Committee differs materially in the case of potential Supreme Court nominees, who have always been regarded as the President's own choice. Consequently, the procedures just described seldom have been applied to Supreme Court candidates. Indeed, the Committee's services were not enlisted in that connection until President Eisenhower nominated William J. Bennan, Jr., to the Court in 1956, and only then *after* the nominee's identity had been made public and transmitted to the Senate Judiciary Committee for action. Thus the A.B.A. Committee preferred to commit itself only to the rankings of "qualified" or "unqualified." This procedure was followed in each of the Supreme Court nominations following Brennan's until Blackmun was appointed in the spring of 1970: nominees Whittaker, Stewart, White, Goldberg, Fortas, Marshall, Fortas again (the aborted promotion), Thornberry (not acted upon by the Senate because its refusal to promote Fortas resulted in Warren's withdrawal of his resignation, hence negating the vacancy), Burger, and Haynsworth and Carswell (both rejected). The Committee stuck to the classification of "qualified" in all but a few instances: in 1963 it ranked Goldberg "highly acceptable" but considered it inappropriate to express ". . . an opinion to the degree of qualification." [9] Yet it did express just such an opinion in the case of Judge Haynsworth in 1969—first and unanimously "highly qualified," then on reconsideration "highly qualified," but only by an 8:4 vote. In the Carswell case the Committee returned to its "qualified" designation (although more than a few observers wondered how he merited that).

In response to a storm of criticism following its actions in endorsing Haynsworth and Carswell (the former twice), the Committee's chairman Lawrence E. Walsh, a Nixon ally and the President's number-two representative at the Paris Peace Talks for some months, announced an impending change in the Committee's Supreme Court nomination classification system. Beginning with the nomination of Judge Blackmun early in 1970, the Committee adopted a new top classification of "high standards of integrity, judicial temperament, and professional competence" and substituted categories of "not opposed" or "not qualified" for the erstwhile dichotomy of "qualified" or "unqualified." It signified a tacit admission that under the latter system almost anyone could have been rated as "qualified." Evidently pleased with the Committee's new classification and its endorsement of Blackmun with the new top category, Attorney General Mitchell yielded to the importunities of Chairman Walsh. On July 23, 1970, Mitchell wrote him that henceforth the Nixon Administration would allow the A.B.A. Committee to screen potential nominees for the Supreme Court *in advance* of their submittal to the Senate Judiciary Committee. Considerable approbation in otherwise critical circles followed the announcement, for it also had become evident that its investigation of Blackmun, in sharp contrast to the sketchy report the Committee had rendered to the Senate in just six days in the Carswell case, had been rigorous: it had interviewed some 200 presumably knowledgeable individuals, including upward of 100 judges and lawyers, and had reviewed all of Judge Blackmun's court opinions in an effort to determine the candidate's qualifications in terms of "integrity . . . judicial temperament and professional competence. . . ."

Yet the era of "good tone" was destined to be short-lived. When Justices Hugo L. Black and John Marshall Harlan announced their resignations in September 1971, the Administration moved rapidly to submit possible nominees to the A.B.A. Committee, starting with Richard H. Poff, Republican Congressman from Virginia. The A.B.A. Committee, after interviewing almost 400 individuals, awarded Congressman Poff the A.B.A.'s highest recommendation. After Poff withdrew there came the much-publicized candidacy of "The Six," whose names reached the press and public even before the Walsh Committee went to work on them. The Attorney General in submitting the names of "The Six" urged speed—the Court had already begun its October 1971 term with but seven sitting members—and requested concentration on the Administration's two top choices, Mrs. Lillie and Mr. Friday. Apparently little or no work was done on the other four candidates, giving rise to later suspicions that they were but decoys.

The A.B.A. Committee, now working almost constantly, interviewed another 400 people in connection with each of the two nominees. The results were distressing. Whatever qualifications Judge Lillie and Lawyer Friday possessed, they were at best marginal in terms of what is required for service on the Supreme Court of the United States. The Committee responded with a unanimous vote of "not qualified" for Mrs. Lillie and a 6:6 tie (6 votes "not qualified," 6 votes "not opposed") for Mr. Friday. The fat was in the fire. When the A.B.A.'s actions, complete with votes, reached the news media only an hour or so after the Attorney General had received them, the Administration barely attempted to conceal its anger. Just who was responsible for the leak is difficult to establish, but the author is satisfied that it did not come from the A.B.A. Committee itself: either it was from personnel in the Justice Department or from members or staff of the Senate Judiciary Committee. There is some evidence that it came from both sources, with the initial divulgence made by the Justice Department. Within a matter of days Attorney General Mitchell addressed a sizzling letter to A.B.A. President Leon Jaworski and Chairman Walsh of the Committee informing them that at least the incumbent Administration would no longer apply to the Committee for its advice on nominees to the Supreme Court, that it would return to the practice of sending nominees directly to the Senate:

> The events of the past week have made it clear that our concern of confidentiality of communications between Justice and the Committee was well founded, and I can only conclude that there is no practical way to avoid unauthorized disclosure of the names submitted and the advice of your committee with respect thereto despite the best efforts of the committe. . . . Like you, I had hoped that the new procedure would be useful and productive. However, under the circumstances, I have concluded that the only fair and proper course is to resume the long-standing practice of submitting the Attorney General's recommendations directly to the President. . . .[10]

The letter ended on a conciliatory note in recognizing the Committee's "wholehearted cooperation," and was signed "Yours sincerely, John," but there was no mistaking its bitter tone. The Committee was equally bitter. It would neither simply accept the blame nor cease its evaluations of Supreme Court nominees—even though that would have to be made at the Senate stage once again. A plainly miffed Chairman Walsh made the latter quite clear: when the President subsequently announced his selections of Messrs. Powell and Rehnquist for the two vacancies (he did not send the Lillie and Friday nominations to the Senate at all) the A.B.A. Committee sprang to action. After its normal investigation it submitted its report to Chairman Eastland of the Senate Judiciary Committee: Powell, unanimously approved with the highest of the three classifications; Rehnquist, with eight votes for the highest classification and four "not opposed" votes. As noted, their confirmation by the Senate in December, 1971 came by votes of 89:1 and 68:26, respectively. One year later the A.B.A. formally requested Mr. Mitchell's successor, Richard G. Kleindienst, not only to revert to the Department's pre-"The Six" arrangements with the Committee, but to broaden the latter's role in advising Presidents on nominations. No action had been taken in the matter by late 1973, either by Kleindienst or by his successor, El-liot L. Richardson. The work of the A.B.A. Committee is but one piece—albeit a prominently perceived one—in a rather large mosaic. Its contribution is indeed essential, yet it should never be-come controlling. One of its most distinguished contemporary members noted perceptively that the Committee "performs a very significant function of saying 'no' to the political muscleboys . . . and it also plays an enormously important one in taking flak for the Senators." [11] But as the Committee sheepishly conceded in its Carswell report "many other factors of a broad political and ideo-logical nature" remain outside its competence. In sum, the bar can be of inestimable help in assessing professional qualifications of judicial nominees, but it must not, on any level, be accorded a veto power. For there remains the crucial constitutional cum polit-ical fact of governance under our representative democracy that judicial nominations are the President's to make and the Senate's to confirm.

That the Senate takes its confirmation role seriously is docu-mented by its refusal to confirm 26 of the 136 Supreme Court nominees forwarded to it in the less than two centuries of our his-tory. True, even when counting the Senate's refusal to vote on the Fortas promotion, only four have been voted down during the pres-ent century, but as the experiences of the Nixon Administration demonstrate, the possibility is ever-present. Yet a return to the nineteenth-century record of one rejection for every three nomi-nees would appear to be highly unlikely nowadays.

Just why were the twenty-six rejected? Among the more promi-nent reasons have been: (1) opposition to the nominating Presi-dent, not necessarily the nominee; (2) the nominee's involvement with a visible or contentious issue of public policy (that is, "poli-tics"); (3) opposition to the record of the incumbent Court which, rightly or wrongly, the nominee had presumably supported; (4) Senatorial courtesy (closely linked to the consultative nominating process); (5) a perceived "political unreliability" of the nominee; and (6) the evident lack of qualification or limited ability of the nominee. Usually several of these reasons—not one alone—

figure in the rejection of a nominee; the purpose of the previous list is merely to suggest some applicable prototypes.

Thus a number of candidates were rejected because of Senate opposition to the nominating Chief Executive. For example, John Quincy Adams's nomination of John J. Crittenden in 1828 was "postponed" by the Senate in a strictly partisan vote of 17:23 two months after the nomination. The "loyalist" Democrats in the Senate thereby foiled Adams's last-minute Whig appointment and preserved the vacancy so that it could be filled instead by the President-elect, strong-party Democrat Andrew Jackson. In 1844 Whig President John Tyler sent six nominations to the upper house—which disapproved five and confirmed but one, the outstandingly qualified Samuel Nelson, Chief Justice of New York's highest court. Of the others, John C. Spencer, an erstwhile Whig who had accepted high Cabinet posts under Tyler and whom the "loyalist" Whig followers of Henry Clay regarded as a traitor, was rejected by a formal roll-call vote of 21:26; and action regarding Edward King—who was nominated twice—Ruben H. Walworth, and John M. Read was postponed by the Senate, chiefly because of the mistaken expectation of the Clay Whigs that their revered leader would defeat James Polk in the Presidential election of 1844. In 1852 action on George E. Badger, one of Whig President Millard E. Fillmore's nominees, was postponed indefinitely (despite the fact that he was then a Whig Senator from North Carolina) and no action at all was taken on his two others, Edward A. Bradford and William E. Micou. The purpose of the anti-Fillmore maneuvers was to preserve court vacancies for incoming Democratic President Franklin Pierce, yet Pierce succeeded in filling only one of them, he too falling victim to similar Senate tactics. Democrat James Buchanan's nomination of Jeremiah S. Black in December 1860, one month before his term ended, fell 25:26, chiefly because Republican Senators wanted to hold the seat for Abraham Lincoln to fill. In 1866 Union President Andrew Johnson nominated his gifted Attorney General, Henry Stanberry, but the Senate's hostility to Lincoln's successor was such as to frustrate every attempt he made to fill a Supreme

Court vacancy. Congress even went so far as to *abolish* the vacancy (thus "icing" Johnson's nominating impotence). A century later, in 1968, the Senate refused to approve Lyndon B. Johnson's simultaneous attempt to promote Abe Fortas to Chief Justice and to replace him with Judge Homer Thornberry of the U.S. Court of Appeals for the Fifth Circuit. Johnson failed largely because most members of the Senate "had had it" with the lame-duck President's nominations. Victory-scenting Republicans also wanted such plums as Supreme Court appointments for themselves; they had not had an opportunity to fill a vacancy on the bench since President Eisenhower's appointment of Mr. Justice Potter Stewart ten years earlier.

A good many illustrations are on record in which nominees failed to receive Senatorial confirmation because of their involvement with public issues. Thus in 1795 the Senate rejected John Rutledge as Chief Justice by a vote of 10:14 (although he had been serving as such for four months on a recess appointment while Congress was not in session). Rutledge had asked President Washington for the appointment on John Jay's resignation but now found his fellow Federalists voting against him because of his vigorous opposition to the Jay Treaty of 1794. The Federalist Senators refused to confirm a public figure who actively opposed the Treaty they had championed so ardently—even though he was able to meet Washington's stiff criteria for service on the highest bench. Their cause was aided by an all-but-unanimous denunciation by the Northern Federalist press. In 1811 James Madison's nomination of Alexander Wolcott fell 9:24 because the Federalist Senators, eagerly backed by the press, opposed Wolcott's vigorous enforcement of the embargo and non-intercourse acts when he was U.S. Collector of Customs in Connecticut. There was, however, also some genuine question as to Wolcott's legal qualifications.

The rejection of James K. Polk's nomination in 1845 of fellow Democrat George W. Woodward of Pennsylvania—although in part due to opposition by Pennsylvania's Independent Senator Simon Cameron on the basis of "Senatorial courtesy"—was largely a result of what was termed Woodward's "gross nativist

American sentiments." Chiefly because of these alleged sentiments, which were particularly offensive to Irish-Americans, five
Democratic Senators joined Cameron and a phalanx of Whigs to
defeat the nomination by a vote of 20:29. The President, however,
saw the action as a power-play calculated to weaken his Administration at the very outset. On December 15, 1869, Republican
President Ulysses S. Grant nominated his eminently qualified and
popular Attorney General, Ebenezer R. Hoar. The debate over his
nomination dragged on for seven weeks until February 3, 1873,
when Hoar was finally rejected by a vote of 24:33. He had antagonized most of the Senators by his consistent refusal to back Senatorial nominations for Judgeships; by his publicly uncompromising
insistence on "non-political" appointments throughout the government; and by his early championship of civil service reform.
Moreover, he had made enemies of fellow Republicans by his outspoken opposition to the proposed impeachment of President Andrew Johnson. Few professional politicians appreciated Judge
Hoar's high standards of excellence and assertive political independence; and the Court was deprived of an unusually promising
candidate.

Another issue-oriented rejection was that of John J. Parker,
U.S. Fourth Circuit Court of Appeals Judge (Hoover, 1930). A
prominent and distinguished Republican leader in North Carolina
for many years and an outstanding jurist, Judge Parker fell victim
to the sustained opposition of the American Federation of Labor
and the National Association for the Advancement of Colored
People. Still, the Senate would not have had the votes to defeat the
nomination—Parker lost by a two-vote margin, 39:41—had they
not been aided by the anti-Hoover Progressive Republicans, including such prominent and influential Senators as Robert M.
LaFollette, Jr., of Wisconsin, Hiram Johnson of California, and
George W. Norris of Nebraska. The A.F.L.'s chief grudge against
the nominee stemmed from the impression that he was "unfriendly"
to labor and that it was he who had handed down an opinion af-
firming a lower-court decision upholding "yellow dog" contracts.[12]
A close reading of Judge Parker's opinion in the case indicates

neither approval nor disapproval of yellow dog contracts; rather, it reflects the jurist's belief that he was bound by a United States Supreme Court precedent.[13] Yet the impression of anti-labor bias lingered, fostered by A.F.L. President William Green and other influential labor spokesmen—who, on the other hand, did concede that Judge Parker's integrity, high standards, and professional qualifications were not in question. The N.A.A.C.P. contended that the nominee was generally opposed to Negro participation in politics and especially to Negro suffrage. Thus Walter White of the N.A.A.C.P. leadership pointed out that Judge Parker, while stumping North Carolina as a gubernatorial candidate in 1920, had indeed made an unfortunate remark: "The participation of the Negro in politics is a source of evil and danger to both races and is not desired by the wise men in either race or by the Republican Party of North Carolina." [14] Parker had uttered the statement in response to repeated taunts and charges by his Democratic opponents that he intended to enfranchise Negroes and to alter the North Carolina Constitution to accommodate "them." Ironically, it would be Judge Parker (he continued to sit on the Fourth Circuit bench after his rejection) who would write some of the earliest and most significant pro-Negro opinions on desegregation. Among them was *Rice* v. *Elmore* in 1947, in which he sustained U.S. District Court Judge J. W. Waring's outlawing of South Carolina's machinations to bar Negroes from primary elections.[15]

The next outright rejections were Judges Haynsworth and Carswell almost forty years later. Although their involvement with civil rights did play a considerable role in their rejections, especially in that of Carswell, the margin of defeat lay elsewhere: in Haynsworth's case in the question of judicial ethics; in Carswell's case in professional qualification.

The Senate's refusal to accept closure in 1968 in order to vote on the promotion of Mr. Justice Fortas has also been variously attributed to his "record" on the high bench on such contentious issues as obscenity and criminal justice. In fact, although the issues were dramatically vocalized by such powerful and committed opponents to the nomination as Senators Strom Thurmond (R.-S.C.)

and John L. McClellan (D.-Ark.), they were not an important reason for the nomination's failure. It was fought with such ardor
largely because of deep-seated opposition to the jurisprudential
philosophy of the "Warren Court"—an approach to constitutional
interpretation that resulted in the inevitable disaffection of numerous groups and individuals, both public and private. The Court's
stance and record of "judicial activism" on such emotion-charged
issues as desegregation, reapportionment and redistricting, criminal justice, separation of Church and State, civil disobedience, and
freedom of expression was bound to offend as well as to please.

Coming, as it did conveniently, at the close of the Johnson Administration, the Fortas nomination readily served as target and
symbol of the pent-up frustrations against the Warren Court—but
against the Court as a unit rather than against the individuals. One
of the famous episodes surrounding the attacks against Fortas occurred early in the hearings of the Senate Judiciary Committee,
when Senator Thurmond shouted at Fortas: "Mallory! Mallory! I
want that name to ring in your ears." Thurmond's reference was
to Andrew Mallory, a nineteen-year-old black from South Carolina who was arrested in 1954 on a charge of choking and raping
a thirty-eight-year-old Washington woman while she was doing
her laundry. After a seven-hour interrogation by the police *prior*
to his arraignment, Mallory had confessed. The trial was delayed
for a year because doubts had been raised that he understood the
proceedings against him, but ultimately Mallory was sentenced to
the electric chair. He appealed to the Supreme Court on the
grounds of coerced confession. In what became the celebrated case
of *Mallory* v. *United States* in 1957,[16] the Court unanimously reversed Mallory's conviction on the grounds that the failure of the
police to bring him before a magistrate forthwith constituted an
"unnecessary delay" (in violation of federal rules of criminal-law
procedure) thereby giving "opportunity for the extraction of a
confession." Released, Mallory resumed a life of drifting and
crime, culminating in his 1960 arrest in Philadelphia and subsequent apprehension for burglary, assault, and rape. He was convicted on the assault count and served eleven years in jail, but

barely six months after his release in 1971 he attacked and robbed a couple in a Philadelphia park. When discovered by two policemen, he aimed a gun at one and was killed by the other in the process. It was the so-called "Mallory Rule" as pronounced by the Supreme Court that Senator Thurmond referred to in his outburst at Justice Fortas. Yet the latter had never been connected with the case and had not even been appointed to the Court until 1965, eight years after the Mallory decision! (The Mallory Rule itself was modified by Congress in the Omnibus Crime Control Act of 1968.) Other, similar charges were leveled at the nominee, some of them concerning decisions in obscenity cases rendered long before Fortas ever sat.

Senatorial courtesy, fourth in our list of reasons for Senate refusal of Supreme Court nominations, has already been discussed. A fifth reason is broadly stylable as "political unreliability," as perceived by the Senate. Perhaps the most obvious example of the application of this reason is another among the several unsuccessful Grant nominations—that of former Attorney General Caleb Cushing, who was the President's third choice,* to assume the Chief Justiceship in 1874, following the death of Salmon P. Chase. Cushing's age—seventy-four—was noted prominently during debate, but the real reason for his rejection was the Senate's not-entirely-erroneous belief that Grant's close personal friend was a political chameleon. Indeed, Cushing had been in turn a Regular Whig, a Tyler Whig, a Democrat, a Johnson Constitutional Conservative, and finally, a Republican. He had proved himself a first-rate legal practitioner and scholar; nevertheless, with opposition from almost all political factions augmenting daily, Grant withdrew Cushing from consideration.

A final reason for Senate refusal of a nominee is simply real or apparent lack of qualification to sit on the Supreme Court. Of course the concepts of "quality" and "ability" are subject to di-

---

* Senator Roscoe Conklin of New York, a close political and personal friend, was Grant's first choice. But Conklin turned down the offer, and the Senate refused to act on Grant's second choice, his Attorney General, George H. Williams.

verse analysis; yet a number of ascertainable standards and guidelines clearly exist. A nominee's age, experience, and record in and out of public life are all available guidelines. Ulysses S. Grant, in choosing his Attorney General George H. Williams to fill the vacancy caused by the death of Chief Justice Chase, thus evoked an entirely justifiable storm of adverse reactions. Williams had seen service in the Senate and had been territorial Governor of Oregon, but his record as Attorney General was undistinguished and his talents as a lawyer were clearly mediocre (it was alleged that he had unnecessarily lost several important cases in private as well as public litigation). Both the bar and the press were severely critical of his achievements and his promise. Stunned and hurt by this reaction and despairing of a lengthy confirmation battle, Williams asked President Grant to withdraw his nomination in early January 1874.

It is fair to conclude that Presidents have avoided nominating patently unqualified individuals to the high tribunal (see Appendix A) although a number of rather weak nominations have slipped past the Senate, such as James C. McReynolds (Wilson), Pierce Butler (Harding), Sherman Minton (Truman), and Charles E. Whittaker (Eisenhower).[17] The one nominee on whose lack of qualification almost all fair-minded observers now agree is G. Harrold Carswell. With the calm hindsight of history, President Nixon's choice still merits the characterization of a spite nomination. It is fortunate that the Senate simply would not accept Carswell.

Would any of the twenty-six who failed in being confirmed have been approved had they been members of the Senate at the time of their nomination? The evidence is persuasive that they would have: the Senate almost invariably treats as a *cas d'honneur* the Presidential designation of a sitting member and normally, although not so predictably, of a past colleague in good standing. Among the many illustrations are Senators James F. Byrnes (D.-S.C.) and Harold H. Burton (R.-Ohio). Byrnes, highly respected and very much a member of the Senate's "inner club," was confirmed unanimously without even being scrutinized by the Committee on the Judiciary when President Roosevelt nominated him in 1941.[18] Burton's nomination, although that of a Republican by a Democratic President (Truman), was unanimously confirmed in 1945 on the same day it reached the Senate, then controlled by a Democratic majority.

That the special treatment accorded Senatorial colleagues is normally reserved to those actually serving is demonstrated by the case of ex-Senator Sherman Minton of Indiana. Minton, who had been defeated for re-election in 1940 largely because of his ardent espousal of the New Deal, was serving as a judge on the U.S. Court of Appeals for the Seventh Circuit when President Truman selected him for the Court in 1949. In part because of his support of Roosevelt's Court-packing bill, the Senate Judiciary Committee voted 5:4 to ask him to testify before it. Minton refused, pointing to his position as a jurist and questioning the propriety of testifying lest conflicts arise concerning pending litigation. The Committee relented and reported his nomination favorably, 9:2. But led by prominent Republicans, the Senate took a formal vote on recommittal of Minton's nomination—which was defeated 45:21; thereafter, he obtained quick confirmation, 48:16.

A notable exception to the unwritten rule of the all but automatic approval of Senatorial colleagues was Franklin D. Roosevelt's controversial nomination of Senator Hugo Lafayette Black (D.-Ala.) in August 1937. Black's nomination was referred to the Judiciary Committee for full hearings, an action not taken since 1888. The initial reasons for that action, over the strong objections by the Chairman of the Committee, Senator Henry Ashurst (D.-N.M.) were Black's strong support of the President's Court-packing bill, his ardent New Deal partisanship, and his ruthless public investigations of the utility lobby. The attempt to increase the size of the Court was anathema to a majority of the Senate and the bar. And the controversy was compounded and exacerbated by rumors that Black had once been—and some alleged still was—a member of the Ku Klux Klan in his native Alabama. Even so, the Committee ultimately approved the nomination by a vote of 13:4 (two Democrats and two Republicans voting against him), and the

Senate confirmed him 66:15 (nine Republicans and six Democrats voting nay). Meanwhile reporter Ray Sprigle of the *Pittsburgh Post-Gazette* came up with evidence that Black had indeed belonged to the K.K.K. Black faced the charges squarely: in a candid dramatic broadcast to the American people he admitted a two-year K.K.K. membership in the mid-1920s but pointed to his established liberal record and vowed to be a fair and impartial jurist. During a tenure on the Court lasting more than a third of a century he kept his word.

The last test of the Senate's refusal to refer nominations to the Judiciary Committee came with Burton in 1945; no U.S. Senator has since been nominated. It was precisely the recognition of that rule that prompted leading supporters of President Nixon to urge him to nominate a Senator after Judge Haynsworth's rejection in 1969. Evidently the President briefly toyed with the idea of nominating John Stennis (D.-Miss.) or Sam Ervin (D.-N.C.), both southern Senators generally supportive of his "strict construction" views, but in his determination to teach the Senate a lesson he chose Carswell. Yet it will be recalled that one of the six he had under consideration in 1971 was Senator Robert C. Byrd (D.-W.Va.)—a man infinitely less qualified to serve on the Court than his colleagues Stennis and Ervin. Whether or not Nixon seriously contemplated the Byrd nomination, there is little doubt that his colleagues would have given their approval. Yet those same colleagues would have been far less likely to approve of someone of equally marginal qualifications from outside the halls of the Senate.

3

Why They Get to the Supreme Court:
Qualifications and Rationalizations

It may suprise some to learn that no legal or constitutional requirements for a Federal Judgeship exist. This is especially surprising given that each state in the union has requirements for
some judicial posts. There does exist, however, an unwritten prerequisite for a post on the federal bench—a bachelor of laws degree. No one can become a member of the Supreme Court today
without that degree, although it is not necessarily mandatory either
to have practiced law or to have been a member of the bar. Yet as
we observed earlier the A.B.A. Standing Committee on Federal
Judiciary not only demands trial experience of a candidate for the
judiciary; it also requires some fifteen years of legal practice to
qualify the candidate for a passing rating. As a matter of historical record, no non-lawyer has ever served on the Supreme Court
of the United States.

To date, all except three presidents—William Henry Harrison
(1841), Zachary Taylor (1849–50), and Andrew Johnson
(1865–68)—have succeeded in appointing at least one of their
nominees to the highest court, although nine appointed but one
each: James Monroe (1817–25), John Quincy Adams (1825–29),
John Tyler (1841–45), Millard Fillmore (1850–53), Franklin
Pierce (1853–57), James Buchanan (1857–61), James A. Garfield

(1881), William McKinley (1897–1901), and Calvin Coolidge (1923–29). Of the three who appointed none at all, Harrison and Taylor died soon after reaching office, and Johnson, who saw several nominees blocked by the Senate, was the victim of an implacably hostile Congress.

Table I lists the number of Justices who were confirmed by the Senate and actually served on the Supreme Court and the Presidents who appointed them. If we count Justices Edward D. White, Charles Evans Hughes, and Harlan F. Stone once (each served as both Associate Justice and as Chief Justice), exactly one hundred Justices had served on the Court as of the 1973–74 term, the result of 103 successful appointments.

TABLE I

Number of Presidential Appointments of Supreme Court Justices Actually Serving on the Court (1789–1974)

PRESIDENT	PARTY	DATES SERVED	NUMBER OF APPOINTEES WHO ACTUALLY SERVED *
Washington	Federalist	1789–97	10
J. Adams	Federalist	1797–1801	3
Jefferson	Democrat–Republican	1801–1809	3
Madison	Democrat–Republican	1809–17	2
Monroe	Democrat–Republican	1817–25	1
J. Q. Adams	Democrat–Republican	1825–29	1
Jackson	Democrat	1829–37	6 (5) †
Van Buren	Democrat	1837–41	2 (3) †
W. H. Harrison	Whig	1841	0
Tyler	Whig	1841–45	1
Polk	Democrat	1845–49	2
Taylor	Whig	1849–50	0
Fillmore	Whig	1850–53	1
Pierce	Democrat	1853–57	1
Buchanan	Democrat	1857–61	1
Lincoln	Republican	1861–65	5
A. Johnson	National Union	1865–69	0

PRESIDENT	PARTY	DATES SERVED	NUMBER OF APPOINTEES WHO ACTUALLY SERVED *
Grant	Republican	1869–77	4
Hayes	Republican	1877–81	2
Garfield	Republican	1881	1
Arthur	Republican	1881–85	2
Cleveland	Democrat	1885–89 1893–97	4 **
B. Harrison	Republican	1889–93	4
McKinley	Republican	1897–1901	1
T. Roosevelt	Republican	1901–1909	3
Taft	Republican	1909–13	6
Wilson	Democrat	1913–21	3
Harding	Republican	1921–23	4
Coolidge	Republican	1923–29	1
Hoover	Republican	1929–33	3
F. D. Roosevelt	Democrat	1933–45	9
Truman	Democrat	1945–53	4
Eisenhower	Republican	1953–61	5
Kennedy	Democrat	1961–63	2
L. B. Johnson	Democrat	1963–69	2
Nixon	Republican	1969–	4
			103

* William Smith (1837) and Roscoe Conkling (1882) were nominated and confirmed but declined to serve; hence they are not included here.
† Jackson nominated Catron, but he was not confirmed until Van Buren had taken over.
** Two in each term.

In view of what is minimally required of a Supreme Court nominee, it is hardly astonishing that many men have come to the bench with no previous judicial experience and that very few of them have had extensive judicial experience. Among the one hundred Justices who had served on the Court by late 1973, only twenty-two had had ten or more years of experience on any tribunal—federal or state—and forty-two had had no judicial experience at all. Yet as Table II indicates, many of the most illus-

trious men in the history of the Court were judicially inexperi-
enced. Among them were eight of the fifteen Chief Justices: *
Charles Evans Hughes, John Marshall, Harlan F. Stone, Roger B.
Taney, Samuel B. Chase, Morrison R. Waite, Melville W. Fuller,
and Earl Warren; and such outstanding Associate Justices as Joseph Story, Samuel F. Miller, Joseph P. Bradley, Louis D. Brandeis, Felix Frankfurter, and Robert H. Jackson.

In a learned essay calling for selection of Supreme Court Justices "wholly on the basis of functional fitness," Mr. Justice
Frankfurter keenly argued that judicial experience, political affiliation, and geographic, racial, and religious considerations should
not play a significant role in the selection of jurists. He felt that a
Supreme Court jurist should be at once philosopher, historian, and
prophet—to which Mr. Justice Brennan, in a conversation with
this writer, proposed to add "and a person of inordinate patience." Justice Frankfurter viewed their task as requiring "poetic
sensibilities" and "the gift of imagination," as exhorting them to

> pierce the curtain of the future . . . give shape and visage to
> mysteries still in the womb of time. . . . [the job thus demands]
> antennae registering feeling and judgment beyond logical, let
> alone quantitative proof. . . . One is entitled to say without qual-
> ification that the correlation between prior judicial experience
> and fitness for the Supreme Court is zero. The significance of the
> greatest among the Justices who had such experience, Holmes
> and Cardozo, derived not from that judicial experience but from
> the fact that they were Holmes and Cardozo. They were thinkers,
> and more particularly, legal philosophers.[1]

As supporting witness, Frankfurter was fond of calling on Judge
Learned Hand, the author of one of the most incisively thoughtful
statements on the subject:

> I venture to believe that it is as important to a judge called upon
> to pass on a question of constitutional law, to have a bowing ac-

* Hughes and Stone are included in the list because neither had had judicial experience at the time of their appointments as Associate Justices.

TABLE II

*Prior Judicial Experience of U.S. Supreme Court
Justices and Their Subsequent Service*

JUSTICE	YEAR NOMINATED	NUMBER OF YEARS OF PRIOR JUDICIAL EXPERIENCE			YEARS OF SERVICE ON SUPREME COURT
		FEDERAL	STATE	TOTAL	
Jay *	1789	0	2	2	6
J. Rutledge *†	1789 and 1795 *	0	6	6	2 **
Cushing	1789	0	29	29	21
Wilson	1789	0	0	0	9
Blair	1789	0	11	11	7
Iredell	1790	0	½	½	9
T. Johnson	1791	0	1½	1½	2
Paterson	1793	0	0	0	13
S. Chase	1796	0	8	8	15
Ellsworth *	1796	0	5	5	4
Washington	1798	0	0	0	31
Moore	1799	0	1	1	5
Marshall *	1801	0	0	0	34½
W. Johnson	1804	0	6	6	30
Livingston	1806	0	0	0	17
Todd	1807	0	6	6	20
Story	1811	0	0	0	34
Duval	1811	0	6	6	24
Thompson	1823	0	16	16	20
Trimble	1826	9	2	11	2
McLean	1829	0	6	6	32
Baldwin	1830	0	0	0	14
Wayne	1835	0	5	5	32
Taney *	1836	0	0	0	28
Barbour	1836	6	2	8	5
Catron	1837	0	10	10	28
McKinley	1837	0	0	0	15
Daniel	1841	4	0	0	19
Nelson	1845	0	22	22	27
Woodbury	1845	0	6	6	6
Grier	1846	0	13	13	24
Curtis	1851	0	0	0	6
Campbell	1853	0	0	0	8
Clifford	1858	0	0	0	23

TABLE II (*Continued*)

Prior Judicial Experience of U.S. Supreme Court
Justices and Their Subsequent Service

JUSTICE	YEAR NOMINATED	NUMBER OF YEARS OF PRIOR JUDICIAL EXPERIENCE			YEARS OF SERVICE ON SUPREME COURT
		FEDERAL	STATE	TOTAL	
Swayne	1862	0	0	0	19
Miller	1862	0	0	0	28
Davis	1862	0	14	14	15
Field	1863	0	6	6	34½
S. P. Chase *	1864	0	0	0	9
Strong	1870	0	11	11	10
Bradley	1870	0	0	0	22
Hunt	1872	0	8	8	10
Waite *	1874	0	0	0	14
Harlan, Sr.	1877	0	1	1	34
Woods	1880	12	0	12	7
Matthews	1881	0	4	4	8
Gray	1881	0	18	18	21
Blatchford	1882	15	0	15	11
L. Q. C. Lamar	1888	0	0	0	5
Fuller *	1888	0	0	0	22
Brewer	1889	6	22	28	21
Brown	1890	16	0	16	16
Shiras	1892	0	0	0	11
H. E. Jackson	1893	7	0	7	2
White *	1894 and 1910 *	0	1½	1½	27
Peckham	1895	0	9	9	14
McKenna	1898	5	0	5	27
Holmes	1902	0	20	20	30
Day	1903	4	3	7	19
Moody	1906	0	0	0	4
Lurton	1909	16	10	26	5
Hughes *††	1910 and 1930 *	0	0	0	17
Van Devanter	1910	7	1	8	27
J. R. Lamar	1910	0	2	2	6
Pitney	1912	0	11	11	10
McReynolds	1914	0	0	0	27
Brandeis	1916	0	0	0	23
Clarke	1916	2	0	2	6

JUSTICE	YEAR NOMINATED	NUMBER OF YEARS OF PRIOR JUDICIAL EXPERIENCE			YEARS OF SERVICE ON SUPREME COURT
		FEDERAL	STATE	TOTAL	
Taft *	1921	8	5	13	9
Sutherland	1922	0	0	0	16
Butler	1922	0	0	0	17
Sanford	1923	14	0	14	7
Stone *††	1923 and 1941 *	0	0	0	23
Roberts	1930	0	0	0	15
Cardozo	1932	0	18	18	6
Black	1937	0	1½	1½	34
Reed	1937	0	0	0	19
Frankfurter	1939	0	0	0	23
Douglas	1939	0	0	0	
Murphy	1940	0	7	7	9
Byrnes	1941	0	0	0	1
R. H. Jackson	1941	0	0	0	13
W. Rutledge	1943	4	0	4	6
Burton	1945	0	0	0	13
Vinson *	1946	5	0	5	7
Clark	1949	0	0	0	18
Minton	1949	8	0	8	7
Warren *	1953	0	0	0	16
Harlan	1955	1	0	1	16
Brennan	1956	0	7	7	
Whittaker	1957	3	0	3	5
Stewart	1958	4	0	4	
White	1962	0	0	0	
Goldberg	1962	0	0	0	3
Fortas	1965	0	0	0	4
Marshall	1967	3½	0	3½	
Burger *	1969	13	0	13	
Blackmun	1970	11	0	11	
Powell	1971	0	0	0	
Rehnquist	1971	0	0	0	

* Indicates Chief Justice and date of his appointment or promotion.
† Rutledge's nomination was rejected by the Senate in December 1795, but he had served as Chief Justice under a recess appointment for four months.
** Actually Rutledge never served as Associate Justice, although he did perform circuit duty before his resignation in 1791.
†† Indicates no judicial experience when appointed as *Associate* Justice.

quaintance with Acton and Maitland, with Thucydides, Gibbon, and Carlyle, with Homer, Dante, Shakespeare, and Milton, with Machiavelli, Montaigne, and Rabelais, with Plato, Bacon, Hume, and Kant as with books that have been specifically written on the subject. For in such matters everything turns upon the spirit in which he approaches the question before him. The words he must construe are empty vessels into which he can pour nearly everything he will. Men do not gather figs of thistles, nor supply institutions from judges whose outlook is limited by parish or class. They must be aware that there are before them more than verbal problems; more than final solutions cast in generalizations of universal applicability. They must be aware of the changing social tensions in every society which make it an organism; which demand new schemata of adaptation; which will disrupt it, if rigidly confined.[2]

What a pity that a man of Hand's intellect and pen never became a member of the Supreme Court—he would have graced it from every point of view.

Yet the matter of judicial experience, although periodically ignored or downgraded by some Presidents, rarely lies dormant long. To Franklin D. Roosevelt judicial experience was of little importance; to Dwight Eisenhower it was crucial: after his initial appointment of Earl Warren as Chief Justice, Eisenhower insisted that future nominees have judicial background, no matter how limited. Of the nine men who served on the Court as a result of F.D.R.'s appointments (or promotion to Chief Justice in the instance of Harlan F. Stone), six had had no judicial experience when they ascended the bench: Chief Justice Stone and Associate Justices Stanley F. Reed, Felix Frankfurter, William O. Douglas, James F. Byrnes, and Robert H. Jackson. Of the three with experience, Wiley B. Rutledge had served on the Court of Appeals for the District of Columbia for four years, and Hugo Black and Frank Murphy on state tribunals for one and a half and seven years, respectively. Harry Truman had a mixed record: of his four appointees, Harold H. Burton and Tom C. Clark had no judicial experience at all, but Fred M. Vinson and Sherman Minton had seen five and eight years, respectively, of service on lower federal courts. The four men Eisenhower appointed following Warren—Associate Justices John M. Harlan, William J. Brennan, Jr., Charles E. Whittaker, and Potter Stewart—all had had judicial experience, although the total number of such years for the four was but fifteen. Neither Associate Justices Byron R. White nor Arthur J. Goldberg, appointed by John Kennedy; nor Abe Fortas, appointed by Lyndon Johnson, had served below the Supreme Court, although L.B.J.'s last successful appointee, Thurgood Marshall, had been a federal appellate judge for three and a half years. Of President Nixon's four selections to date, Chief Justice Warren E. Burger and Associate Justice Harry A. Blackmun had served on lower federal tribunals for thirteen and eleven years, respectively, but Associate Justices Lewis F. Powell and William H. Rehnquist had served on no court. Thirteen appointees with no judicial background were sent to the Court by the six most recent Presidents, and with the exception of one or two, all possessed at least some qualifying attributes: broad experience in the public sector, strong personality and strength of character, capacity for hard work, political savoir faire, a modicum of intellectualism, and verbal as well as written articulateness. To raise judicial experience to the level of either an express or implied requirement would render a distinct disservice to the Supreme Court.

Fortunately, Congress has hardly been of one mind on the necessity or even the desirability of judicial experience as a prerequisite for appointment to the Court. Rarely does a session of Congress go by that does not see proposed legislation embodying such a requirement, usually specifying from five to ten years of prior service. In the Ninetieth Congress (1969–71) some fifteen such bills were sponsored by members on both sides of the aisle in both houses. But they all failed to be enacted, as had thirteen such bills in the Eighty-ninth Congress (1967–69). A majority of the members of Congress—two-thirds of whom are lawyers—continue to agree that judicial experience is not essential. Clearly they recognize that the Supreme Court is not a trial court in the sense of the federal district courts; that it does not deal with a particular constituency as do the federal district courts and, to a considerably lesser degree, the federal courts of appeals. Further, experience gained in the lower courts may be of little significance in the Supreme Court as their procedural and jurisdictional frameworks are really quite different. The private litigation at common law so prevalent in the lower courts is practically absent at the bar of today's Supreme Court, which is almost exclusively occupied with questions of public law.

Returning again to Frankfurter and Hand, today's business of the Supreme Court is what Judge Hand categorized as the "application of rather fundamental aspirations," what he styled "moods" that are embodied in constitutional provisions such as the due process clauses of the Fifth and Fourteenth amendments. Evidently these clauses were deliberately designed in Mr. Justice Frankfurter's words, "not to be precise and positive directions for rules of action." According to him:

> The judicial process in applying them involves a judgment on the processes of government. The Court sits in judgment, that is, on the views of the direct representatives of the people in meeting the needs of society, on the views of Presidents and Governors, and by their construction of the will of the legislatures the Court breathes life, feeble or strong, into the inert pages of the Constitution and the statute books.[3]

Indeed this is a function calling for a combination of philosopher, historian, and prophet—but it also calls for other vital attributes that enter into the judicial process.

A glance at the personnel of the 1973–74 Court will perhaps serve to underscore that judicial experience is not necessarily vital to a Supreme Court jurist. Of the nine men—Messrs. Burger, Douglas, Brennan, Stewart, White, Marshall, Blackmun, Powell, and Rehnquist—who commenced the 1973–74 term of Court, only five could point to judicial experience on lower courts, and in three instances it was for but a brief period.

Yet all of the members of that Court had come to the high tribunal with considerable experience in public life, frequently of an administrative-executive nature. In order of seniority of service on the bench: Mr. Justice William O. Douglas, an army private in World War I, had practiced law for a few years, taught it for almost a decade, and had been both a member and Chairman of the federal Security and Exchange Commission when in 1939 F.D.R. appointed him to the Court at age forty-one (only four Justices were appointed at an earlier age). Mr. Justice William J. Brennan, Jr., an army colonel in World War II, had practiced law for fifteen years and had served for seven years on three state courts in New Jersey, including the State Supreme Court, before he was appointed in 1956. Mr. Justice Potter Stewart, who saw three years of service overseas during World War II, had practiced law for more than a decade, had been a member of the City Council of Cincinnati, and had served on the U.S. Court of Appeals for the Sixth Circuit for six years when he was appointed in 1958. Mr. Justice Byron R. White, Rhodes scholar and All-American football star, had been Mr. Chief Justice Vinson's law clerk, had practiced law for fourteen years, and was Deputy Attorney General of the United States when John Kennedy sent him to the Court in 1962 at age forty-five. Mr. Justice Thurgood Marshall—the first black to reach the highest court and a nationally known civil rights leader—had practiced law for three decades, much of it constitutional law at the bar of the Supreme Court, and had served for three and a half years on the U.S. Court of Appeals for the Second Circuit. When he was appointed in 1967 to the Supreme Court he held the position of U.S. Solicitor General. Mr. Chief Justice Warren E. Burger, appointed in 1969, had practiced law for twenty-three years, had been politically active in his native Minnesota, and for three years had held the post of Assistant Attorney General, heading the Civil Division, before becoming a federal jurist in 1956. With thirteen years on the U.S. Court of Appeals for the District of Columbia, he had had the most extensive judicial background. Mr Justice Harry A. Blackmun, appointed to the Court in 1970, had a record similar to that of his fellow Minnesotan Burger, having practiced law in a Minneapolis firm for twenty-five years when in 1959 he was named to the U.S. Court of Appeals for the Eighth Circuit. Mr. Justice Lewis F.

Powell, Jr., appointed to the Court late in 1971, had a long and distinguished record as a legal practitioner and civic leader in Virginia—including the chairmanship of the Richmond public school board in the late 1950s—and had been President of the American Bar Association. Mr. Justice William H. Rehnquist had clerked for Mr. Justice Robert H. Jackson, had practiced law and been active in Arizona politics for many years, and was serving as Assistant Attorney General of the United States, in charge of the office of Legal Counsel, at the time of his elevation to the Court in December 1971.

If for the sake of argument one were to grant the necessity of *judicial* experience as a requirement for all Supreme Court nominees, the rich non-judicial backgrounds of the men just described would not compensate for their lack of actual experience on lower benches. But almost all Supreme Court jurists have had extensive *legal* experience. Moreover, all of the one hundred individuals who actually served on the Court, with the sole exception of Mr. Justice George Shiras, Jr. (1892–1903), had engaged in at least some public service at various levels of government or had actively participated in political enterprises. Nevertheless, unlike the jurists of France, for example, who are trained and schooled as jurists, a great many American jurists have no judicial background. And in the considered judgment of a majority of the members of the bar as well as most non-legally trained students and observers of the Court, it is not a vital prerequisite to a successful judicial career. Table III indicates the occupations (at the time of appointment) of those (using the full figure of 103 here) who have served on the Supreme Court.

Discounting rare individual exceptions, the caliber of the Supreme Court has been universally high. No other part of the American government can readily match its general record of competence and achievement. Yet there is nothing particularly astonishing about the essentially upper-middle-class "establishment" components that by and large have tended to characterize the members of the Court. A fusing of the background characteristics

TABLE III

Occupations * *of Supreme Court*
Designees at Time of Appointment †

Federal Officeholder in Executive Branch	22
Judge of Inferior Federal Court	21
Judge of State Court	21
Private Practice of Law	18
U. S. Senator	8
U. S. Representative	4
State Governor	3
Professor of Law	3
Associate Justice of U. S. Supreme Court **	2
Justice of the Permanent Court of International Justice	1

* Many of the appointees had held a variety of federal or state offices, or even both, prior to their selection.
† In general the appointments from state office are clustered at the beginning of the Court's existence; those from federal office are more recent.
** Justices White and Stone, who were *promoted* to the Chief Justiceship in 1910 and 1930, respectively.

of the one hundred individuals who have sat on the Court thus produces the following profile:

NATIVE-BORN (there have been but six exceptions, the last, Austrian-born Felix Frankfurter); WHITE (the first nonwhite, Thurgood Marshall, was appointed in 1967); MALE (there have been no women to date); GENERALLY PROTESTANT (six Roman Catholic and five Jewish Justices); FIFTY to FIFTY-FIVE years of age at the time of appointment; ANGLO-SAXON ETHNIC STOCK (all except six); UPPER-MIDDLE to HIGH SOCIAL STATUS; REARED IN AN URBAN ENVIRONMENT; MEMBER OF A CIVIC MINDED, POLITICALLY ACTIVE, ECONOMICALLY COMFORTABLE FAMILY; B.A. and LL.B. DEGREES (usually from prestigious institutions); SERVICE IN PUBLIC OFFICE.

Present-day egalitarian trends may well operate to alter that profile somewhat: assuredly a woman will be appointed to the Court in the near future, and the continuation of a "black seat" seems all

but certain. Yet a dramatic alteration of the pattern is highly unlikely. With the indicated exceptions, the described composite is
not only more or less self-operating, but most members of the
American body politic would not welcome any drastic change in
it. Notwithstanding the frequent attacks on the Supreme Court as
an institution, its personnel has generally been held in high esteem
by the average citizen.

The only person who knows with certainty why an individual is
appointed to the Supreme Court is the President of the United
States himself. But historians and students of the judicial process
can come close to the truth by interpreting the facts at their dis-
posal; thus a study of the records of the thirty-four Presidents who
have sent men to the Supreme Court—an evaluation of their reasons for making the choices they did—points to several criteria
that have been predominant in influencing Presidential decisions.
The following four have probably been the most important: (1)
objective merit, (2) personal friendship, (3) balancing representation on the Court, and (4) political and ideological compatibility.

When a President considers the objective merit of a candidate,
he attempts to determine whether he or she possesses the ability
and background requisite to a mastery of the vital and complicated issues that reach the Supreme Court. To achieve that end he
might look to the candidate's basic intellectual acumen, reputation
for legal scholarship, and competence in a particular area of the
law. He might consider his experience as a judge, lawyer, legislator, or executive and he might note his integrity and morals, his
judicial temperament, and his work habits. Even age may be relevant. If the nominee is too young he may be lacking in judgment,
wisdom, and experience; if too old, visions of retirement, illness,
or death may intervene.

Personal friendship is difficult to measure, but assuredly it has
influenced a considerable number of nominations. In Taft's choice
of Horace H. Lurton; in Wilson's of Louis D. Brandeis; in Truman's of Harold H. Burton; and in Kennedy's of Byron R. White
—to cite some obvious illustrations—personal friendship figured
prominently. Other examples were Truman's appointments of Mr.

Chief Justice Fred M. Vinson and Associate Justices Tom C. Clark and Sherman Minton. It was probably the crucial consideration in the case of Minton, although the Indianan was a good Democrat who had seen eight years of service, however colorless, on the federal appellate bench. Most obvious and most recorded in recent years was Lyndon Johnson's choice of Abe Fortas. Long Fortas's intimate personal friend, L.B.J. consistently urged him to accept a vacancy. Perhaps prophetically, Fortas was consistently reluctant. But he ultimately bowed to the President's entreaties and, with considerable lack of enthusiasm, accepted appointment to the seat vacated by Mr. Justice Goldberg when he resigned to become United States Ambassador to the United Nations in 1965.

Balancing geographical and religious representation has also influenced Presidents in their choice of Supreme Court nominees. Of the four factors, religious representation is the least defensible and the most emotion-charged. Yet no matter how undesirable it may be in theoretical terms, it is not only here to stay but, viewed against the backdrop of present-day group consciousness, it will very likely be joined by the new close regard for race and sex.

The widespread notion that all sections of the land should be "represented" on the bench—to date the Justices have come from thirty-one of the fifty states—cannot be readily dismissed (see Table IV). It has considerable appeal as a matter of political equity. It was a primary consideration among almost all of the nineteenth-century Presidents; thus Lincoln's successful search for "an outstanding trans-Mississippi lawyer" (Samuel F. Miller) and a Californian (Steven J. Field, a Democrat) and Cleveland's insistence on geographic appropriateness, best exemplified by his choice of a Chief Justice (Melvin Fuller). Among recent Presidents strongly influenced by the "geography factor" Richard Nixon stands out. Yet after the Haynsworth and Carswell rejections, he abandoned his much-publicized quest for a "Southern strict-constructionist," choosing Judge Harry A. Blackmun of Minnesota—not only a Northerner but a resident of a state already "represented" on the Court by Blackmun's close friend, Mr. Chief Justice Burger.

On the other hand, a determined President will not permit geography to stand in the path of a desired appointment. Woodrow Wilson proved this with his insistence on the confirmation of Brandeis, notwithstanding the presence of Oliver Wendell Holmes on the bench, a fellow citizen from Massachusetts; so did Hoover when he finally appointed Cardozo in the face of the Court presence of fellow New Yorkers Stone and Hughes.

TABLE IV

The 31 States from Which the 103 Supreme Court
Appointments Were Made

New York	15	Louisiana	2
Ohio	9	Minnesota	2
Massachusetts	8	North Carolina	2
Virginia	7	Iowa	2
Tennessee	6	Michigan	2
Pennsylvania	6	New Hampshire	1
Kentucky	5	Maine	1
Maryland	4	Mississippi	1
New Jersey	4	Kansas	1
South Carolina	3	Wyoming	1
Connecticut	3	Utah	1
Georgia	3	Texas	1
Alabama	3	Indiana	1
California	3	Missouri	1
Illinois	3	Colorado	1
		Arizona	1

The religious factor is based upon the notion of a "Roman Catholic seat" and a "Jewish seat" on the Supreme Court. A development of dubious communal wisdom, the concept of religious-group representation has become one of the facts of American political and judicial life (see Table V)—although it has been less of an emotional problem in the courts than in the makeup of election slates in minority-conscious cities, for example.

Six men have occupied the "Catholic seat" to date: Chief Justice Roger B. Taney (Jackson, 1835); and Associate Justices Edward D. White (Cleveland, 1894—he was promoted to Chief

Justice by Taft, 1910), Joseph McKenna (McKinley, 1898); Pierce Butler (Harding, 1922); Frank Murphy (Roosevelt, 1940), and William J. Brennan (Eisenhower, 1956). With the exception of the seven years between Mr. Justice Frank Murphy's death in 1949 (when President Truman deliberately ignored the unwritten rule of the "reserved" seat and nominated Protestant Tom C. Clark to the vacancy created by Murphy's death) and the nomination of Mr. Justice William J. Brennan, Jr., in 1956, a Roman Catholic has been on the Supreme Court continually since White's appointment.

TABLE V

Acknowledged Religion of the 100 Individual Justices of the Supreme Court (at time of appointment)

Episcopalian	26
Unspecified Protestant	24
Presbyterian	17
Roman Catholic	6
Unitarian	6
Baptist	5
Jewish	5
Methodist	4
Congregationalist	3
Disciples of Christ	2
Lutheran	1
Quaker	1
	100

The "Jewish seat" was established in 1916 with the appointment of Louis D. Brandeis. That tradition was broken when in 1969 President Nixon successively nominated three Protestants (Haynsworth, Carswell, and Blackmun) to succeed Fortas. In 1971 Nixon had two opportunities to appoint a Jewish Justice, but he again nominated two more Protestants—Lewis F. Powell, Jr., and William H. Rehnquist. Questioned on the continued "oversight" at one of his infrequent news conferences, Nixon gave the appropriately logical response: that merit, rather than religion, should and must govern [4]—a laudable aim provided it is indeed invoked. The five occupants of "the Jewish seat" to date have been: Louis D. Brandeis (Wilson, 1916), Benjamin N. Cardozo (Hoover, 1932), Felix Frankfurter (F. D. Roosevelt, 1938), Arthur J. Goldberg (Kennedy, 1963), and Abe Fortas (L. B. Johnson, 1965).

In June 1967 Lyndon Johnson designated Thurgood Marshall, the first black ever to be nominated to the Supreme Court. The President, leaving no doubt that the nominee's race was probably the major factor in his decision, told the country: "I believe it is the right thing to do, the right time to do it, the right man and the right place." [5] It is fair to conjecture that there is scant, if any, doubt, that there now exists a "black seat" on the bench that is at least as secure as the Catholic seat and the Jewish seat. It is also highly likely that a "woman's seat" will be established, too— probably within this decade. The Presidential campaign of 1972 featured public assurances by both candidates that a woman would be appointed: George McGovern promised that "the next vacancy" would go to a woman, and Nixon, already on record with his abortive Mildred Lillie nomination, spoke repeatedly of his desire to nominate "a qualified woman."

Political and ideological compatibility often go hand in hand in influencing Presidential choices for the Supreme Court. Among the points a President is almost certain to consider are the following: (1) whether his choice will render him more popular among influential interest groups; (2) whether the nominee has been a loyal member of the President's party; (3) whether the nominee favors Presidential programs and policies; (4) whether the nominee is acceptable (or at least not "personally obnoxious") to his home-state Senators; (5) whether the nominee's judicial record, if any, meets the Presidential criteria of constitutional construction; (6) whether the President is indebted to the nominee for past political services; and (7) whether he feels "good" or "comfortable" about his choice.

It is an unwritten law of the judicial nominating process that the President will not normally select an individual from the ranks of the political opposition. To lessen charges of Court-packing, however, this rule is purposely relaxed now and then—but only within "political reason," which seems to have meant roughly to the tune of 10 per cent of all appointments to district and appellate tribunals and 15 per cent to the Supreme Court. In at least thirteen instances, the appointee to the Supreme Court, including two to the post of Chief Justice, came from a political party other than that of the President: Whig President John Tyler appointed a Democrat, Samuel Nelson, and Republican Presidents Abraham Lincoln, Benjamin Harrison, William H. Taft, Warren G. Harding, Herbert Hoover, Dwight D. Eisenhower, and Richard M. Nixon appointed nine Democrats—Taft alone three! The nine Justices and their nominators were Stephen J. Field (Lincoln); Howell E. Jackson (Benjamin Harrison); Horace H. Lurton, Edward D. White (promoted to Chief Justice), and Joseph R. Lamar (Taft); Pierce Butler (Harding); William J. Brennan (Eisenhower); and Lewis F. Powell, Jr. (Nixon). And Democratic Presidents Woodrow Wilson, Franklin D. Roosevelt, and Harry S Truman appointed three Republicans: Louis D. Brandeis (Wilson); Harlan F. Stone (promoted to Chief Justice by F.D.R.), and Harold D. Burton (Truman). To this list some would add F D R 's selection of Felix Frankfurter, who labeled himself an Independent.

There will always be some crossing of party lines, particularly at the lower court levels, in order to maintain at least the appearance of judicial non-partisanship and to placate the opposition, but the practice may be safely viewed as the exception rather than the rule (as Table VI and the following statistics indicate).

TABLE VI

Avowed Political Affiliation of the 103 Supreme Court Justices (at time of selection)

Federalists	13
Whig	1
Democrats	49
Republicans	39
Independent	1

Many a President has been told by his political advisers to stay on his side of the fence, where surely there are just as many qualified and deserving lawyers as on the other side. "Think Republican," Republican National Chairman Rogers C. B. Morton urged President Nixon at the latter's first opportunity to fill seats on the Supreme Court.[6] As Table VII amply demonstrates, Morton's sentiments are not confined to his political party!

TABLE VII

Percentages of Federal Judicial Appointments Adhering to the Same Political Party as the President, 1888–1973

PRESIDENT	PARTY	PERCENTAGE
Cleveland	Democrat	97.3
B. Harrison	Republican	87.9
McKinley	Republican	95.7
T. Roosevelt	Republican	95.8
Taft	Republican	82.2
Wilson	Democrat	98.6
Harding	Republican	97.7
Coolidge	Republican	94.1
Hoover	Republican	85.7
F. D. Roosevelt	Democrat	96.4
Truman	Democrat	90.1
Eisenhower	Republican	94.1
Kennedy	Democrat	90.9
L. B. Johnson	Democrat	93.2
Nixon	Republican	93.7

If the percentage of "other party" Supreme Court appointees has been higher than that of the lower federal courts, it is because the President recognizes that what matters more than anything else is the ideological compatability of the candidate—what Theodore Roosevelt referred to as the nominee's "real politics."

Whatever the merits of the other criteria attending Presidential motivations in appointments may be, what must be of overriding concern to any nominator is his perception of the candidate's real politics. The Chief Executive's crucial predictive judgment concerns itself with the nominee's likely future voting pattern on the bench, based on his or her past stance and commitment on matters of public policy, insofar as they are reliably discernible. All Presidents have tried to thus pack the bench to a greater or lesser extent.

In the public eye, Court-packing has been most closely associated with Franklin D. Roosevelt. Having had not a single opportunity to fill a Court vacancy in his first term (1933–37), and seeing his domestic programs consistently battered by the Court, the frustrated President attempted to get his way all at once. His Court-packing bill, however, died a deserved death in the Senate.

It is not surprising that Court-packing and the name of President Roosevelt have become synonymous. Yet even such popular heroes as Jefferson, Jackson, and Lincoln followed similar courses of action in the face of what they considered "judicial intransigence and defiance." Their approach was not so radical as Roosevelt's, but they very likely would have been sympathetic to his efforts. George Washington, though broadly regarded as far-removed from "politics," insisted that his nominees to the Court meet a veritable smorgasbord of qualifications. In fact, every President who has made nominations to the Supreme Court has been guilty of Court-packing in some measure. It is entirely understandable that a President will choose individuals who he hopes will share his own philosophy of government and politics, at least to the extent of giving him a sympathetic hearing. Theodore Roosevelt, for example, in discussing the potential candidacy of Horace H. Lurton with Henry Cabot Lodge, put the issue well:

> The nominal politics of the man has nothing to do with his actions on the bench. His real politics are all important . . . . He is right on the Negro question; he is right on the power of the federal government; he is right on the Insular business; he is right about corporations, and he is right about labor. On every question that would come before the bench, he has so far shown himself to be in much closer touch with the policies in which you and I believe.[7]

Lodge concurred in substance, but he replied that he could see no reason "why Republicans cannot be found who hold those opinions as well as Democrats." [8] Consequently, he strongly urged the candidacy of a Republican, whom T.R. then duly nominated: William H. Moody, Attorney General of Massachusetts.

Thus, concern with a nominee's real politics is a fundamental issue, and examples abound. It prompted Republican Taft to give half of his six appointments to kindred souls who were Democrats; Republican Nixon to appoint Democrat Powell; Democrat Roosevelt to promote Republican Stone; and Democrat Truman to appoint Republican Burton. Yet there is no guarantee that what a President perceives as real politics will not fade into a mirage. Hence Charles Warren, eminent chronicler of the Court, observed realistically that "nothing is more striking in the history of the Court than the manner in which the hopes of those who expected a judge to follow the political views of the President appointing him are disappointed." [9] Few have felt the truth of that statement more keenly than Teddy Roosevelt did with Oliver Wendell Holmes, Jr., whose early "anti-administration" opinions in antitrust cases (notably in *Northern Securities* v. *United States*) [10] were entirely unexpected. A bare 5:4 majority in that case did uphold the Government's order under the Sherman Anti-Trust Act dissolving the Northern Securities Company, a brainchild of E. A. Harriman and J. J. Hill—the rich and powerful owners of competing railroads who had organized the company in order to secure a terminal line into Chicago. Roosevelt had won that important litigation, but he was furious about his recent appointee's "anti-antitrust" vote in the case and stormed: "I could carve out of a banana a Judge with more backbone than that!" [11] Holmes reportedly merely smiled when told the President's remark and noted his intention to "call the shots as I see them in terms of the legal and constitutional setting." Later, during T.R.'s second term of office (1905–9) Holmes expressed his sentiments to a labor leader at a White House dinner with characteristic directness: "What you want is favor, not justice. But when I am on my job, I don't give a damn what you or Mr. Roosevelt want." [12]

James Madison was similarly chagrined with his appointment of

Mr. Justice Joseph Story, having refused to heed his political mentor Thomas Jefferson. Jefferson warned him that Story was an inveterate Tory who would become a rabid supporter of Mr. Chief Justice Marshall, and he was right: Story not only instantly joined Marshall's approach to constitutional adjudication and interpretation, he even out-Marshalled Marshall in his nationalism. Perhaps even more chagrin was felt by Woodrow Wilson when his appointee James C. McReynolds proved himself at once to be the antithesis of almost everything his nominator stood for and believed in.

More recently, Harry Truman observed that "packing the Supreme Court simply can't be done . . . I've tried and it won't work. . . . Whenever you put a man on the Supreme Court he ceases to be your friend. I'm sure of that." [13] Future Presidents may well be advised to heed the admonition of Zechariah Chafee, Harvard's famed expert on the judicial process, who contended that in order to forecast the behavior of a future jurist it is wiser to consider the books in his library than the list of clients in his office.

There is indeed a considerable element of unpredictability in the judicial appointing process. To the often-heard "Does a person become any different when he puts on a gown?" Mr. Justice Frankfurter's sharp retort was always, "If he is any good, he does!" In the tellingly colorful prose of Alexander M. Bickel, "You shoot an arrow into a far-distant future when you appoint a Justice and not the man himself can tell you what he will think about some of the problems that he will face." [14] And late in 1969, reflecting upon his sixteen years as Chief Justice of the United States, Earl Warren pointed out that he, for one, did not "see how a man could be on the Court and not change his views substantially over a period of years . . . for change you must if you are to do your duty on the Supreme Court." [15] It is a duty that in many ways represents the most hallowed in the governmental process of the United States.

Who the one hundred individuals to sit on the Court were; why they were appointed (and why some were not); and who chose them is the concern of the rest of this book.

4

The First Forty Years:
From George Washington
Through John Quincy Adams
(1789 - 1829)

George Washington, whom the experts (see Appendix B) still regard as second only to Lincoln in terms of greatness,[1] made few mistakes during his eight years in office. Both judicious and secure, he knew what he wanted and readily admitted to staffing both the judicial and the executive branches with reliable, cautious, conservative adherents to the Federalist cause. It was his opportunity to appoint ten members to the Supreme Court, a judicial body of unknown practical power. In choosing his candidates, Washington, probably more than any other President to date, not only had a clear set of criteria for Court candidacy but adhered to them predictably and religiously: (1) Support and advocacy of the Constitution; (2) Distinguished service in the Revolution; (3) Active participation in the political life of state or nation; (4) Prior judicial experience on lower tribunals; (5) Either a "favorable reputation with his fellows" or personal ties with Washington himself; (6) Geographic "suitability." Of these criteria evidently the most important to him was advocacy of the principles of the Constitution—the more outspoken the better. Perhaps more than many of his contemporaries he recognized the potential strength and influence of the Judicial Branch, keenly sensing the role it would be called upon to play in spelling out constitutional basics and penumbras. In his letters of commission to the first six nominees to the first Supreme Court in 1789, he wrote: "The Judicial System is the chief Pillar upon which our national Government must rest." [2] That Pillar needed strong men—proponents of the Federalist philosophy of government. Indeed, seven of those whom the President sent to the bench had been participants in the Constitutional Convention of 1787.

John Jay of New York—lawyer, jurist, diplomat, soldier, political leader—at forty-four years of age was Washington's first appointment and his choice for Chief Justice. Jay had not been in Philadelphia during the summer of 1787. Yet he had contributed to the *Federalist Papers* and had been influential in Hamilton's cliff-hanger struggle to secure New York's ratification of the Constitution.

Another among the original choices, however, had been a key figure at the Convention, John Rutledge of South Carolina—a former Governor of that state and a judge of its Chancery Court. As Chairman of the Committee on Detail, which composed the first draft of the Constitution, he was regarded as one of the central personalities behind the creation of a *United* States of America. In fact Washington referred to Rutledge rather extravagantly and incorrectly as the individual who "wrote the Constitution." [3] He had seriously considered appointing Rutledge as the first Chief Justice—which is what Rutledge and his supporters had really craved—but opted for Jay because he wanted to honor the key state of New York, whose ratification of the Constitution had proved so decisive. Rutledge was confirmed as Associate Justice in 1791 but had stepped down from the bench before the Court actually convened in order to assume the Chief Justiceship of South Carolina. When Jay resigned as Chief Justice in 1795, Washington again chose Rutledge as his nominee, but the Senate rejected the nomination chiefly because of Rutledge's pronounced opposition to the Jay Treaty.

Pennsylvania's James Wilson was also a key member of the Convention. One of the outstanding lawyer-scholars of his time, Wilson was greatly instrumental in strengthening the role of the judicial branch and was widely regarded as the Father of the judicial article of the Constitution. He had fought successfully for a judiciary independent of both the states and of the national Legislative and Executive branches. He had argued in favor of the establishment of lower ("inferior") federal courts; advocated judicial appointment by the President; and had fortuitously convinced his fellow delegates that judicial independence would be impaired if the President—at the request of Congress—were able to remove Justices from the bench (a proposal that a good many future Presidents, including the incumbent, would have loved to have had available!). At the ratifying convention of his home state, he was among those most influential in obtaining its consent to the Constitution. Wilson not only proposed his own nomination to the President in writing but expressed a preference for the Chief Justiceship. Jay, of course, was named Chief Justice, but the President, who was initially torn between Wilson and the latter's fellow Pennsylvanian, Chief Justice Thomas McKean, chose Wilson as an Associate Justice. It would be a fortunate decision, indeed, for McKean later became a rabid states' rights advocate who rejected the power of judicial review by the federal courts, the United States Supreme Court in particular.

John Blair of Virginia, at fifty-seven the second-oldest member of the Supreme Court, had also been a participant at the Convention, although he had figured much less prominently than Wilson. But Blair had proved himself an excellent "team man" when, subordinating his own strong personal preferences, he had cast his lot with Washington and Madison to carry the Virginia delegation and the Convention for the establishment of the electoral college just as the Convention seemed hopelessly deadlocked over the method of selecting the President. Ultimately Blair, Washington, and Madison were the only members of the Old Dominion delegation to vote for the Constitution in its entirety.

William Cushing, Chief Justice of the Supreme Judicial Court of Massachusetts, completed the group of five chosen for the Court in 1789. Fifty-seven, he was the oldest appointee. Although he had not attended the Constitutional Convention, he had been active in the cause of the Constitution, having initially persuaded Massachusetts to send delegates to Philadelphia. In 1788 he had served as Vice-President of his state ratifying convention, emerging as its most dominating single figure. As a sitting member of the Supreme Court he became Washington's second choice (after Rutledge had been rejected) for Chief Justice to succeed Jay in 1795. The Senate confirmed him; but Cushing, who was now sixty-four years old, pleaded advanced age and declined the post one week after his confirmation early in 1796—without ever having taken his place at the Court's helm.

The last of the original six justices was James Iredell, former Attorney General of North Carolina, the youngest member of the first Court at age thirty-eight. Although he had not been a Convention participant, he has been an influential proponent of ratification; very likely it was because of his massive public "educational" campaign that North Carolina approved the Constitution. Actually, Iredell was Washington's second choice for the position: he had first nominated, and the Senate had confirmed, his close friend and former private military secretary, Robert Hanson Harrison. But Harrison was chosen Chancellor of Maryland just a few days after his confirmation, and he decided to accept the state post—notwithstanding Washington's and Hamilton's warmly urgent pleas to decline it. Iredell, however, would prove to be a source of considerable satisfaction to Washington during his service on the high bench—so much so that the President seriously considered his promotion to Chief Justice when Cushing stepped aside.

Washington's pattern of seeking men with Convention participation or support continued with his remaining four appointments. In 1791 he chose Thomas Johnson of Maryland, a former Governor of that state and a lower federal judge at the time of appointment. There was no doubt as to Johnson's adherence to Federalist principles. He had been a delegate to the Constitutional Convention and had faithfully supported the finished document. Reluctant to accept appointment to the Court because of his aversion to circuit-riding, Johnson saw his fears realized when he began to serve, and resigned in less than a year's time. His replacement was William Paterson, the forty-four-year-old Chancellor of New Jersey and former state Attorney General and U. S. Senator. A strong Federalist "with such consistency as possible to a small-state man," [4] Paterson had been one of the foremost leaders of the Constitutional Convention, offering the "small state," or New Jersey Plan, for equal representation of all states in the national legislature. One of his most significant services to the new Union was his work—second only to Oliver Ellsworth's—on behalf of the Judiciary Act of 1789, which implies the judicial review that was so vital to Washington's visualization of a strong federal judicial system.

A signer of the Declaration of Independence and a hero of the Revolution, Chief Justice Samuel Chase of Maryland, fifty-five, was the President's initial choice to fill the vacancy caused by the Senate's rejection of Rutledge as Chief Justice in 1796, but wisely he did not designate the acid-tongued, outspoken Chase. Instead he named him to the Associate's seat vacated by Blair in the early summer of 1795, which had not yet been filled. Washington had been widely cautioned about Chase's character and temperament, but the President knew him well and eventually decided that his service to the causes of independence warranted his appointment. Chase had opposed the adoption of the Constitution on grounds that were rather nebulous, and he had voted against its adoption at the Maryland ratifying convention. But subsequently he had seen the light, "recognized" the merits of the Constitution, and become a zealous, vocal backer of the Union. Once on the high bench, Chase immediately began to make a speciality of attacking Republicans and rendered himself thoroughly obnoxious to them: in 1796 he predicted that under Jefferson "our republican institution will sink into a mobocracy, the worst of all possible governments"; [5] and he charged Jefferson, both before and after his election as President, with "seditious attacks on the principles of the Constitution." For these attacks the House of Representatives impeached Chase on grounds of "high crimes and misdemeanors." Fortunately for the cause of judicial independence and the principles of separation of powers, when the Senate voted on the charges brought by the House on March 1, 1805, enough Republicans joined the Federalists to acquit the colorful figure by a four-vote margin. It was just as well that Washington did not live to see the controversies that surrounded his appointee—he would have been chagrined and embarrassed.

In 1796, one year before the end of his second term, Washington made his last appointment: Oliver Ellsworth of Connecticut, a staunch Federalist, state jurist, federal legislator, diplomat, and the principal author of the Judiciary Act of 1789. Like the other Washington appointees, Ellsworth was an influential spokesman in behalf of Union, and had been a delegate to the Philadelphia Convention. He had also been particularly effective in bringing about Connecticut's ratification of the Constitution. During the Philadelphia debates he emerged as an early and articulate exponent of the Supreme Court's inherent power of judicial review, which he, like Washington, saw as an essential constitutional check upon potential legislative excesses. Yet Ellsworth remained at the helm for but a brief time. Notwithstanding grave inherent questions of the propriety and constitutionality of assigning non-judicial functions to a sitting jurist, John Adams had appointed him Envoy to France early in 1799. While still there late in 1800 Ellsworth resigned because of ill health—thus setting the stage for the appointment of John Marshall by the lame-duck Adams.

In addition to insisting on strong Federalist credentials, Washington searched for men who had rendered service during the Revolution and, if possible, men who had been active in the affairs of their home states and communities. Seven of his appointees had been delegates to the Constitutional Convention, the exceptions being John Jay, William Cushing, and James Iredell. But Jay, in addition to having written the New York Constitution of 1777, had been a member of the Second Continental Congress and had been appointed "chief foreign relations officer" of the Confederacy. Cushing had served as Chief Justice of Massachusetts during the difficult and crucial period of 1777–89. Iredell too had served North Carolina—as Attorney General, as a member of the

Council of State, and as a Superior Court judge. Six of the President's choices—John Jay, Oliver Ellsworth, Samuel Chase, William Paterson, Thomas Johnson, and John Rutledge—had all been members of the Continental Congress at various times. Chase, Paterson, and Wilson were signers of the Declaration of Independence. And, to the President's particular delight, several of the ten had experienced active involvement in the field during the Revolutionary struggles. For example, Paterson had served as an officer in a company of Minute Men, and Cushing, indomitably energetic, had ridden circuit and held court in Massachusetts during the entire Revolutionary era. The President was perhaps proudest of all of Thomas Johnson: in 1777 when General Washington was literally struggling to keep his army on its feet Governor Johnson of Maryland had recruited a force of 1800 men, personally leading them to Washington's camp. Indeed, for three successive terms as Governor, Johnson displayed an uncanny ability to supply food, arms, and supplies as well as men to the embattled Continental Army.

Yet Washington sought still other attributes in his candidates—among them previous judicial experience—and with the exception of Wilson and Paterson all came to the Court with such background. In fact, his eight other appointees had sixty-three years of collective judicial experience. Four had served on the Supreme Court of their state (Jay, Ellsworth, Chase, and Cushing), and the remaining four had been jurists on other high state courts: Iredell on the Superior Court of North Carolina; Rutledge on the South Carolina Court of Chancery; Johnson as Chief Judge of the General Court of Maryland; and Blair on both the General Court and the High Court of Chancery of Virginia. As for Paterson and Wilson the "mitigating circumstances" were clearly acceptable: Paterson was a co-author of the federal Judiciary Act of 1789 and while Governor of New Jersey had codified its laws and updated the rules of practice and procedure in its courts. Wilson, one of the country's most widely acclaimed legal scholars and a superb practioner at the bar, had emerged as an expert on the judiciary in the Constitutional Convention.

Geography must also be noted as one of the elements that strongly influenced Washington's appointments. He regarded it as extremely important in the light of his constant endeavor to be President of *all* the states of the fledgling nation, and repeatedly stated his desire to see each "section" of the land "represented" on the Supreme Court. On several occasions Washington "rewarded" a strategic state. For example, in commenting on Iredell's appointment, the President frankly stated: "he is of a State of some importance in the Union that has given no character to a federal office." [6] And perhaps the decisive consideration in his appointment of Jay rather than Rutledge as Chief Justice was that Jay hailed from New York, a critical state which had so narrowly and recently ratified the Constitution. Rutledge, Wilson, and Jay had been Washington's three "finalists" for the post. The President eliminated Wilson because of what he regarded as a lack of "appropriate" administrative and political experience, leaving the New Yorker and the South Carolinian as contenders. Since Washington himself, Secretary of State Thomas Jefferson, and Attorney General Edmund Jennings Randolph were all Virginians, Washington determined that yet another top federal office occupied by a Southerner would clearly be unwise. Hence Rutledge had to settle for an Associate Justiceship, from which he resigned seventeen months later.

Washington died too soon to see the full on-the-bench record of his ten Federalist appointees, but he would have been well pleased with their performances. Practically no anti-Federalist decisions were rendered by them or their Federalist successors; and none of them wrote what could be called an anti-Federalist dissenting opinion. It was a pity that the first President could not witness the momentous decisions of the Court under the firm guidance of the great John Marshall, who by his opinions and decisions as Chief Justice did so much to bring to fruition Washington's dreams for the Republic.

John Adams was of considerably less stature than Washington, but the second President did what he could to follow what was indeed a "tough act." History and most historians have been kind to

Adams, even ranking him as a "near great" President. Overshadowed by the talented, shrewd, and ambitious Hamilton and by the memories of Washington's Administration, he proved to be a weak leader and poor administrator, often taking the easy way out. Yet he managed to keep a shaky peace with France, despite Hamilton's hawkishness and plotting.

Adams appointed but three men to the Court: * Bushrod Washington, Alfred Moore, and John Marshall. His criteria for nomination are identifiable but considerably less numerous than Washington's. The pre-eminent requirement was that candidates be of strong Federalist persuasion. Thus George Washington's nephew, Bushrod, although only thirty-six years old at the time of his selection, had amply proved his Federalist loyalty during his career in the Virginia House of Delegates; Moore had had extensive judicial as well as executive experience in his native North Carolina and was widely regarded as one of the most gifted and persuasive Federalist lawyers in the states; and Virginian John Marshall in general personified the Federalist creed.

As with his predecessor, a potential appointee's home state was of genuine importance to Adams. There had been no "Virginia seat" on the Court since Mr. Justice John Blair's resignation in 1795, and Adams, determined to avoid a potentially explosive situation, offered to John Marshall the post caused by James Wilson's death in 1798. Yet Marshall declined to serve, pleading financial exigencies. The President now turned to Washington, who had studied law under James Wilson, the man whose seat he would now take on the high bench. And when James Iredell of North Carolina died in 1799, Adams selected that state's Alfred Moore.

On the other hand, Adams did not insist that his nominees have previous judicial experience; in fact neither Washington nor Marshall had. In Adams's eyes public service was more important, and all of his appointees fit that criterion well: Washington had served as a state legislator; Moore had been North Carolina's Attorney General and a judge of its Supreme Court; and Marshall had been

---

* There were four, if one counts the Senate-confirmed re-appointment of John Jay as Chief Justice late in 1800, which Jay declined.

Congressman, Cabinet officer, soldier, and diplomat. In sum, whereas President Washington followed a well-publicized set of six criteria in his quest to staff the Court, his successor contented himself with four: Federalist loyalty, appropriate geographic base, public service, and a good reputation.

Adams's great achievement was his appointment of John Marshall. No one has had a more profound impact on Court and Constitution than the crafty, hedonistic, and brilliant Virginian. In 1971–72 a poll of sixty-five experts on constitutional law ranking all Supreme Court Justices from 1789 to 1969 (see Appendix A) was unanimous in categorizing Marshall as "great," the sole Justice to receive such recognition. (Next were Brandeis with sixty-two votes and Holmes with sixty-one.) Ironically, Marshall had played second fiddle to John Jay, Adams's initial selection for the Chief Justiceship vacated by Oliver Ellsworth late in 1800. But Jay, whom Adams had not consulted before forwarding his name to the Senate, declined to serve—allegedly for reasons of health but more accurately because he loathed circuit-riding and quite prophetically doubted that Congress would act reasonably soon to relieve the Justices of that fatiguing and often unpleasant chore. Further, he felt that the young Court lacked "energy, weight, and dignity." [7] Adams's associates now urged him to return to a man frequently mentioned as worthy of Supreme Court status, Samuel Sitgreaves of Pennsylvania—especially since no Pennsylvanian was then on the Court. But Adams demurred—and he did so even more firmly when they suggested two prominent candidates of the Hamiltonian faction of the Federalist party: General Charles C. Pinckney of South Carolina, who had declined an appointment offered by Washington in 1791, and sitting Associate Justice William Paterson of New Jersey. Adams wanted his own man, one of whose loyalties he could be absolutely certain, especially because he had lost the election of 1800 and "that Radical" Jefferson was about to succeed him. On January 20, 1801, with but minimal consultation and practically no fanfare Adams sent to the Senate the name of his forty-five-year-old Secretary of State, John Marshall, Virginia lawyer and Thomas Jefferson's distant cousin and avowed political enemy to whom Jefferson liked to refer as "that gloomy malignity." [8]

The Senate, although still Federalist, was not pleased with its fellow partisan's nomination. Most of its leaders would have preferred Paterson, despite his link with the party's Hamiltonian wing. Indeed there is considerable evidence that they stalled for at least a week in the hope that Adams could be persuaded to substitute Paterson after all. But Adams, now a lame duck and no longer subject to the kind of political strictures that might otherwise have caused him to waiver, remained firm. The Senate, recognizing Marshall's ability and the danger of a low-ranking "spite" nomination should it reject Marshall (or the danger of leaving the vacancy for the eager incoming Jeffersonians) yielded and voted confirmation on January 27, 1801. No Federalist could possibly have had any cause for regret: Marshall's record on the Court proved to be blue-ribbon Federalism in every respect. Moreover, he would serve the Court and his country longer (thirty-four and a half years) than any other member of the Supreme Court except Mr. Justice Stephen J. Field (1863–97) and Mr. Justice William O. Douglas (1939–), and he did so with an excellence and a distinction that deserves to be categorized as *sui generis*. In 1826 Adams could proudly and justly say: "My gift of John Marshall to the people of the United States was the proudest act of my life. There is no act of my life on which I reflect with more pleasure. I have given to my country a Judge equal to a Hale, a Holt, or a Mansfield." [9]

In John Jay's view the young Supreme Court was an "inauspicious" body, characterized by little work, dissatisfied personnel, and a lack of popular esteem and understanding. Jay so thoroughly disliked his job as first Chief Justice that he not only spent one year of his brief tenure (less than four) in England on a diplomatic mission, but he twice ran for Governor of New York. On the second try he won the Governorship and happily resigned the Court; he later (1800) declined to succeed Oliver Ellsworth as Chief Justice. Ellsworth too had few regrets as he left his post for a diplomatic mission in France. Marshall's helmsmanship brought about a change in the Court's posture and position that was as far-reaching as it was dramatic. Completely dominating his Court —what few dissents there were came almost solely from William Johnson, a Jefferson appointee—Marshall delivered the opinion for the Court in 519 out of a total of 1215 cases between 1801 and 1835, and he wrote 36 of the 62 decisions involving constitutional questions.[10] It is simply beyond dispute that he, more than any other individual in the history of the Court, determined the character of America's federal constitutional system. It was Marshall who raised the Court from its lowly if not discredited position to a level of equality with the Executive and the Legislative branches —perhaps even to one of dominance during the heyday of his Chief Justiceship.

John Marshall called his constitutional interpretations as he saw them, always adhering to the following creed: ". . . It is a constitution we are expounding . . . intended to endure for ages to come and, consequently to be adapted to the various crises of human affairs." [11] Yet he hastened to add that "judicial power, as contradistinguished from the power of law, has no existence. Courts are the mere instruments of the law, and can will nothing." [12]

Thus "willing nothing," Marshall handed down four of the most momentous decisions in the nation's history: (1) *Marbury* v. *Madison* (1803) [13]—judicial review, supremacy of the United States Constitution; (2) *McCulloch* v. *Maryland* (1819) [14]—implied powers of Congress, reaffirmation of the supremacy of the Constitution, federal immunity from involuntary state taxation, federal government held to derive its power directly from the people rather than from the states; (3) *Dartmouth College* v. *Woodward* (1819) [15]—inviolability of contracts; and (4) *Gibbons* v. *Ogden* (1824) [16]—plenary federal authority over interstate and foreign commerce. In Mr. Justice Cardozo's words: "Marshall gave to the constitution of the United States the impress of his own mind; and the form of our constitutional law is what it is, because he moulded it while it was still plastic and malleable in the fire of his own intense convictions." [17] Truly the Marshall Court led the federal government and gave it the means to develop and work. Under Marshall's guidance the Federalist dreams of a powerful nation found articulation and sanction. The Federalists gave way to the Republican-Democrats at the century's turn, but the broad outlines of the Federalist philosophy were secure. The many years of Jeffersonianism, whatever its success at the non-judicial policy-making level proved to be, did not reverse the Federalist doctrines of the Marshall Court. Indeed the six men appointed by Jefferson, Madison, and Monroe—all loyal Republican-Democrats—entered nary a dissent to the key Federalist rulings of Marshall's Court.

Yet Jefferson's arrival on the canvas of government and politics represented a major departure from the *Weltanschauung* of the Administrations of his predecessors. Not entirely comfortable as Chief Executive, the stately Virginian was above all a great leader of the legislature, a superb Congressional party chief and party organizer. He would have been an ideal British Prime Minister, then as well as now. Jefferson has been rated as "great" by the experts, yet the man himself had doubts about his accomplishments in that office, and he did not wish to see his Presidency memorialized on his gravestone in the cemetery at Monticello. "And not a word more," read his instructions asking that the following accomplishments be chiseled into the stone: "Here was buried Thomas Jefferson, Author of the Declaration of American Independence, Of the Statute of Virginia for Religious Freedom, and the Father of the University of Virginia." Jefferson's first opportunity to appoint a Supreme Court Justice came in 1804 when Associate Justice Alfred Moore resigned—after barely five years on the bench—because of ill health. The President, eager to designate only solid Republican-Democrats, made it clear that any candidate would have to meet at least two criteria: loyalty to the Jeffersonian cause and "appropriate geographical provenance." There was no question about the first; only true-blue Republican-Democrats were considered. As for the second, since both the Second and Sixth circuits were not "represented" on the Court, the nominee had to come from New York, South Carolina, or Georgia. There was no dearth of worthy candidates and Jefferson looked to several highly qualified and faithful-to-the-cause South Carolina attorneys. His choice devolved upon a young lawyer, thirty-two-year-old William Johnson, who had already been a judge of the South Carolina Supreme Court. Johnson was the only Republican-Democratic member of the Court to stand up against Marshall on occasion. He also stood up against Jefferson, thus demonstrating early the spirit of independence that has so often characterized members of the Supreme Court.

On Mr. Justice Paterson's death in 1806, President Jefferson's second appointment went to forty-nine-year-old Henry Brockholst Livingston of New York. He had been very much in the running at the time of Johnson's appointment; Jefferson had long been attracted by Livingston's consistent loyalty to Republicanism, his proved legal scholarship, and his effective public needling of the Federalists. Moreover, along with Aaron Burr, George Clinton, and his cousins Edward and Robert R. Livingston, Henry Livingston was a part of the New York political faction that had joined Jefferson's supporters from Virginia to form the "Virginia-New York Alliance" so important in Jefferson's election. Not quite in Johnson's class as a jurisprudential figure, Livingston nonetheless would prove himself to be an able, thoughtful, delightfully humorous, and learned member of the Court during his seventeen years there.

Jefferson would have had to content himself with two appointments only, had not Congress created a seventh seat on the Supreme Court in 1807. The mounting population and resultant escalating judicial business in Kentucky, Ohio, and Tennessee dictated the creation of the additional post and the new Seventh Circuit. Ever conscious of the need to mend political fences, Jefferson now adopted the unique strategy of officially requesting each member of Congress to suggest to him two individuals for the vacancy, indicating first and second choices. Delighted to be thus involved, Congress caucused repeatedly, debating the relative merits of three men: John Boyle and James Hughes, both of Kentucky, and U.S. Representative George W. Campbell of Tennessee, ultimately asking Jefferson to designate Mr. Campbell. But the President demurred—he had serious doubts, and appropriately so, as to the constitutionality of appointing a sitting member of the Legislative Branch to an office created during his incumbency, and he was also less than enthusiastic about Campbell's expertise as a lawyer. But still wishing to abide by his determination to select someone entirely congenial to Congress, he chose Thomas Todd of Kentucky who, alone among the names advanced by Congress, was listed as either the first or the second choice of every one of the ten members of Congress from the three states of the new circuit.

Todd—who was forty-one years old and serving as Chief Justice of the Court of Appeals of Kentucky at the time of his appointment—established but a modestly distinguished record on the Court, writing only a few opinions. The choice of Todd was in considerable measure a testimonial to the importance Jefferson attached to the geographic suitability of a Supreme Court nominee. His three appointees came from different circuits, each circuit having a valid claim to "representation" in Jefferson's eyes.

Jefferson was also greatly concerned with his candidates' record of public service, preferably judicial service. Lawyer Johnson lacked judicial experience, but he had seen legislative service capped by the Speakership of the House of Representatives of South Carolina; Livingston had served three times in the New York State Assembly and was a hard-working member of the New York Supreme Court; and Todd had served both as a member and as Chief Justice of the Kentucky Court of Appeals.

Jefferson's fervent hope that his three appointments would serve to break the Marshallian-Federalist stranglehold on the course of Supreme Court decisions was not realized, although Johnson—a concerned humanitarian—provided a measure of success for him. Johnson, along with Story and Marshall the only outstanding Justices until the Taney Court period (Taney succeeded Marshall in 1836 and served until 1864), displayed considerable intellectual independence while on the Court and, disdaining Marshall's bossy displeasure, insisted on writing a good number of separate opinions. Yet the major thrust of his jurisprudence was the enhancement of national power particularly in foreign and interstate commerce and in treaty matters. Livingston and Todd, despite a joint total of almost four decades on the bench, went along with Marshall with all but complete docility. Todd, for one, during whose career 644 cases were decided by the Court, wrote exactly fourteen opinions. His sole dissent was his first written opinion as a Justice—a five-line comment penned in the 1810 term.[18] No wonder that Jefferson, now back in Monticello and establishing his beloved University of Virginia, would in 1820 refer to the Court (on which then still served all of his three appointees) as "a subtle corps of sappers and miners" consisting of "a crafty chief judge" and "lazy or timid associates." [19]

James Madison, who succeeded Jefferson to the Presidency in 1809, did not find the office congenial. The "Father of the Constitution," a first-rate statesman and diplomat, and a superb intellect, Madison neither liked the political process nor was he adept in it. He proved the maxim that great statesmen are by no means great —or even good—politicians. He was essentially uncomfortable in the Presidency and proved to be indecisive and inept in the very area he had been deemed an expert: foreign affairs. Moreover, he failed where Jefferson had been so strong: in his relationship with and ability to manage Congress. But he did give the country Joseph Story—second only to Marshall in influence and power and one of the truly great Justices of the Supreme Court.

It was midway in Madison's first term that two vacancies occurred on the Supreme Court. The last two surviving Washington appointees, Justices William Cushing and Samuel Chase, had died in the fall of 1810 and mid-1811, respectively. Jefferson's party looked forward to their replacements with great expectations, for here was the first chance to turn the Federalist majority on the bench into a minority. All knowing eyes were on the President, who was bombarded with advice from many Republican-Democratic quarters—most notably from Jefferson. Publicly espousing the two cardinal Jeffersonian criteria of party loyalty and geography, Madison began his search soon after Cushing's death, but it would not end until November 1811. To fill Cushing's seat, Madison first turned to Jefferson's able Attorney General, Levi Lincoln of Massachusetts, whose dedication to Republicanism was beyond question and for whom Jefferson strongly lobbied. Madison warned that the candidate might well decline for reasons of age or health—he was sixty-two and plagued by very poor eyesight—but Jefferson continued to press for the nomination, and in October 1810 the President asked Lincoln to accept it. Late in November Lincoln responded negatively, yet Madison chose to disregard the refusal and formally nominated him on January 2, 1811. The Senate confirmed him on the following day and sent his commission to him forthwith. But Lincoln, now facing blindness, felt he had to persist in his decision—much as he would have relished becoming a thorn in Marshall's side.

Madison waited a month, then nominated another proved and prominent New England Republican-Democrat leader, Alexander Wolcott of Connecticut, an attorney of little distinction who had long served as United States Collector of Customs, making himself obnoxious to the Federalists through what they regarded as his extreme partisanship both in and out of office. As mentioned earlier, the Senate rejected him decisively 9:24. Within ten days the President had selected another candidate—another Republican-Democrat, but one who had begun to show a measure of political independence—his Minister to Russia, John Quincy Adams. Adams was then eminently acceptable to both political parties, and the Senate confirmed him unanimously as soon as the nomination reached it. But to Madison's consternation, Adams declined the appointment, pleading insufficient legal acumen and too much political ambition. Madison now resolved to sit back and wait—it was not until seven months later, in mid-November 1811, that he sent to the Senate the controversial name of Joseph Story of Massachusetts, passing over Jefferson's hard-pushed candidacy of his former Postmaster General, Gideon Granger of Connecticut.

What finally prompted the President's selection of Story is unclear, although Story's uncle, Isaac Story, was a long-time friend of Madison's. What is clear is that Jefferson and almost the entire

Republican-Democratic leadership opposed the thirty-two-year-old legal whiz, a personal friend of John Marshall who had given every indication of leaning toward Federalism. He also had refused to support Jefferson's controversial Embargo Act of 1807. All this bothered Madison considerably less than Jefferson— indeed the President was much more inclined to look sympathetically at some aspects of Federalist policy than was Jefferson, although Jefferson himself was a pronouncedly more adamant anti-Federalist out of office than he was in office. It is often easier to be a dogmatic critic than a dogmatic fashioner of policy. Story's nomination sent Jefferson into a rage. He pronounced him a "pseudo-Republican," a "political chameleon," an "independent political schemer." [20] Jefferson particularly feared Story's admiration for the Chief Justice personally and for his propertarian views. Later he would see some of his worst fears confirmed.

The Senate was not especially enchanted with the Story nomination either, yet its members were ready to end the impasse which had caused the vacancy of one Supreme Court seat for more than a year and another for several months. The country too had tired of what looked like an appointment charade, and there was general relief when the Senate quickly and without a record roll call confirmed the controversial young New Englander on November 18, 1811, three days after Madison had sent his name over.

Story's nomination was to be one of the most fortuitous appointments in the history of the country. Both in terms of intellectual leadership and jurisprudential commitment, he proved himself to be an outstanding Justice. Standing with Marshall for almost a quarter of a century and continuing for another decade after Marshall's death until his own in 1845, Story was perhaps even more determined than Marshall to further the national posture in the face of mounting storm signals to the Union. To be sure Story was neither a democrat nor a confirmed majoritarian and thus proved to be the intellectual antithesis of the Republican-Democratic creed. Yet the role this great common-law jurist played in the stabilization of the Republic and in its growth and security was second only to Marshall's. He left lasting monuments to constitutionalism, nationalism, and legal scholarship with his famed lectures at the Harvard School of Law; his co-sponsorship with Chancellor James Kent of New York of the American equity system; his work on copyrights and patents; his elucidation of property, trust, partnership, insurance, commercial, and maritime law. His *Commentaries on the Constitution,* published in 1833, remains an indispensable work in the study of constitutional law and history.

On the same day the Senate confirmed Joseph Story it also approved the nomination of fifty-eight-year-old Gabriel Duval of Maryland, a faithful Republican-Democrat, to fill the vacancy caused by the death of his fellow Marylander Samuel Chase. Of less stature and surrounded by infinitely less controversy than Story, Duval nontheless proved to be a competent if unexciting jurist, fulfilling Madison's expectations both on grounds of political compatibility and legal acumen. He had served with distinction on his state's highest court for six years, and in 1802 had become Comptroller of the Treasury in the Jefferson and, subsequently, Madison administrations. Looking every inch the legendary jurist, he spent almost twenty-five workmanlike, quiet years on the bench, resigning at eighty-two, almost totally deaf.

During the six remaining years of his Presidency, Madison had no further opportunities to make a Supreme Court appointment. It was the longest "no vacancy" stretch in the history of the Court; in fact no vacancy arose until 1823, when Mr. Justice Livingston died after seventeen years of service—enabling James Monroe to make his one and only appointment. Monroe, a President of above-average ability and performance, encountered difficulties with Congress similar to those encountered by his friend and colleague Madison. But he was a better administrator, and he knew how to pick excellent associates, especially in the foreign-policy field. Monroe was a good Republican-Democrat but he was even less committed to party doctrine than was Madison, and it was widely doubted that he would be more than casually concerned with a nominee's party loyalty. Yet when his opportunity to select a nominee came at last in 1823, he turned to someone with whom he felt comfortable both politically and personally, Smith Thompson, his fifty-five-year-old Secretary of the Navy. Fortuitously, Thompson also hailed from New York, the deceased Livingston's circuit. Moreover, he met the other criteria Monroe had determined upon for any Supreme Court nominee: personal integrity, judicial or other high public-service experience, and active party service.

Monroe deliberated a while before nominating Thompson— there were other attractive names to consider. Among these was Senator Martin Van Buren of New York, a loyal Republican-Democrat with excellent professional and political credentials and considerable bipartisan support, including that of Secretary of State Adams. Two others were the prominent New York State jurists Ambrose Spencer and James Kent. The latter, widely regarded as second in ability only to the great Marshall, was an avowed Federalist, but one known as a champion of states' rights because of his stance in a series of decisions culminating in the famed Steamboat Monopoly Case of *Gibbons* v. *Ogden* (1824),[21] which would spell out the federal government's plenary power over interstate commerce. Yet the President neither trusted Van Buren's political ambitions nor did he regard Spencer or Kent sufficiently reliable politically. Thompson was the President's choice because he met his criteria and because he liked, respected, and admired him. Thompson had had an extensive career in public service: as a member of the New York Constitutional Convention of 1801; as a New York State legislator; and as an Associate Justice (twelve years) and then Chief Justice (four years) of the New York State Supreme Court. He had studied law under James Kent, whose law practice he had taken over, and he was widely regarded as an excellent legal technician.

After hesitating a while, Thompson accepted the Court nomination in December 1823 and was quickly confirmed by a generally admiring Senate. His twenty years on the high tribunal constituted a diligent and unspectacular but above-average performance. Thompson occasionally stood up to Marshall determinedly, especially during the last seven or eight years of his tenure but, like practically all who served under the great Chief Justice, more

often than not he succumbed to his spell, notwithstanding generic
political differences.

In 1824 John Quincy Adams became President as a result of a
bitterly contested four-way race between himself, William H.
Crawford, General Andrew Jackson, and Henry Clay—all nationalist Republicans. When no one attained the necessary majority of
the electoral college vote (Jackson had received the highest number of electoral votes, 99, and Adams, 84), the election was
thrown into the House of Representatives. There, on the first ballot taken in January 1825, Adams won by a margin of one state
with three decisive states' votes allegedly delivered by Clay—who
had come in fourth—in return for Adams's promise to appoint
him as Secretary of State. (He did.) It proved to be a Pyrrhic victory, for Adams's tenure as President was essentially frustrating
and unfulfilled—notwithstanding his "high average" ranking by
the Presidential historians. The distinguished public servant of
three decades who had been such a brilliant diplomat and courageous legislator—and who would again serve his country as a
member of the House of Representatives after his Presidency—
had little taste for day-to-day Presidential politics. Moreover, he
faced a divided party and a divided legislature and proved himself
incapable of effective party leadership, which inescapably influenced the decision-making processes.

John Quincy Adams had two chances to make Supreme Court
appointments and he succeeded in but one of these. To fill the vacancy created by Mr. Justice Thomas Todd's death in February
1826, Adams nominated Todd's fellow Kentuckian, Robert Trimble, then U.S. District Court Judge for Kentucky (the first Supreme Court appointee with previous federal judicial experience).
Indeed, before his death, Todd had indicated to his colleagues his
devout hope that Trimble, his long-time friend and ex-associate,
would be chosen to succeed him. Although Judge Trimble had an
accurate reputation for furthering the cause of Federalism and was
widely viewed as an ideological Marshallian—having frequently
opted for upholding federal over states' rights—Adams was confident that Trimble's Republican political label would facilitate his

confirmation. The President himself regarded Trimble as amply meeting the criteria he believed to be of significance for elevation to the Court: the "right" geographical background; appropriate judicial experience; a scholarly background in constitutional law; and real politics acceptable to both major political camps in the Senate. Adams's prognosis proved correct, but Trimble's confirmation by a vote of 27:5 did not come until after a month-long acrimonious struggle. He had incurred the displeasure of a number of Senators—including that of John Rowan of his own home state of Kentucky—because of his repeated and articulate insistence on the supremacy of federal over state power while he served on the lower federal bench.

Yet death came to the new Justice barely two years after his confirmation. In line with his criteria for nominees, Adams first offered the post to Charles Hammond, neighboring Ohio's most distinguished lawyer (Ohio, Kentucky, and Tennessee being in the same judicial circuit). Hammond declined the honor, preferring to remain in private practice. The President next turned to his ally of 1824, the colorful Henry Clay of Kentucky who also declined, still having bigger stakes in mind. But Clay, supported by Mr. Chief Justice Marshall, recommended that Adams nominate another able lawyer, a well-known Whig statesman, former Senator John J. Crittenden of Kentucky. Adams, now a lame-duck President, sent Crittenden's name to the Senate late in December 1828. Yet, victorious Andrew Jackson's Democratic supporters in the Senate were not about to award the Supreme Court plum to a Clay Whig, and by a vote of 23:17 "postponed" the nomination in February 1929, thus consigning it to oblivion. It was the end of an era. Within less than a month Jackson would assume the reins of office, and his influence upon the Court and its personnel would prove to be second only to Washington's in its impact upon the young nation's history.

5

The Next Forty Years:
From Andrew Jackson to Andrew Johnson
(1829 - 1869)

Andrew Jackson and his disciples were destined to dominate the political system of the United States until the onset of the Civil War and the accession of Abraham Lincoln. Whatever one's views of Jackson's theory and practice of egalitarianism, "Old Hickory" was unquestionably a great popular hero, a superb leader, and a stunning political practitioner. Pragmatic and assertive, he was not averse to challenging even John Marshall's citadel to the point of outright defiance, as he did in a celebrated Georgia missionary case. In *Worcester* v. *Georgia* (1832),[1] Marshall upheld the landed rights of the Cherokee Indians against sundry hanky-panky by the state of Georgia and certain of its citizens by ruling that the jurisdiction of the federal government in Cherokee Territory was exclusive. Georgia's reaction was predictably hostile, as was that of states' rights champion Jackson, who allegedly said: "Well, John Marshall has made his decision, now let him enforce it." [2] Jackson probably did not make that statement, but he did not stop Georgia from defying the Court's decision. His attitude toward the controversy made it clear that he would not hesitate to take on the Court if he thought that its actions violated the constitutionality of legislation. On the other hand, he stopped short of claiming an inherent prerogative to defy or disregard judicial decisions. Jackson wished to make clear that he was dedicated to co-equality. In his veto message of the proposed re-chartering of the Bank of the United States in 1832 he wrote: "The authority of the Supreme Court must not . . . be permitted to control the Congress or the Executive when acting in their *legislative* capacities but to have only such influence as the force of their reasoning may deserve." [3] Yet "his" Court (he succeeded in making six appointments) would by no means be universally submissive to the attempts that Jackson and his successors made to keep it in line. Indeed, the Taney Court—however pleasing the course of its decisions would be to the Democrats—was hardly a supine Presidential instrument. Roger Brooke Taney, a faithful friend and political ally of Jackson's, was the President's choice to succeed John Marshall. Under Taney's assertive, sophisticated leadership the Court maintained its base of power and, while it unquestionably became states' rights and anti-corporation in orientation, it continued to nurture and secure the Marshall creed of judicial sovereignty—the now well-established role of the Court as the final arbiter of constitutional questions. It is a pity that the Taney Court has not only been widely misunderstood but even maligned. It is simply too facile an excuse to use the Dred Scott decision of 1857,[4] which came in the waning years of Taney's Chief Justiceship, as a basis for that misunderstanding.

President Jackson's criteria for Supreme Court candidacy represented at least some departure from those of his six predecessors —if for no other reason than he made them less explicit. Yet he held to the traditional considerations of geography, public service, and political loyalty, making it clear that political loyalty would have primacy in his decisions. He was determined to reward the party faithful, and if that meant extending his much-vaunted "spoils system" to include nominees to the highest judicial body in the land, so be it. Ironically, Jackson's first selection, Postmaster General John McLean, was hardly a party faithful; yet the appointment was clearly intended to serve political purposes.

The Senate's deliberate refusal to approve John Quincy Adams's nomination of John J. Crittenden to replace Mr. Justice

Trimble presented Jackson with a Supreme Court vacancy at the very outset of his Presidency. He was delighted to oblige, but his choice of the forty-three-year-old McLean, a native of Ohio and one-time judge of the Ohio Supreme Court (from the same judicial circuit as Trimble), was dictated by the contemporary partisan politics concerning personalities as well as the range and degree of federal authority that reflected the intra-party struggle among the Democrats. An ambitious aspirant to high office, McLean had been Postmaster General since the days of the Monroe Administration. He had given the impression of being friendly to both the Adams and Jackson forces during the election of 1828, cultivating many prominent Jacksonians without unduly antagonizing the Adams wing. Jackson, who had kept McLean on in his former post, did not really trust him; indeed, he felt actively threatened by McLean's foot-dragging in patronage matters, especially when the latter resisted his requests to replace Adams supporters with Jackson loyalists in the postal service. Yet Jackson also realized that McLean was immensely popular in the West and he feared the consequences of a public clash so early in his incumbency. Thus when McLean promised not to pursue his political ambitions while a member of the Court, Jackson tendered him the nomination—although not without some misgivings. The Van Buren forces in the Administration were delighted to see the man they considered an adversary safely shelved, for McLean had been a member of the Calhoun faction in the government.

To no one's great astonishment, McLean did not hold to his promise.[5] While on the bench he became a Presidential candidate four times: in 1832 as an Anti-Mason; in 1836 as an Independent; in 1842 as both a Whig and a Free-Soiler; and in 1856 as a Republican (he had officially joined the Republican party). No doctrinaire he![6] But McLean served on the Court for thirty-two years, having remained there until his death in 1861—unpredictable and independent to the end.

There was no doubt whatever of the political loyalty of Jackson's next selection for the Court. When in 1829 Bushrod Washington died after thirty-two years of service, the President turned to Henry Baldwin, age fifty, a popular Pennsylvania Congressman. Long an aggressive and enthusiastic supporter, Baldwin had been instrumental in bringing Pennsylvania into the Jacksonian fold in the election of 1828. The President, alive to Baldwin's services, had rewarded him immediately after the election with the Cabinet post of Secretary of the Treasury. But that nomination was blocked in the Senate by Vice-President John Calhoun chiefly because of Baldwin's avowed championship of a high-tariff policy that was anathema to Calhoun and his supporters. The Calhoun forces then attempted to scuttle Baldwin's nomination to the Court, but they succeeded only in delaying it for two days. On January 6, 1830, the Senate approved him by a vote of 41:2, the sole dissenters being the two Senators from South Carolina, Robert Y. Hayne and William Smith. By choosing a Pennsylvanian rather than a Virginian, Jackson in a sense "atoned" for John Adams's selection of a Virginian (Washington) for the seat held by a Pennsylvanian (Wilson) in 1798—although that was not a major consideration in the selection. Loyalist that he was, Baldwin too would vote "wrong" on the Court on a number of crucial issues championed by Jackson. He even committed the unpardonable sin of siding with the "pro-Bank" forces during Jackson's great struggle over rechartering the Bank of the United States. Still, Baldwin's "deviations" during his fourteen years on the Court were minor in the eyes of the Jacksonian Democrats in comparison to those of McLean and Jackson's next nominee, James M. Wayne.

After Baldwin's appointment in 1830, the Supreme Court's membership remained stable for five years—a relatively long period in view of the vagaries of age and health. During that time Jackson reorganized his Cabinet and began his assault on the Bank of the United States. Presumably party policy had now been clarified and, although Jackson could not eliminate all party factions, he had a firm grip on the majoritarian direction of his Democratic party. His remaining choices for the Court reflected even more of a commitment to party principles than did his first two selections. Nominees James M. Wayne, Roger B. Taney, Philip P.

Barbour, and John Catron had all evinced a close adherence to the Jacksonian creed and had rendered many services to the President. James Moore Wayne, forty-five, former Judge of the Supreme Court of Georgia, was one of those rare Southerners who was also a Unionist. In appointing Wayne to the seat of the recently deceased William Johnson of South Carolina, Jackson not only kept that judicial circuit's "representation" intact but placated the Whigs, who had feared the designation of an avowed states' righter from the South. Wayne was confirmed enthusiastically within two days and Jackson found himself widely praised for a "statesmanlike" appointment, notwithstanding Wayne's loyalist Democratic history. To Jackson's later dismay, Wayne would in a significant number of cases side with the nationalist rather than the states' rights side in decisions involving the interpretation of federal and judicial power.[7]

Within a matter of days after Wayne had taken his seat on the Court, the octogenarian Mr. Justice Gabriel Duval of Maryland resigned. The worst apprehensions of the Whigs and Calhounians were promptly confirmed when President Jackson nominated his close friend and loyal adviser and supporter, Roger Brooke Taney, to the seat. Taney, now fifty-eight, had succeessfully navigated the political shoals from the localism of Maryland politics to national prominence, having served as Chairman of the Jackson Central Committee of Maryland in 1828, as Jackson's Attorney General and, on a recess appointment, as Secretary of the Treasury after the Cabinet reorganization of 1832. It was in the latter post that Taney had incurred the undying enmity of the Whig-Calhounian political axis: he had fully approved of and complied with Jackson's order that all Government deposits be removed from the Bank of the United States—the major controversy of the time. The enraged opposition struck back at Jackson and Taney by rejecting the latter's formal appointment as Secretary of the Treasury, thus forcing him to resign. Jackson vowed revenge, and in a letter to Taney that left little doubt that his political opponents had not heard the last of the matter he wrote: "For the prompt and disinterested aid thus afforded me, at the risk of personal sacrifice which were then probable and which has now been realized, I feel that I owe you a debt of gratitude and regard which I have not the power to discharge. . . ." [8] Duval's resignation gave Jackson his first opportunity to discharge that debt of gratitude. The Senate thwarted him by "postponing" the nomination on the last day of its session—but not before it had voted to do away with the vacant seat entirely, a maneuver that failed of enactment, however, in the House of Representatives.

Enraged, Jackson refused to make another nomination and resolved to try Taney again. Fate played into his hands. On July 6, 1835, after almost thirty-five years on the bench, Mr. Chief Justice John Marshall died in Philadelphia. Jackson now had two vacancies to fill. That one of them would go to Taney was a foregone conclusion. But the President bided his time; he appeared to be considering a host of candidates for both the Associate and the Chief Justice vacancies. All attention focused on his choice for Chief Justice, of course. A strong possibility was the brilliant Justice James Story, but Jackson was not about to promote the man whose record out-Marshalled Marshall. There was wide advocacy of Daniel Webster, but he too personified the old Federalist team. A good many urged the promotion of John McLean, but he had already incurred the displeasure of the President and most Democrats by his iconoclastic behavior on the Court. Jackson kept his counsel until the end of December and then proposed Roger Brooke Taney of Maryland to succeed John Marshall of Virginia and Philip P. Barbour of Virginia to succeed Gabriel Duval of Maryland. Even-Steven geographically—and, "Senate of the United States, here we go again," Jackson might well have chuckled.

Philip Barbour, fifty-three years old when nominated, had himself been rumored in line for the Marshall vacancy. A strong states' rights advocate of the Southern school, he had nonetheless been a loyal Jacksonian on most issues and a conciliating force in the parties. He had seen many years of public service in Congress and on Virginia and federal benches and was as well qualified as he was popular. Yet because it was tied to Taney's confirmation,

Senate approval of Barbour's appointment did not come until
March 15, 1836, by a vote of 30:11. Barbour died after less than
six years on the bench, but he had served diligently and in a manner pleasing to his nominator.

"Judge Story thinks the Supreme Court is *gone,* and I think so,
too," wrote Daniel Webster.[9] The remarkable Chief Justiceship of
Taney would prove both men wrong, indeed. But first Jackson's
favorite nominee would have to run the gauntlet of a hostile and
powerful group of Senators. For close to three months the battle
raged in the upper house, but when the vote finally came, it was
not nearly so close as the bitter debates had led the country to be
lieve. Taney won the nomination by a 14-vote margin, 29:15, opposed to the last by such powerful and influential Senate leaders as
Calhoun, Clay, and Webster, who later would come to respect the
superb performance of the man they had so ardently opposed.
Taney, whom history and the experts have justly accorded the
mark of greatness, was resolved to enhance the role of the states
as governmental and philosophical entities. But shrewd political
tactician and skillful leader that he was, Taney knew how to exercise judicial self-restraint. Not a devotee of overt manifestations of
power, he guided his Court along pathways of conciliation and
compromise virtually devoid of dogmatism and ploys. Thus, not
only were the Court's actions accepted by the majority of political
leaders of the time, but its position as the logical, ultimate, and
fair-minded arbiter of the Constitution was fully secured as well.
Far from assaulting the Marshall-built fortress of judicial power,
the Taney Court secured it and did so with all but general approbation.

Even the Dred Scott decision, monumental aberration though it
was, could not destroy the institution that Taney and Marshall had
fashioned. It is a pity that Taney is so often remembered by that
case rather than by his supreme accomplishments in achieving
governmental concord and constitutional understanding. For with
Dred Scott, the Court, in an attempt to stem the oncoming tide of
civil war, had in effect hastened the war. Ruling that no Negro
could be a citizen; that the Negro was a "person of an inferior

order"; that the Negro was a slave and thus his master's permanent property; that no Negro was a "portion of the American people"; and that the Missouri Compromise was unconstitutional, the decision has generally been regarded as the most disastrous ever handed down by the Supreme Court, "more than a crime . . . a blunder," [10] in the words of one observer not given to wild judgments. Its impact could not be lessened by Mr. Justice James M. Wayne's anxious explanation that "there had become such a difference of opinion that the peace and harmony of the country required the settlement of the slavery issues by judicial decision. . . . In our action we have only discharged our duty as a distinct and efficient department of the Government, as framers of the Constitution meant the judiciary to be. . . ." [11]

Nine opinions (seven in the majority and two in dissent) were written by the members of the court.

One of the opinions on the side of the majority was authored by Andrew Jackson's last appointee, * his fellow Tennessean Mr. Justice John Catron—who, abetted by Mr. Justice Grier, had informed President Buchanan of the thrust of the decision in advance, the only such breach of secrecy on record. Catron's nomination, which was very much in the nature of a repayment for faithful services rendered, had fallen to Jackson as the result of a last-minute law that increased the number of Associate Justices of the Court from six to eight, thus creating a nine-member body. The new positions were earmarked for two newly created circuits in the West and the Southwest. Catron, Jackson's choice for the Western circuit, gladly accepted and readily won Senate approval. A long-time friend of the President's, he had served with him in the War of 1812 and had been a strong ally in the struggle against the forces of nullification later. He was also a strong pro-judiciary figure, having had served as both Judge and Chief Justice of the Supreme Court of Tennessee, during which time his lucidly written opinions had created a favorable public climate on behalf of Jacksonian policies. Catron had been on Jackson's side in most of

---

* Appointed, in fact, on Jackson's last day in office.

the major political disputes during his Presidency—a factor
stressed heavily in a romantic journal allegedly written by Mrs.
Catron, who apparently traveled from Tennessee to Washington to
plead her husband's case with her friend "Andy" Jackson.

William Smith of Alabama was Jackson's choice for the other
new position on the Court. Smith at one time had been a United
States Senator from South Carolina and had cast one of the two
opposition votes against Jackson's nomination of Henry Baldwin
in 1830. But he was now a loyal Jacksonian, and the Senate confirmed him on March 8, 1837. He declined to serve, however,
frankly citing what he regarded as the position's inadequate pay.
Thus the seat remained vacant for incoming President Van Bur-
en's action.

Despite the fact that Jackson's criteria for appointments to the
Court were less visible and less precise than those of the early
Presidents, certain strands of policy were in evidence. Thus, in
each of his eight nominations the President followed the current
strictures of geography: he made a point of representing each circuit, as had his predecessors. Of his choices only Taney and Baldwin lacked judicial experience. Both men had records of long and
distinguished public service, but apparently Jackson was not over-
ridingly concerned with his candidates' record on that score. Political acceptability, on the other hand, was a major consideration.
In fine, Jackson had few equals as a politician.

Martin Van Buren, who had been Taney's colleague in Jackson's Cabinet, was a shrewd and effective political leader in his
own right. He succeeded to the Presidency largely as a result of
Jacksonian dictation. Jackson's Vice-President in his second
term, he had been Secretary of State in the first, and he was the
first Governor of a state (New York) to attain the White House.
Van Buren was thus superbly qualified for the Presidency—
though the charismatic Jackson's was a tough act to follow.
Shrewd, able, and poised, Van Buren might have received a much
higher rating as President had he not fallen heir to an economic
depression—the Panic of 1837. That depression plus his pronounced opposition to the annexation of Texas and his refusal to

give aid to the Canadian rebels, who in the fall of 1837 moved (unsuccessfully) to expel the British from North America, very likely cost him the re-election he deserved.

Van Buren inherited not only an enlarged Court but a practically new and relatively young one. His only two chances to appoint a Justice came almost literally on the first and last days of his Presidency, when William Smith (the Jackson appointee) refused to serve and when Mr. Justice Philip P. Barbour died.* For his first appointment Van Buren selected another Alabaman, Senator John McKinley, fifty-seven, an experienced lawyer who in addition to meeting the required geographic criterion had impeccable political credentials. Although only a recent convert to Jacksonian Democracy, McKinley had established a record of unflagging support of its cause. Thus, during the nullification battle, McKinley had been an eloquent and conspicuous supporter of the Union. Moreover, he was highly regarded by "Old Hickory" himself. These factors alone would have been more than adequate rationale for his nomination, but in addition McKinley had been one of Van Buren's key managers during the Presidential campaign of 1836 and was personally responsible for capturing Alabama's electoral votes. He would not disappoint his nominator during his fifteen years on the high bench.

In February 1841 Mr. Justice Barbour died after less than five years on the bench. For that vacancy the President's choice was Peter V. Daniel, fifty-six, another Jacksonian, and a Van Buren loyalist. At the time Daniel was serving as U.S. District Judge in Virginia, having succeeded his fellow Virginian Barbour in the post. Long an active and powerful member of the "Richmond Junto" (Virginia's ruling Democratic elite), he had served his state government as both a member of the lower house and as Lieutenant Governor. He had worked hard for Jackson in the abortive campaign of 1824 and in the ensuing campaigns as

---

* Some credit him also with the Catron appointment; Catron's name, however, was submitted by Jackson on the day he left office. Van Buren readily accepted the nomination, and the Senate confirmed it on the new President's fourth day in office.

well, and during the Bank and nullification controversies he had stood with and spoken for the President. When Martin Van Buren was nominated, Daniel had continued his effective organizational labors in Van Buren's behalf. Later Daniel became one of his most effective advisers and supporters, although he did refuse the President's tender of the Attorney Generalship. Theirs was a close philosophical-political affinity on the issues of the day: both disliked banks in general, and United States banks in particular; both favored states' rights, but not nullification; and both backed an agrarian conception of government. But before Daniel was confirmed by the Senate he and Van Buren had some anxious moments. The President had but a few remaining days in office (he had lost the 1840 election to Whig William Henry Harrison), and he rushed Daniel's name to the Senate even before there was time to bury Barbour. The victorious Whigs, who were not amused, launched a series of tactical maneuvers to prevent the nomination from reaching the Senate floor. But because of their defective strategy, absenteeism, and crossed signals, the Whigs were ultimately outmaneuvered by the Democrats, who managed a bare quorum with most of the Whigs absent and forced a vote that carried 22:5. Daniel's record on the Court amply justified Van Buren's faith in him: it proved to be as non-deviationist as McLean's was the opposite.

From 1841 to 1845 the country saw the first of what would be two Whig interludes in the Presidency. General William Henry Harrison, the hero of the Battle of Tippecanoe of 1811, rode into the White House at the advanced age of sixty-eight—still a record —on the strength of his personal popularity and his ability to avoid involvement in any controversy or to take a stand on any major issues. Harrison contracted pneumonia shortly after his inauguration (his two-hour-long address, also still a record, was delivered on a freezing day mixed with rain and snow) and died after thirty-one days in the Presidency. His successor, John Tyler, was a generally unhappy President who lacked a personal political base and political support and who was in constant conflict and competition with the powerful Henry Clay and his followers.

Rated "below average" by the experts, he nonetheless performed the significant service of proclaiming himself "President" rather than "Acting President," a manifestation of the meaning of Presidential succession that has stood the test of time.

But also standing the test of time is Tyler's record of five Supreme Court nominations rejected—more than any other President in the history of the Court. During the last thirteen months of his incumbency, Justices Smith Thompson and Henry Baldwin died, and in attempting to fill their seats Tyler made a total of six nominations. Tyler's first nominee for the Thompson (New York) seat was a New York lawyer, John C. Spencer, a Whig who had held two Cabinet posts in the Tyler Administration. But he was an avowed political enemy of Henry Clay and his followers, and it was with more ease than the rejection vote of 21:26 indicates that the Clay faction succeeded in blocking Spencer. Next Tyler selected an able lawyer though again a potentially controversial nominee: Chancellor Reuben H. Walworth of New York, whom the Senate Whigs cordially disliked. Before the Senate could act, Mr. Justice Baldwin died, leaving the second seat vacant. To Baldwin's Pennsylvania seat Tyler resolved to nominate James Buchanan, also of the Keystone State. When Buchanan declined the honor, Tyler chose a distinguished Philadelphia lawyer and legal scholar, Judge Edward King. It was now June, and the Whig Senators, thinking they had victory in their grasp in the forthcoming Presidential election, moved to "postpone" both the Walworth and King nominations by votes of 20:27 and 18:29, respectively. The angry and frustrated Tyler in turn re-nominated King in December, but the Senate would not act, and the President withdrew both nominations in January 1845.

He was not through, however, especially after Jackson Democrat James K. Polk defeated the Clay Whigs in the Presidential race of 1844. Having pretty well broken with the Whigs, Tyler now selected Samuel Nelson, fifty-two, an able and dignified lawyer and long-time Justice and Chief Justice of the Supreme Court of New York who had been an elector for President Monroe in 1820. A clear writer and incisive scholar, his forte was commercial law, one of the most litigated areas of the law of the times. This time Tyler hit paydirt: within ten days, and with only scattered Whig opposition, Nelson won confirmation to the seat that had been vacant for fourteen months. By no means outstanding on the Court, he would nonetheless serve diligently and perceptively for almost three decades—generally in a manner anticipated by and pleasing to the Jacksonians.

Tyler had still one more chance: the Baldwin seat remained unfilled, given a series of Senate "postponements." He nominated a well-known Philadelphia lawyer with supporters in both the Whig and Democratic camps, a one-time United States Attorney of proved legal acumen and political deftness, John Meredith Read. But it was now mid-February, and a weary Senate adjourned without acting on the nomination—thus handing Tyler his fifth failure. It was widely expected that the incoming President Polk would have more luck.

James Knox Polk, the underdog victor in 1844 over the aging but still powerful Henry Clay, is best remembered for his aggressive pursuit of America's Manifest Destiny to extend westward to the Pacific and southward to the Rio Grande, if not farther. His successes in that ambitious endeavor—the acquisition of California, the conquest of Oregon, and the securing of Texas—found wide-ranging support in the country. Forceful and a fine administrator and legislative leader, Polk was given to crafty and devious methods that frequently brought him major policy victories. Accordingly, history has been increasingly supportive of his over-all record and his achievements. Not surprisingly, the experts have ranked him in the "near great" category, eighth in the over-all standings.

Polk's Supreme Court nominees, however, were little more than mediocre. There were three: one was rejected, one lived but little more than five years after his appointment, and one served in routine fashion for a quarter of a century. Polk made his decisions based on now well-established criteria: demonstrated party loyalty, compatibility, and geographic suitability—although party loyalty was less important to him than it had been to his political lode-stars, Andrew Jackson and Martin Van Buren.

Polk made his first nomination after six months in office: he was in no particular hurry and domestic appointments took a back seat to foreign policy matters. To the still-vacant seat of the deceased Mr. Justice Baldwin he nominated James Buchanan—to whom Tyler had offered the job in 1844. This time Buchanan appeared to want the position but asked for time to give his final answer. After pondering the matter for a couple of months, the politically ambitious Buchanan again decided to reject the offer. In the interim Mr. Justice Story—second only to Marshall in distinction and accomplishments on the Court until that time—had announced his resignation at the end of the term of Court. Worn out and disillusioned by what he viewed as the declining quality and influence of his beloved tribunal, Story proposed to devote full time to his Harvard Law School Professorship; but in September 1845 he died, shortly before he was to leave the bench. He had served magnificently for almost thirty-four years. Thus Polk had another opportunity to nominate. At this point he decided to forget the jinxed Baldwin vacancy for a while and to concentrate on Story's slot.

The President's choice for Story's "New England" seat on the Court was fifty-six-year-old Levi Woodbury, U.S. Senator from New Hampshire. Woodbury, a solid Democrat but a conservative one highly acceptable to the Whigs, was an eminently qualified public servant who had served in all three branches of government: Legislative (as Senator), Executive (as Governor of New Hampshire, Secretary of the Navy under Jackson, and Secretary of the Treasury under Van Buren), and Judicial (as a judge on New Hampshire's Supreme Court). Few men had come before the Senate with such extensive credentials; and his confirmation was so taken for granted that Polk gave him a recess appointment in September, which was confirmed as soon as the Senate reconvened the following January. A long-time supporter of the governmental and jurisprudential commitments of Mr. Chief Justice Taney, Woodbury embraced Taney's conviction that rather than looking eternally to the British judicial system the legal profession in the United States should develop an "American" legal system. But only five and a half years later death cut short his promising career.

Meanwhile Polk still had the old Baldwin vacancy to fill! Since Secretary of State Buchanan would not take the position, the President turned to a jurist on the lower Pennsylvania bench, George W. Woodward. Although a member of a distinguished family and a proved Democrat, Woodward had acquired a reputation as an extreme "American nativist" and was staunchly opposed by several Democratic Senators, among them Simon Cameron of his home state. Cameron's resolute opposition and the negative votes of five other Democrats along with a solid "no" vote by the Whigs resulted in Woodward's rejection 20:29 late in January 1846. The exasperated Polk let six months go by, and then *again* asked James Buchanan to take the job. Flattered and never one to be unduly decisive, the latter accepted—only to turn it down for the third time two months later! Next the President selected Robert Cooper Grier of Pennsylvania, the fifty-two-year-old President Judge of the Allegheny County (Pittsburgh) District Court.

It was now August 1846, and Henry Baldwin had been in his grave for twenty-eight months. It was about time to fill his seat, and the Senate responded by confirming Grier in less than a day. It was not a difficult task for the upper house, for Grier was a conservative Democrat and a cautious constitutionalist who was generally acceptable to all factions of the party. His long service on the bench proved to be predictably low key, and his performance was average. He loved being on the Supreme Court and resigned only when (having become a mental and physical wreck) he yielded to the combination of liberalized retirement provisions for Justices and the repeated entreaties of his colleagues—who at one stage sent a delegation headed by Mr. Justice Steven J. Field to urge him to step down. Grier is probably best remembered for that episode and the ignoble role he played—with Justice Catron

—in informing President-elect Buchanan of the thrust of the Dred Scott decision in advance of the Court's public announcement.

Polk's successor, General Zachary Taylor, was the third Whig President. Taylor was firm, forthright, and honest, but this professional soldier was ill-qualified and ill-prepared for the political process. He lived only sixteen months after his inauguration in March 1849 and was the second of three Presidents to date who made no appointments to the Supreme Court. His successor, Vice-President Millard Fillmore (the last Whig President) worked hard and with considerable determination to preserve the endangered Union. He had but one chance to appoint a member of the Court, yet his choice was an excellent one: Benjamin R. Curtis. Three other attempts to fill a later vacancy were frustrated by the Senate.

Fillmore's initial opportunity came in the fall of 1851 when Mr. Justice Levi Woodbury died. The President gave much thought to a successor, for he was genuinely concerned about mounting attacks on the Court because of what abolitionists termed its "pro-Southern" stance in the slavery and fugitive slave issues. Accordingly he wanted to find a man who had not only strength of character and the potential for judicial presence but also an understanding of contemporary history and politics. Moreover, he specified that the nominee had to be a Whig, a comparatively young man, and a New Englander.

All these criteria he found in Benjamin Nathan Curtis of Massachusetts, who came not only highly recommended but enthusiastically backed by the still enormously influential Daniel Webster (although Webster's first choice had been Rufus Choate, who declined to be considered). A superb commercial lawyer—the *Massachusetts Law Quarterly* referred to the forty-one-year-old Curtis as "the *first* lawyer of America" [12]—Curtis was a follower of the legal philosophy of Marshall and Story. Yet he had never campaigned for Court membership, and while he was being considered for the position he continued to let his constitutional shots fall where they might, including support of the constitutionality of the hated and embattled Fugitive Slave Act of 1850. That he personally might have been opposed to the Act was not at issue: at issue was his posture in constitutional interpretation and application, a role that did not permit the intrusion of personal political, or result-oriented rulings. His belief that the majority of the Court had permitted political expediency to govern in the Dred Scott decision—for which he had written one of the two dissenting opinions—was one of the main factors that prompted him to resign after the decision had been rendered early in 1857. Mr. Justice Curtis, whose confirmation had been delayed by leading abolitionists in the Senate for the then-inordinately long period of more than two months, thus served barely six years on the Court. But he left a lasting mark, having displayed careful judgment and judicial independence. He did this not only in his dissent in the *Dred Scott Case,* but also in a series of crucial opinions dealing with the nature of the federal power over interstate and foreign commerce, of which the most significant was his pronouncement of a proper concurrent state power to legislate in the absence of federal action.[13] Fillmore could be proud indeed of his one appointment.

In the summer of 1852 Mr. Justice John McKinley died after fifteen colorless years on the bench—during which time, because of illness, he was as much absent as he was present. Fillmore attempted to fill the vacancy with dispatch not only because he was eager to see a full bench—one with additional Whig sympathizers —but because the Presidential election of 1852 did not look very promising either for his candidacy or for a Whig victory. He was a good prophet: neither was he selected (General Winfield Scott became the candidate) nor did his party win (the Democrats won under Franklin Pierce). Fillmore's first choice to succeed the late Alabaman was Edward A. Bradford of Louisiana, a well-known, able lawyer from the same circuit. The Senate, however, was about to adjourn, and it was in no mood to expedite a Fillmore nomination. When it reconvened after Pierce's victory, Fillmore named a U.S. Senator: George E. Badger of North Carolina. A conservative Whig who was not readily identifiable as either pro- or anti-slavery, Badger was nonetheless a clearly identifiable Whig who had served as Secretary of the Navy in the Harrison and

Tyler Cabinets. The Democratic majority in the Senate was not about to deprive the victorious incoming President of the choice of his own man, even though rejecting one of its own members would be little short of political sacrilege. Senator Badger, however, saw his nomination permanently "postponed" by one vote, 25:26. Finally, the lame duck Fillmore turned back to Louisiana and to another well-known lawyer, William C. Micou. Predictably, the Senate simply refused to act on Micou's nomination, and the McKinley seat remained vacant for the incoming Franklin Pierce to fill.

The only incumbent President to date to be resolutely denied a second crack at the Presidency by his own political party, Franklin Pierce—New Hampshire's one contribution to the Presidency —was a tragic figure both personally and politically. A man of mediocre talents at most, he did his best—which was simply not enough to fend off the approaching Civil War. He had the misfortune of presiding over the assault on the Missouri Compromise in favor of the ill-starred Kansas-Nebraska Act of 1854. Designed to apply the doctrine of "popular sovereignty" to questions of the extension of slavery to the territories, it was largely the creation of Pierce's potential rival, the powerful Senator Stephen A. Douglas of Illinois. Pierce's often pathetic efforts to "do right" by both North and South brought about more rather than less alienation; and his party leadership role was tenuous throughout his term. No wonder, then, that he is ranked close to the bottom of the scale among our Presidents.

But the sole Supreme Court appointment he made proved to be an excellent one: John Archibald Campbell of Alabama, whose name he sent to the Senate shortly after his inauguration in 1853. A highly visible, brilliant young lawyer, the forty-one-year-old Campbell was respected nation-wide as an expert in both civil and common law, and was noted for his uncanny ability as an advocate in trial courts. Although he had no judicial experience he had served two terms in the legislature of his state and twice had been tendered nominations (which he declined) to the Alabama Supreme Court. A strong advocate of states' rights and a "strict constructionist," Campbell nonetheless opposed secession and favored improving the lot of the slaves. He thus received support from practically all sides of the political spectrum. In what probably still stands as an unique action, the entire incumbent membership of the Court wrote to Pierce in behalf of Campbell and deputized Associate Justices Catron and Curtis to deliver the letters to the President personally.[14] It is thus understandable that Pierce did not seriously consider anyone else for the nomination and that the Senate confirmed Campbell promptly. Campbell served the Court nobly and promised a distinguished career but, in 1861—although personally opposed to secession and the war—he felt duty-bound to resign and join the Confederate cause.

Franklin Pierce was followed by Pennsylvania's James Buchanan, who had passed up several opportunities to serve on the Supreme Court in favor of pursuing the Presidency. At last attaining it in 1857 at the age of sixty-six, he was destined to be plagued by a divided, disloyal Cabinet and by a hostile, negative Congress that refused to act on any of his many desperate proposals designed to stem the tides of war. Unlike his activist successor Abraham Lincoln, Buchanan disdained a strong show of Presidential force: if Congress would not provide the tools of authority, he would not forge them himself. No wonder then that Buchanan—who is now ranked even below Pierce by the experts—would greet Lincoln on Inauguration Day in 1861 with these pathetic words: "My dear sir, if you are as happy in entering the White House as I shall feel on returning to Wheatland [his house in Lancaster, Pennsylvania], you are a happy man, indeed." [15]

Buchanan had two opportunities to make Supreme Court nominations, but he succeeded with only his first, Nathan Clifford of Maine, still the sole appointment from that state. The vacancy was caused by the dramatic resignation of Mr. Justice Benjamin R. Curtis of Massachusetts following the Dred Scott decision in 1857. Although what he regarded as inadequate remuneration also played a role in his withdrawal from the high bench, Curtis acted chiefly because he felt that the Court had become an instrument for personal and political aggrandizement and that under Chief Justice Taney it could not be expected to be restored to its former high station of judicial and public esteem. The country was startled and troubled by Curtis's resignation and anxiously looked to Buchanan for his replacement nomination. The President, after initially wavering on the geographic consideration, determined to remain within the First Circuit and considered a number of New Englanders. Yet he felt more comfortable personally and politically with Nathan Clifford, with whom he had served in President Polk's Cabinet when Clifford was Attorney General. Democrat Clifford, then fifty-four years old, was an able lawyer and legal scholar who had also been a distinguished representative in both the Maine and United States lower houses.

But his political posture was a complicated one—one that combined an apology, even a defense, of slavery with a record of firm support of Jacksonian egalitarianism. It was hardly astonishing that his nomination would run into bitter opposition from abolitionist and allied forces in the Senate, where a five-week-long battle ensued, marked by acrimonious debate. Only the closing of Democratic party ranks plus the absence of two of his most prominent Northern opponents, Senators Charles Sumner of Massachusetts and Simon Cameron of Pennsylvania, and a last-minute change of mind by Democratic Senator Philip Allen of Rhode Island, brought about Clifford's confirmation by a 3-vote margin: 26:23. Until he died twenty-three years later, Clifford served on the Court competently and diligently but without particular distinction.

President Buchanan's second chance to make a nomination came when Mr. Justice Peter V. Daniel died on May 30, 1860, after nineteen years on the Court. Although the jockeying for Presidential nominations was already in full swing and Buchanan wanted no part of another term, he still had a number of months in office and his Democratic colleagues looked to him for an acceptable appointment. Understandably the South wanted someone from its own region. Daniel was a Virginian, and the high tribunal was now evenly divided between four Southerners and four Northerners. Just as understandably the North sought to gain the balance of power over the pro-slavery forces on the Court. Characteristically Buchanan moved slowly. There is some evidence that Buchanan, still dreaming of maintaining peace, considered a number of moderate Southerners for the post, but he eventually decided against them. He then toyed with the idea of leaving the post vacant for his successor to fill, especially since the next term of Court would not commence until December 1860—after the election. At last he hit upon what he viewed as a viable compromise: he would send up a fellow Pennsylvanian, Jeremiah S. Black, a good Democrat acceptable to the South but not a Southerner, a strong Union man but not an abolitionist. Black, an able and knowledgeable lawyer, was well known in public circles: he had had extensive judicial and executive experience as Justice and Chief Justice of the Pennsylvania Supreme Court and as U.S. Attorney General; and at the time of his nomination he was Secretary of State. Buchanan's plan might well have worked at an earlier stage, but now it was too late: the date was February 5, 1861—less than a month before Lincoln's succession; the embittered loser to Lincoln in the 1860 Presidential campaign, Stephen A. Douglas, was opposed to Black; a good many Southern Senators had already left their seats as a result of secession; and the victorious Republicans certainly were not going to lend a helping hand to fill a vacancy that Mr. Lincoln would presumably be delighted to attend to shortly. Still the confirmation vote was close indeed—Black lost by only one vote, 25:26. Although he briefly considered submitting yet another candidate, Buchanan decided to stop. The path was clear for President Lincoln.

If earlier evaluations had often placed Abraham Lincoln second to George Washington in stature, historians now consistently accord him the top rank among his fellow Chief Executives. Lincoln, the personification and the symbol of the Union, more than any other person was responsible for its ultimate preservation; and in attaining that goal he demonstrated qualities of personal and political leadership that have become almost legend. He was not instinctively tough or heavy-handed, but he could be both when necessary: not even the letter of the Constitution was spared to the ideal of Union.

Lincoln had five chances to appoint Supreme Court Justices during little more than four years in office. He visualized the Court as a partner in the nation's preservation—not an easily realized vision, for the Court was at best a "toss-up" in terms of its stance on Lincoln's policies. The Court did, however, support the President in the crucial decisions dealing with his war-time policies, notwithstanding the battle between Lincoln and Chief Justice Taney concerning the constitutionality of the Presidential suspension of the writ of *habeas corpus*—so excitingly dramatized in the case of *Ex parte Merryman* in 1861.[16] John Merryman, a militant Maryland secessionist had been imprisoned by Union forces. Taney issued a writ of *habeas corpus,* which Merryman's custodian, General George Cadwalader, ignored in view of Lincoln's action. Taney, unsuccessful in bringing Cadwalader into Court, wrote a brilliant opinion rejecting Lincoln's asserted right and arguing for exclusive Congressional control over suspension. He sent a copy to the President who disdained the ruling, denying any illegal or unconstitutional action, but later ordered Merryman released and turned over to civilian authorities. (He was indicted for treason but the case against him was ultimately dropped.) The very inconclusiveness of that struggle enunciated the principled posture of the two protagonists. Just before his death in 1954 Mr. Justice Robert H. Jackson would comment: "Had Mr. Lincoln scrupulously observed the Taney policy, I do not know whether we would have had any liberty, and had the Chief Justice adopted Mr. Lincoln's philosophy as the philosophy of law, I again do not know whether we would have had any liberty." [17]

The Civil War dominated all aspects of Lincoln's Presidency. Clearly, then, the effect a proposed Court member might have on the conduct of the war was of paramount importance to him. All other considerations were secondary. Even so, he regarded as desirable and perhaps even essential geographic suitability, political loyalty, and payment of political debts. He assigned lesser importance to judicial background. Almost immediately on taking office

Lincoln had been presented with three vacancies on the Court: the still unfilled seat of the deceased Mr. Justice Daniel; that of Mr. Justice McLean, who had died in April 1861 after thirty-two years of service; and that of Mr. Justice Campbell, who had resigned that April to join the Confederacy. Yet the President's probably inexcusable delay in making any appointments for almost a year seriously imperiled the Court's ability to function effectively, especially since Mr. Justice Catron and Mr. Chief Justice Taney were ill for much of 1861. At this early stage of the war, however, Lincoln was determined to appoint to federal posts only those men whose views on slavery and the war were not suspect—men who would not alienate the Border states and the upper South, which Lincoln hoped to induce to return to the Union quickly.

Noah H. Swayne, an eminent fifty-seven-year-old Ohio lawyer, was Lincoln's first nominee and met all of the President's criteria. Swayne's anti-slavery convictions (he had freed his slaves and moved North from Virginia), his loyalty to the Union, and his solidly conservative Republicanism rendered him eminently acceptable on political grounds. Yet his Southern heritage was certain to be a point in his favor in the Border states. From Lincoln's point of view Swayne was the ideal candidate: a born Southerner yet an abolitionist and a strict Quaker. Swayne's excellent ties with the financial and business community whose support was crucial to the Northern war effort also influenced Lincoln; further, replacing McLean with a fellow Ohioan would repay the huge debt Lincoln owed Ohio Republicans for their vital third-ballot support at the Republican party's National Convention in 1860. Swayne amply lived up to his nominator's expectations, but his work on the Court during his tenure of more than two decades deserves but an average rating.

Lincoln's second appointment was intimately linked with the politics of judicial redistricting then alive on Capitol Hill. With the admission of new states into the Union, the existing judicial circuits had become increasingly large and unwieldy in terms of work loads, particularly since individual members of the Court were still being called upon for occasional circuit riding. As more territories of the South and the West became formal components of the United States, Congress resolved to readjust the physical boundaries of the existing circuits. To that end the five old Southern circuits were reduced to three; Indiana was moved to the Ohio circuit; Illinois was grouped in the Eighth Circuit with Michigan and Wisconsin; and a new trans-Mississippi circuit, the Ninth, was created, including Minnesota, Iowa, Kansas, and Missouri. This boundary game effectively removed from consideration two active candidates for the Daniel vacancy, Republican Senator Orville H. Browning of Illinois and Caleb B. Smith of Indiana, Lincoln's Secretary of the Interior. Lincoln then turned his attention to Samuel Freeman Miller of Iowa, at forty-six probably the outstanding trans-Mississippi lawyer of the time.

The President did not really know Miller—in fact, at this point he relied heavily on the recommendations of others. A native Kentuckian with a medical as well as a law degree, Miller had left the South because of his opposition to slavery. He was a loyal Republican with impeccable political and professional credentials, and he was from the right geographic region. All these factors were brought to Lincoln's attention by one of the most vigorous nomination drives in the history of the Court. Numerous insistent voices chorused Miller's qualifications; the President heard not only from western Governors, the Iowa Attorney General, and the Iowa Supreme Court but also from prominent figures in the world of law and politics throughout the country, capped by a petition from Congress containing the names of 129 of 140 members of the House and all but 4 Senators! Lincoln gladly forwarded Miller's name to an eager Senate which confirmed it unanimously within half an hour on July 16, 1862. Scholarly, skillful, and creative, Miller justified Lincoln's and his supporters' faith during twenty-eight productive years. He was to become one of the outstanding Justices to grace the bench, recognized as such with a "near great" rating by the Court experts. It is a pity that his labors are so often exclusively characterized by his contentious 5:4 majority opinion in the *Slaughterhouse Cases* of 1873.[18] It held, in interpreting the privileges and immunities clause of the Fourteenth Amendment, that there is a "citizenship of the United States and a citizenship of a state, which are distinct from each other," thus turning aside for many a decade the belief that the basic freedoms in the Bill of Rights cannot be encroached upon by state governments.

With the new circuit now staffed, and given the war-time contraction of the Southern circuits, Lincoln was free to fill Campbell's seat without feeling any obligations toward the latter's native Alabama. In fact, the President could now select someone from his own state to "represent" the Eighth Circuit. The three most likely and assertive ones were Republican Senator Orville H. Browning, Judge Thomas Drummond of the U.S. District Court, and Judge David Davis of the Illinois Circuit Court. The race soon narrowed to Browning and Davis. Both men were as well qualified as Drummond, but they were closer to Lincoln and their political supporters were more powerful. Lincoln bided his time, however. For a while he considered solving the dilemma by appointing Davis to a Cabinet post and sending Browning to the Court, but Davis made it clear that he would have none of such an arrangement. Ultimately the President was aided by a cooling among Browning's fellow Republican Senators, who accused their colleague of appeasing secessionist elements in Illinois, and by the attacks made on Browning by the influential Illinois publisher, Joseph Medill. To the relief and delight of Davis's allies, who had incessantly reminded the President of their candidate's staunch services on behalf of the Republican party and its leader, Lincoln turned to Davis in December of 1862.

Davis and Lincoln had been close personal and political friends for many years. Recognizing Lincoln's ability and promise, Davis had worked hard to see him elected to the U.S. Senate in 1858. At the 1860 Convention, it was Davis who was instrumental in marshalling the crucial Illinois Republican forces behind Lincoln. And as Lincoln's campaign manager, Davis had worked tirelessly. Clearly the President was greatly indebted to his nominee. Yet Davis was also eminently qualified. From the appropriate geographic area, he had extensive legal and judicial experience, including fourteen years on the Illinois bench; he was politically wise and shrewd; he was a loyal Republican and philosophical Lincolnian; even his age—forty-seven—was ideal. He was quickly confirmed with near unanimity and, at least during Lincoln's lifetime, supported Lincoln's constitutional interpretations. Intriguingly it was Davis who, scarcely a year after the President's death, wrote the *Ex parte Milligan* opinion,[19] in which a unanimous Supreme Court containing all five Lincoln appointees held unlawful the military commission authorized by the President to operate judicially in areas where civil courts were open and functioning.

In March 1863, with the enthusiastic backing of Abraham Lincoln, Congress created a Tenth Circuit consisting of California and Oregon to which Nevada was later added, allegedly because of the anticipated increase in Court business in the West. The increase in the number of Justices from nine to ten suited Lincoln's purposes admirably: his fourth Court appointee would bring at least some security to the prospects of a favorable judicial stance in the enormously significant Civil War litigation now on the Court's docket. It was widely expected that the President would nominate someone from the new circuit—someone familiar with its needs and problems, but also someone who could be counted upon strongly to back the cause of Union. Lincoln found his man in the camp of the Democrats—Stephen J. Field of California, easily the most distinguished jurist in the Pacific States. In addition, he was enthusiastically backed by California's powerful Governor, Leland Stanford. Although Field had been a Buchanan Democrat as recently as 1860 Lincoln correctly perceived his real politics to be akin to his own. The forty-six-year-old Field, who had served as both an Associate Justice and Chief Justice on the Supreme Court of California, had played a crucial role in keeping the state loyal to the Union and had often eloquently espoused the Union's cause in public. Moreover, he was the brother of David Dudley Field, the prominent abolitionist who had become a trusted adviser to Lincoln after playing a key part in Lincoln's nomination for the Presidency. The President nominated Field on March 7, 1863, and the Senate confirmed him unanimously three days later. It was the same day on which the Union blockade of the South (initiated by Lincoln in 1861) was upheld by the Supreme Court in the Prize Cases,[20] in a cliff-hanger vote (5:4).

Stephen Field served the Court for just over thirty-four and one-half years, second-longest to date. He did not disappoint Lincoln during the two years that remained to the President, but the development of Field's jurisprudence once the Civil War was over might have caused Lincoln a good many second thoughts. Although the experts have justly rated Field "near great" rather than "great," the Californian's role and influence on the bench were far-reaching and often decisive. Strong-willed, creative, intellectual, and result-oriented, a classical property-rights advocate, Stephen Field became the Court's personification of laissez-faire economics.

On October 12, 1864, Mr. Chief Justice Taney died at the age of eighty-eight, having served for almost three decades. Alone, tired, and disillusioned, he succumbed not realizing how much he had meant to his government and his people. He and Marshall had presided over the Court for almost sixty-five years. Who could now replace him? From the outset Abraham Lincoln's former Secretary of the Treasury, fifty-six-year-old Salmon Portland Chase of Ohio, was a major contender for Taney's seat. Insanely ambitious and conniving, Chase, who had been Governor of Ohio as well as U.S. Senator, was unquestionably able, but Lincoln had never liked or trusted him and was not comfortable with him. Hence while certainly not ruling Chase out, Lincoln delayed in filling the vacant chair—unquestionably in the hope of finding someone more in line with his expectations of character and personality. Among the other men he considered were sitting Associate Justices James M. Wayne and Noah H. Swayne and, to a lesser extent, Associate Justice David Davis; Secretary of War Edwin M. Stanton; Secretary of State William H. Seward; Secretary of the Treasury W. P. Fessenden; former Attorney General Edward Bates; former Secretary of the Interior Caleb B. Smith (a perpetual candidate); and former Postmaster General Montgomery Blair, plus a host of distinguished lawyers throughout the land, notably William Strong of Pennsylvania and William M. Evarts of New York.

Had Lincoln been able to select whom he really wanted and deemed most personally deserving as well as promising, he would have chosen Montgomery Blair, whose candidacy was ardently embraced and furthered by Secretary of State Seward and Secretary of the Navy Gideon Welles. Blair, a noted attorney from St. Louis with extensive public and private experience in government and at the bar, was a political moderate with long-time family roots in the original Free Soil contingent of the Republican party and a bitter foe of Chase. Bright, scholarly, and humane, he was among the eminent counsel who had argued on the losing side in the *Dred Scott Case*. The President knew Blair well and was keenly aware of his devotion to principle and courage. Yet he was not convinced that Blair possessed sufficient strength, leadership, or ability to unify disparate groups within the party. Lincoln quite correctly and disapassionately recognized that Chase did have all of these qualifications. Moreover, the President had not the slightest doubt of Chase's dedication to the Union cause. Deeply troubled and concerned, Lincoln delayed his decision for eight weeks, during which time he carefully weighed his step—a period well described by such perceptive chroniclers as Carl Sandburg and David M. Silver.[21]

The President finally concluded that in the interest of national unity and security the nod would have to go to Chase. If only Chase were not so politically ambitious! He had spent much of his time in the Lincoln Cabinet scheming for personal political gain; he was ruthless, stubborn, self-seeking, perhaps even malicious; and Lincoln was convinced that even as Chief Justice, Chase would remain an active candidate for the Presidency. He had sought the Republican candidacy in both 1856 and 1860 (and while on the bench in 1868 would seek the candidacy for *both* parties). But three overriding reasons finally prompted the President to send Chase's name to the Senate: First, he had no doubt that Chase's policy views on the war and future Reconstruction were sound and reliable. Second, if anyone could heal the widening breach in the Republican party, it would be Chase, even from the high bench. Third, Chase held an important "I.O.U.": although he had been Lincoln's rival for the Presidency in 1860 and had even angled for it in 1864, he had campaigned hard and effectively for Lincoln's election. Without even referring Chase's name to committee, the Senate confirmed its ex-colleague on the same day the nomination reached it.

Lincoln's shrewd evaluations of the new Chief Justice proved to be generally correct: Chase's political ambitions were, of course, never stilled by his new post. Yet he voted "Lincoln" on all war and related issues during Lincoln's lifetime and, while yielding on some issues, he stood up to Congress on a good many others during Reconstruction. On the other hand, Lincoln would have been as displeased as Congress was with Chase's 1870 opinion for a 4:3 Court that—employing tortured constitutional reasoning—struck down the Legal Tender Act of 1862 [22] which made "green-backs" legal tender in payments of debts. One other Lincoln appointee, Stephen J. Field, joined the Chase-led majority—which saw both a due process violation and a contract violation in the "fiat money." (But within fifteen months, the other "Lincoln men" who had dissented from the first decision—Swayne, Miller, and Davis —would joint two Grant appointees to overrule it in the *Second Legal Tender Cases*.[23] In retrospect Chase's greatest contribution probably was his superbly skillful and shrewd handling of Andrew Johnson's impeachment trial by a hostile Senate. The assertive, no-nonsense leadership he exercised as the presiding officer during the proceedings in the upper chamber was nothing less than brilliant, and may well have saved the institution of the Presidency itself.

Andrew Johnson, whose misfortune it was to fall heir to an office for which he was only marginally qualified, temperamentally ill-suited, and politically out-of-step (although a Union Democrat, he never became a Republican after joining the Lincoln ticket), entered it at a moment in history that called for a combination of

Washington, Jefferson, Jackson, and Lincoln. He was not made of such stuff. With a kind of stubborn courage, he often needlessly inflamed a powerful Republican Congress that already was not too kindly disposed toward him. The ultimate result was his impeachment of February 24, 1868, by a vote of 128:47. Charged by the House with eleven largely spurious articles of impeachment centering on his summary removal of Edwin M. Stanton, his disloyal Secretary of War, he went on trial in the Senate on March 30. In late May the President escaped conviction by one vote on Article Eleven—a catch-all provision through which the House managers hoped to obtain the necessary Senate votes to convict Johnson—and thereby effectively on the entire charge, the vote of 35:19 falling just one short of the constitutionally required two-thirds majority. He was saved by the courageous "nay" votes of seven Republican Senators who, as John F. Kennedy wrote eight decades later in his *Profiles in Courage,*[24] "looked into their open graves," and committed political suicide by casting their ballots with the Democratic minority in favor of Andrew Johnson's acquittal.

President Johnson's one opportunity to appoint a man to the Supreme Court came on the death of Mr. Justice Catron in May 1865. Vacillating for almost a year, Johnson finally chose Attorney General Henry Stanbery, an Ohio Republican of considerable legal skill and a well-liked public figure. But it is doubtful that the Senate would have approved God himself had he been nominated by Andrew Johnson. Not only did it fail to act on the Stanbery nomination, but it also passed a bill that abolished the Catron seat, reducing the Court's membership from ten to nine. An added proviso stipulated that after the next vacancy the Court be further reduced to eight members. This maneuver, it was hoped, would accomplish two things: first, it would block further Johnson nominations and, second, it would increase the voice of the presumably "safe" Lincoln appointees. The Radical Republicans' scheme was indeed crowned with success: Johnson never had another crack at a nomination, for when Mr. Justice James M. Wayne died in 1867 after more than three decades on the Court, the vacancy was statutorially abolished. On the other hand, the presumably "safe" Court certainly did not prove to be a supine servant of Radical Republican construction or Reconstruction, as it demonstrated in a series of post-war decisions that ran counter to Radical pleasure.[25] Yet its repeated dodging of major questions of constitutionality concerning the Reconstruction Acts [26] between 1867 and 1869 was proof-positive that the Court did not wish to embark upon a major struggle with Congress over the delicate and emotion-charged issues of Reconstruction.

The Balance of the Nineteenth Century: From Ulysses S. Grant to William McKinley 1869–1901

As President of the United States, General Ulysses S. Grant, the North's Civil War hero, has been rated all but unanimously as a failure by the experts. Grant was one of those strange paradoxes in American history: a leader enthusiastically backed by the people in the face of a visibly disgraceful performance in office. Not only was he unanimously nominated twice by the Republican party on the first ballot, not only was he easily elected in 1868 with a large popular majority and re-elected with an even larger majority in 1872, but he almost broke the two-term tradition in 1876, leading all other Republican nominees through the first thirty-five convention ballots! Ignorant about and bored by the political process; prejudiced, undignified, vacillating, and naïve; conducting government through a bevy of cronies who betrayed his confidence, he presided over two Administrations wracked by scandal and corruption. Yet the four Supreme Court members whom Grant appointed were generally able, and in two instances even superior, individuals.

Grant may have been bored by government and politics, yet he carefully heeded the entreaties of prominent Republican leaders at his side, led by Ebenezer Rockwood Hoar, his first Attorney General. They made clear to the President the need to pack the Court

with Republican loyalists; consequently, he resolved at the outset
that a safe Republican record would be a basic requirement for
nomination, to which he added geographic suitability. Other qualifications appeared not to matter; no discernable pattern of selection can be found in the eight nominations * Grant forwarded to
the Senate. Thus, it is hardly astonishing that all except one of his
appointees (Ward Hunt) would vote contrary to the heart of the
libertarian legislation growing out of the three Civil War amendments that Grant presumably favored.

To the re-created ninth seat on the Court—a "gift" to Grant by
Congress—the President nominated his Secretary of War, the
popular, outspoken, and independent Ebenezer R. Hoar. Hoar was
superbly qualified, but after seven weeks of debate and delay the
Senate rejected him, 24:33, on February 3, 1870. The majority
were still furious with Hoar for his refusal to back their strictly
partisan suggestions for lower-court nominees; his active labors on
behalf of a merit civil service system for the federal government;
his opposition to Andrew Johnson's impeachment.

While the Senate was still arguing over Hoar, Grant was presented with a second opening: the aged and ill Robert C. Grier at
last yielded to his colleagues' urgent pleas and resigned in mid-December 1869, after twenty-three years on the Court. Grant thought
he might be able to strike a compromise with the Senate's opponents to the still-pending Hoar nomination by acceding to a petition signed by a large majority of both the Senate and the House
in favor of Lincoln's Secretary of War, the impetuous Edwin M.
Stanton. Grant was not happy with this nomination, but he felt
reasonably certain that it would help Hoar's cause in obtaining the
other vacancy. He was quite wrong: although the Senate eagerly
approved Stanton by a vote of 46:11 on December 20, one day
after it officially received his name, it refused to budge on Hoar.
Ironically, four days later the fifty-four-year-old Stanton suc-

---

* One of the reasons that the President had so many opportunities to make
nominations was that Congress had restored the Court's membership to
nine within a month after the maligned Johnson's return to Tennessee.
Only four of his eight nominees, however, ultimately served on the Court.

cumbed to a coronary thrombosis—and the President still had two seats to fill!

Grant now acted quickly. Four days after Hoar's defeat, he sent to the Senate two nominations: for the Grier seat, William Strong of Pennsylvania, and for the "new" ninth, Joseph P. Bradley of New Jersey. Strong, whom Grant had actually wanted to nominate instead of Stanton, was a distinguished and experienced state jurist who had been very much in the running for the Chief Justiceship in 1864. Enthusiastically backed by Hoar, many prominent Pennsylvanians of both major political parties, and incumbent members of the Court, the sixty-two-year-old Strong was easily confirmed by the Senate within ten days, the nine opposition votes coming chiefly from Southerners who felt their region should have received the nod.

Things did not go so smoothly for the scholarly, thoughtful Bradley, five years Strong's junior. Also backed by Hoar and certainly Grant's best appointee, he had been initially recommended for the post by Mr. Justice Grier himself—even though Grier was a Democrat and Bradley a Republican. Before he was finally confirmed six weeks later by a vote of 46:9, Bradley came under heavy fire from Eastern "hard money" interests who quite correctly regarded him as dedicated to a "soft money" economic philosophy. Yet Bradley had excellent business connections and, although he had no previous judicial experience, he had practiced a variety of law for many years, obtaining considerable prominence as one of the foremost railroad attorneys in the nation. He would not disappoint the conservative business community during his more than two decades on the bench, nor would he let Grant and the Republicans down in the legal tender controversy. And as a member of the Electoral Count Commission in the disputed Presidential Election of 1876 he cast the decisive ballot in each of twenty disputed electoral votes, thereby awarding the election to Republican Rutherford B. Hayes over Democrat Samuel J. Tilden.[1]

Assuredly Bradley was Grant's most fortuitous appointment in terms of ability and party loyalty. But he was not a happy choice in terms of advancing civil rights legislation—as exemplified by his votes in such crucial decisions as those attacking the Enforcement Acts of 1870–71 [2] and the Civil Rights Acts of 1871 and 1875.[3] Indeed, he wrote the opinion striking down the latter by ruling that Congress could not use the Fourteenth Amendment enforcement clause to prevent discrimination by private persons —not even in such privately owned public accommodations as hotels, theaters, buses, and trains. Nonetheless, Bradley's over-all performance, characterized by judicial ingenuity, craftsmanship, lucidity, and eloquence, was of such caliber as to earn him a "near great" ranking by the Court's leading students. Together with Associate Justices Miller, Field, and Harlan he provided the intellectual leadership on the high bench in the latter decades of the nineteenth century.

When Mr. Justice Samuel Nelson resigned in November 1872 after almost three decades of dedicated and able service, President Grant designated a fellow New Yorker, Ward Hunt, to replace him. Then sixty-two, Hunt came to the Court with a wealth of legislative and judicial experience and the added attraction of having been one of the organizers of the Republican party in 1856— although he had begun his career as a Jacksonian Democrat and had been elected as such to state and municipal offices. But he had become disenchanted with the Democratic party's national posture in post-Jackson days and through the Free-Soil movement had eagerly embraced the fledgling Republicans—on whose ticket he successfully ran for a seat on the New York Supreme Court. Backed by the influential Hoar and the entire New York Congressional delegation as well as the state's and nation's business community, Hunt was an ideal candidate from Grant's point of view. Within a week he had been confirmed, 53:11. He proved to be at once the most judicially loyal and least effective of Grant's appointees during his relatively brief tenure of nine years on the Court.

On May 8, 1873, after but eight and a half years in his post, Mr. Chief Justice Salmon P. Chase died, still harboring ambitions for the elusive Presidency. Grant, now in his second term, turned the process of his last appointment into somewhat of a comic opera, offering the Chief Justiceship to no fewer than seven individuals!

When he began his quest for Chase's replacement, he was quite aware that at least two of the sitting Associate Justices—Samuel F. Miller and Joseph P. Bradley—were interested in being promoted and further, that they were eminently capable of performing the job. Yet he ruled them out immediately: it was his way of keeping the peace and harmony on the Court, and perhaps on that score he had reasoned wisely. He then began to consider other possibilities and after six months of dawdling finally offered the post to the shrewd, outspoken Senator Roscoe Conkling of New York, his close friend, policy confidant, and political supporter. The youthful Conkling, to his credit, declined at once—he was neither interested in the position nor was he sufficiently qualified for it.

It was now November and Grant, realizing that he had to take some action, turned to his Attorney General, George H. Williams of Oregon, an honest but only marginally capable individual. Williams's nomination ran into immediate flak from the bar, press, and public—who all quite rightly deemed him to be lacking in stature—but Grant persisted in pushing the fifty-year-old Oregonian until the Judiciary Committee approved his nomination. The full Senate, however, demurred, and the President withdrew Williams's name early in January 1874 at the nominee's own request. Almost as if to sass the Senate, Grant now came up with the name of his good friend, seventy-four-year-old Caleb Cushing. Unquestionably highly qualified and possessed of a superb mind, Cushing, in addition to being far too old for the position, had made many enemies in and out of public life by virtue of his changeable political record: he had been a Whig, a Tyler Whig, a Democrat, a Johnson Constitutional Conservative, and he was now a Republican! The opposition was widespread and rampant, focusing not only on Cushing's shifting political persuasions, but on an exchange of letters that had once taken place between him and Jefferson Davis. Grant was not long in withdrawing his nomination.

He then offered the Chief Justiceship to three others, Senator Timothy P. Howe (Wisconsin), Senator Oliver P. Morton (Indiana), and Secretary of State Hamilton Fish—but he did not formally nominate any one of them; he seemed to enjoy the suspense. Finally, recognizing that the time for experimenting was over, he yielded to continuing clamor from the Midwest and settled upon another Ohioan, the undistinguished, non-controversial, quietly efficient, well-liked Morrison Remick Waite.

The fifty-eight-year-old man the Senate confirmed 63:6 on January 21, 1874, two days after he was nominated—and more than eight months after Chase's death—had been recommended to the President at the very outset of his quest for a successor to Chase. Grant had in fact known Waite when the latter served, with others, as Counsel before the Geneva Arbitration Commission of 1871 that considered the *Alabama* claims and deposits. An expert in real estate and titles, Waite was not too well known beyond Ohio. But there he was respected as hard-working, able, and conscientious, a man with great integrity and an expertise in constitutional law. Widely called "His Accidency" because of his seventh-fiddle nomination and described by Mr. Justice Field as a "man that would never have been thought of for the position by any person except President Grant . . . an experiment which no President has a right to make with our Court," [4] Waite was nonetheless an effective, tactful, and hard-working leader of a difficult Court and deservedly earned the very high rating accorded him by most Court observers.

But if Grant had expected Waite to lead the way in the liberal interpretation of the Civil War amendments, he was badly mistaken. The new Chief Justice, like Bradley and Strong, gave a restrictive rather than liberal construction to the amendments, particularly to the Fourteenth Amendment, whose "due process of law" and "privileges and immunities" clauses became the special targets of illiberal reading. Thus Waite, echoing the devastating *Slaughterhouse Cases* [5] of three years earlier, wrote in 1876 that the Fourteenth Amendment "adds nothing to the rights of one citizen as against another. It simply gives an additional guarantee against any encroachment by the States upon the fundamental rights which belong to every citizen as a member of society." [6] On the other hand, Waite wrote the majority opinion in the famed *Granger Cases* of 1877,[7] which wrought a revolution in constitutional law: Waite's opinion in the leading Granger case of *Munn v. Illinois* recognized that the due process of law clause of the Fourteenth Amendment, while a barrier against illegal governmental assaults on property, did not forbid the exercise of governmental (here, state) police power to regulate those categories of business "affected with a public interest." He went on to point out that "when private property is affected with a public interest it ceases to be *juris privati* only," and he concluded with the often repeated admonition tha for "protection against abuses by legislators, the people must resort to the polls, not the courts." Despite this landmark decision—for which he is best remembered— Waite's career on the Court was basically that of a constitutional and economic conservative.

Rutherford Birchard Hayes, the nation's nineteenth President, entered the White House under a cloud after his rather dubious victory in the "Stolen Election of 1876." Yet there is no doubt that the three-time Governor of Ohio and two-time member of Congress was an excellent President, and that he richly merits the somewhat delayed recognition that Presidential historians now bestow in ranking him just below the "near greats." He was not a brilliant man, but he was strong, public-spirited, perceptive, effective, and—so vital after the shadowy and shady Grant era—a bright symbol of rectitude, morality, and honesty. Despite the blot on his election, a Democratic Congress during most of his regime, and considerable back-biting and factionalism in his own party, he gave the country strong leadership and restored to the Republican party much of the good will and faith that Grant's performance had wiped out. Unquestionably Hayes's most memorable and far-reaching executive move was his immediate recall of federal troops from the South. In thus fulfilling a campaign promise, he in effect wrote *finis* to both military and political Reconstruction. Conciliatory and sensitive, he strove mightily to "bind up the wounds."

During his four years at the helm, Hayes had three opportunities to nominate men to the Supreme Court. Two of these men, John Marshall Harlan and William B. Woods, he saw confirmed; the third, Stanley Matthews, whom he nominated in the waning days of the Administration, was not acted upon before Hayes left office, but President Garfield would successfully re-submit his name. If Woods, who died after little more than six years in office, was mediocre at best, Matthews was an excellent Justice and Harlan was among the greatest. Even if Hayes did not approve of all aspects of Harlan's jurisprudence or of his advanced libertarian opinions on the Bill of Rights and the Civil War amendments, he might well be proud of the ex-Kentucky slaveholder who had come aboard to fight for the Union cause. All of Hayes's nominations reflected, of course, his spirit of compromise and reconciliation. Thus his choice of nominal Republicans who were presumably moderate to conservative and broadly acceptable to the South was hardly surprising. The geographic factor that had once figured so prominently appeared to be of little importance to Hayes; he did not hesitate to substitute Kentucky (Harlan) for Illinois (Davis), and Georgia (Woods) for Pennsylvania (Strong). For his last nomination he did, however, stay with Ohio (Matthews) for Ohio (Swayne). Mr. Justice David Davis's resignation prior to Hayes's assumption of the Presidency provided him with an immediate vacancy to fill. In mid-October he proposed to the Senate the forty-four-year-old Harlan, a man to whom he was deeply indebted politically.

Harlan had been an indispensable ally to Hayes both during the Republican Convention and the election campaign of 1876. He had headed his state's delegation to the Convention, throwing Kentucky's votes to Hayes at a critical point in the balloting. During the campaign, he was largely responsible for important political work in the Border states. And he also served as a member of the Commission investigating Louisiana's disputed electoral returns in the 1876 election: his vote helped to adjudge the results in Hayes's favor. Yet it would be wrong to attribute Harlan's nomination solely to political considerations—indeed, at the time of his selection Harlan could have been looked upon as both non-partisan and bipartisan, a characterization not at all inconsistent with his political history. Both a Democrat and a Whig before the Civil War, he had been an unsuccessful Whig candidate for Congress in 1859 and a Presidential elector on the Bell-Everett Constitutional Union party ticket in 1860. A staunch defender of the Union, he reluctantly converted to Republicanism, yet initially opposed the Civil War amendments and supported General George B. McClellan rather than Lincoln for the White House in 1864. But he was directly responsible for rejuvenating Kentucky's Republican party; he ran twice for the Governship, although unsuccessfully; and because he had been a firm Grant backer in 1868, his name was prominently mentioned as a Vice-Presidential candidate on the Grant ticket in 1872. Harlan's ancestors were Southern slaveholders; but by now Harlan had become a firm devotee of the Civil War amendments, which he more than any other public figure on the nineteenth-century Supreme Court would amply and poignantly demonstrate by word and deed, though almost invariably in dissent.[8] An ideal choice for Hayes in terms of public service, ability, and political compromise, Harlan still ran into considerable bipartisan, bi-regional Senatorial opposition. But after a month-long delay he was confirmed. For almost thirty-four years John Marshall Harlan would grace the tribunal he loved. Grandfather of the future Associate Justice, Harlan became "the brilliant precursor in liberalism and dissent of Justice Holmes." [9] As long as conscience will govern men and women they will remember his outcry in solitary dissent from the Court's 1896 opinion in *Plessy* v. *Ferguson,* which upheld the "separate but equal" doctrine: "Our Constitution is color-blind, and neither knows nor tolerates classes among citizens." [10]

Hayes's second nomination, designed to replace Mr. Justice William Strong, who had resigned in December 1880 after a decade of routine service, was fifty-six-year-old Judge William B.

Woods of Georgia. Mr. Justice Woods shared several characteristics with Harlan, but he would prove to be in a totally different class as a jurist. Like Harlan a confirmed Unionist who served with the Federal Army, he too had reluctantly become a Republican. An ex-resident of Ohio, he had moved to Alabama and then to Georgia, where he was serving as a U.S. Circuit Judge when Hayes appointed him to the Supreme Court—the first Southerner to get the nod since the resignation of James A. Campbell in 1852. Although Woods—whose appointment was recommended strongly by Mr. Chief Justice Waite—had lingering and fond attachments to the North, his professional loyalties were to the South. Thus he was precisely the kind of candidate Hayes sought as a conciliation, one who could help bind bitter sectional wounds. Less visibly controversial in the Senate's eyes than Harlan, Woods was confirmed within five days by a solid 39:8 margin just before Christmas Eve.

An avowed one-term President, Hayes was already a lame duck when in late January 1881 he nominated his Kenyon College classmate and fellow Union Army combatant, Stanley Matthews of Ohio, to the Court vacancy created by the retirement of the aged Mr. Justice Noah H. Swayne, who had given almost two decades of diligent service. Hayes might have been willing to wait for the incoming Garfield, but illness had thinned the ranks of the Court and, after all, Matthews was not only his good friend and political ally, but he was cast in the mold Hayes perceived as highly desirable in the pursuit of sectional peace and compromise. Like Harlan and Woods a political maverick, Matthews had supported Democrat Polk but also the politically versatile Salmon P. Chase. He was firmly opposed to slavery, yet he faithfully sought to enforce the Fugitive Slave Act in his capacity as United States Attorney for Ohio (Ohio was a frequent terminus of the Underground Railway). President Grant, apprised of Matthews's political savoir faire and his experience as a state legislator and Presidential elector, had appointed him to the sensitive and crucial post of counsel for the Republican faction arguing Hayes's case before the Electoral Count Commission of 1876–77. Matthews had proved his mettle, persuasively arguing that the Commission and Congress should not "go behind the election returns," but should instead shun a probing of motives, accepting the certified results by legally constituted state authorities. He had thus been of no small aid to his old friend President Hayes.

What caused the two men untold difficulties, however, was Matthews's avowed association with corporate financial and railroad interests, both as a practicing attorney and as a Senator from Ohio. When the President nominated Matthews to the Court he was Midwestern Chief Counsel to Financier Jay Gould. The Senate exploded in anger, its Committee on the Judiciary flatly refusing to report the nomination out for floor action. It was perhaps the first clear instance of overriding opposition to a nominee on the grounds of economic affiliation. The Matthews nomination was understandably dead.

To the surprise of a good many, however, the incoming President renominated Matthews almost immediately after taking the oath of office. James Garfield had never really sought the Presidency; if there was ever in our Presidential history a dark-horse draft, it was that of the long-time Ohio Congressman and ex-General whose selection was desired neither by those who nominated him nor by Garfield himself. A decent but gullible and weak man, Garfield was President for six months only. Four of these months were spent actively in office, the last two in a courageous but futile struggle for life against the bullet a disappointed office-seeker, Charles J. Guiteau, shot at the President as he was about to entrain for a Williams College reunion.

Why Garfield really nominated Matthews is not entirely clear, although considerable evidence points to the political and financial influence of Gould and his associates as well as Garfield's desire to heal party wounds. The clout of the Gould-led group might well explain the shift of Senatorial votes that resulted in Matthews's razor-thin confirmation, 24:23, after two months of acrimonious debate. The opposition thus barely fell short of preventing what the *New York Times* had characterized as one of Hayes's "most injudicious and objectionable acts" and "a sad and inexcusable error" on Garfield's part.[11] Yet the history of the Court has proved that appointees often rise above associational and philosophical predispositions, and Stanley Matthews was one of those men. Although he died less than eight years after he reached the Court, his record demonstrated an entirely open mind on such crucial questions as governmental regulation of the economy—and of business as well as labor. Far from establishing a slavish ideological attachment to a laissez-faire economy, he frequently joined other fair-minded independents on the bench such as John Marshall Harlan and Mr. Chief Justice Waite in regulatory opinions that confounded prognosticators.

In 1881, on Garfield's death, Chester A. Arthur of New York came to the Presidency with almost everyone predicting doom and failure: his selection as Vice-President had been steeped in political hacksmanship and spoilsmanship, nurtured by the nether Roscoe Conkling wing of New York's Republican party. His public career had been limited to the notoriety surrounding his removal from a New York Port customs office post by President Hayes and, while his reputation as a shrewd attorney was widespread, he was much better known as a Conkling machine politician. No wonder the nation stood horrified in anticipation of his performance as Chief Executive! Yet in what was one of the most dramatic character reversals in the country's history, President Arthur not only turned his back on his spoilsmen-cronies but authored the great Pendleton Civil Service Reform Act of 1883 —a monument to the principle of public office based on merit rather than patronage. Moreover, he gave proof of solid, intelligent administrative expertise, generally acquitting himself with aplomb. Historians accord him no more than an "average" rating, but that is considerably higher than he could have expected had he not altered his erstwhile approach to government and politics.

Arthur had three opportunities to nominate Justices for two vacancies, and the two men whom he would see appointed—Horace Gray and Samuel Blatchford—were admirably in line with his new-found regard for meritorious service. Arthur's first vacancy was a holdover from his predecessor's term: the aged and ill Mr.

Justice Nathan Clifford had died shortly after Guiteau's attack on Garfield, and the slot had simply been left empty. Two months after assuming office, President Arthur nominated the fifty-three-year-old Horace Gray, a distinguished and experienced jurist with almost two decades of service on the Supreme Court of Massachusetts, including eight as Chief Justice. One of the youngest graduates in the history of Harvard College, Gray was an eminent legal scholar and historian whose selection was universally applauded. As a federalist Republican with an acute appreciation of limited states' rights, Gray was a fiscal and economic conservative. Yet he would not be averse to siding with such Justices as Waite, Harlan, and Matthews (his father-in-law, but only three years his senior) in upholding selective government regulation of the economy. He fully lived up to Arthur's expectations and served diligently for more than twenty years, demonstrating an enormous capacity for research and writing.

Barely two months after Gray's appointment, Mr. Justice Ward Hunt, who had been ill for five of his ten years on the bench, resigned his post. It was widely expected that President Arthur would tender the nomination to Senator George F. Edmunds, a brilliant lawyer and influential public servant from Vermont (a state that to this day has never been "represented" on the Supreme Court). But to the consternation of most observers, Arthur had a "relapse" and offered the post to his one-time political mentor and boss, Senator Roscoe Conkling of New York (who, it will be remembered, had been tendered the Chief Justiceship by Grant in 1873 but, to general relief, had refused it). This time, however, Conkling accepted the Associate Justiceship. But he pondered the matter for several days, during which time the press had a field day in lambasting nominator as well as nominee. True to its tradition of never rejecting one of its own, the Senate confirmed Conkling with a comfortable 39:12 margin on March 2, 1882. Yet to audible sighs of relief, Conkling formally declined five days later, with the *New York Times* and the *Nation,* among others, suggesting that he did so because there was not enough money in the post of Justice of the United States Supreme Court.

In thus paying homage to his political spoilsman and teacher, Arthur had only narrowly been spared a potentially disastrous appointment. The President now fortunately reverted to his merit principles, selecting the well-qualified Samuel Blatchford of New York, a state and federal judge and a specialist in admiralty law. Sixty-two years old, a moderate Republican, and a non-controversial public figure who had amply proved his mettle in public service, Blatchford's career on the Court was in the mold of his colleague Gray. What he lacked of Gray's quickness and astuteness he made up in productivity, becoming one of the Court's most avid opinion writers during his eleven years of service. Well might Arthur be pleased with his two appointees, both in terms of performance and expectations. He had selected two professionally experienced moderate Republicans of judicial temperament and open-mindedness and both had served diligently and thoughtfully without rocking the ship of state.

Rather generously ranked "near great" by the experts (although they placed him at the lowest level in that category) Grover Cleveland of New York was both our twenty-second and twenty-fourth Presidents, serving 1885–89 and 1893–97. He actually received a majority of the popular vote three times, for he also bested Benjamin Harrison by almost 100,000 votes in the election of 1888, but the vagaries of the electoral college caused him to lose that election. The sole Democrat to serve between the Presidencies of James Buchanan and Woodrow Wilson, Cleveland was an economic conservative of such intensity that Wilson had cause, if only half-jokingly, to regard himself as the first President of the Democratic party since 1860.[12] Cleveland was a courageous, conscientious, and principled President, honest and incorruptible during a time in which graft, conspiracy, and corruption found favor at the highest levels. Energetic and pragmatic rather than imaginative or intellectual, he was essentially a "no"-sayer no matter how powerful and ardent the interest or the pleader. He did "what was right"—as he so often stated—and that even extended to his public election campaign acknowledgment of an illegitimate son, whose existence had given rise to the infamous

1884 campaign slogan: "Ma! Ma! Where's my Pa? Gone to the White House, Ha! Ha! Ha!"

Cleveland was neither a social nor an economic reformer. His basically conservative economic-proprietarian philosophy was clearly reflected in the four appointments he made to the Court during his two terms as President. With the exception of a few of the judicial votes to be cast by his third appointee, Edward D. White,[13] Cleveland's choices lived up to his expectations amply. The President's criteria were easy to behold: a Democrat in good standing (no Democrat had been appointed since Stephen J. Field in 1862); an individual known to him personally; an economic-proprietarian of generally conservative bent; and a non-Populist from an appropriate geographic area.

Lucius Quintus Cincinnatus Lamar of Mississippi was the first Democrat to be selected in a quarter of a century. The President called upon him in late 1887, following the death of Mr. Justice William B. Woods of Georgia after little more than five years in office. There were other "firsts" that characterized the Lamar choice: Woods was but a transplanted Ohioan who had fought with the Union, whereas Lamar was a real Southerner—the first sent to the Court since Campbell's appointment by Pierce in 1853. He was also the first appointee with active service in the Confederate Army, and he was the first with a background of legislative and executive service in both the Union and the Confederate governments. The ex-General—who had surrendered at Appomatox as a Colonel—had written the Mississippi Ordinance of Secession, had served in the Confederate Congress, and had been the Confederate Envoy to Russia. Yet he labored hard and successfully to facilitate adoption of the Compromise of 1877 by the South. Elected to the House of Representatives in 1872 and to the Senate in 1876, he became Cleveland's Secretary of Interior in 1885 and quickly won the President's admiration, confidence, and affection, particularly because of his integrity and sound judgment. A Democratic leader in his native Mississippi, he had earned universal respect as a gentleman and a scholar in the Southern tradition (at the University of Mississippi, he had taught mathematics, law, ethics, and metaphysics); as a brilliant orator; and as an honest, scrupulously fair man. He was Cleveland's first and apparently only serious choice for the vacancy, despite his age, sixty-two, and Confederate affiliations. Led by angry Northern Republicans, the confirmation battle raged on for six weeks, finally ending with Lamar's approval by a four-vote margin (32:28) in January 1888, aided by the cross-over of three Republican votes. Death came to him only five years later.

Two months after Lamar's confirmation, Mr. Chief Justice Morrison R. Waite died after a stewardship of fourteen years. Cleveland thus became only the sixth President and but the second Democrat to confront the awesome responsibility of filling the highest judicial post in the nation. Waite, who had served ably and intelligently with a fine nose for compromise and conciliation, was conservative but not dogmatic, and he had effectively presided over an often seriously divided but enormously able Court. To whom would the President turn? Determined to adhere to his perceived and announced criteria, Cleveland moved cautiously but with considerable dispatch. He was offered a plethora of suggestions, including some self-serving ones by Associate Justice Field, who ardently aspired to the top post. But Cleveland, who did not want Field, was determined not even to consider anyone who did not represent the Midwest (preferably Illinois, a state not then "represented" on the high bench and the state with more litigation than any other except New York); who was not a solid, active Democrat; and who was not one with whom he could be comfortable ideologically and personally. He considered the promotion of Associate Justice Miller, an Iowan, but that superb, powerful jurist was seventy-two years old; also Kentucky's able barrister John G. Carlisle, but Kentucky was already "represented" by the great John Marshall Harlan. His initial choice devolved upon a fifty-four-year-old Illinois lawyer, John Scholfield, strongly recommended by their close mutual friend, Melville Weston Fuller. Scholfield refused the honor, however. Cleveland now turned to Fuller himself, an active Illinois Democrat whose business connections made him acceptable to Republicans. A native of Maine,

Harvard Law student, well-to-do corporation lawyer, prominent Episcopal layman, and at fifty-five the "right" age, Fuller shared most of the President's generally conservative social, economic, and political ideas. He had given a number of indications that he would become even more conservative in his Darwinian commitments to sound money, free trade, states' rights, and absence of government "paternalism" in the economic sector.

Fuller's confirmation was delayed for two and a half months, an uncommon hiatus due almost entirely to the personal Senatorial vendetta by the Republican Chairman of the Senate Judiciary Committee, George F. Edmunds of Vermont. Edmunds claimed that Cleveland had promised the nomination to one of his constituents, but in the end Edmunds capitulated—faced with wholesale Republican defections—and Fuller was approved by a vote of 41:2 in late July 1888. During his twenty-two years as Chief Justice, Fuller not only ran true to form, he presided over and was supported by a Court that became a veritable bastion of economic laissez faire, espousing a policy of preserving in extremis the notion of "freedom of contract," which he and most of his associates found in the "vested rights" inherent in the "property" concept of the due process of law clauses of the Fifth and Fourteenth amendments. Indeed, the Fuller Court would go down in history as the incarnation of free enterprise, of the equation of laissez faire with constitutionally protected rights. Fuller himself wrote few opinions, and few memorable phrases of quotations crept into those opinions. He was less interested in being a Justice *qua* jurist than he was in providing the Court with administrative and organizational leadership. This he achieved with great success and he is generally regarded as one of the two or three best presiding officers in the Court's history. Yet in terms of his contributions to over-all jurisprudence, the non-intellectual Fuller is quite justly ranked by the experts as little more than average, roughly on a par with his predecessor once-removed, Salmon P. Chase.

Four months after Grover Cleveland returned to the Presidency in 1893, following the Harrison interregnum, Mr. Justice Samuel Blatchford died after a decade on the Court. It was Cleveland's third opportunity to make an appointment. This time, however, he nominated three men before he was able to fill the vacancy. According to his principle, Cleveland wanted to replace New Yorker Blatchford with another New Yorker. The state's astute and powerful Senator David B. Hill advanced numerous suggestions to the President. But Hill was a member of an anti-Cleveland patronage faction in New York's Democratic party, at odds with the President on patronage matters, and the President refused to heed the Senator, despite the latter's threats to invoke Senatorial courtesy. When Cleveland thus proposed William B. Hornblower, a conservative corporation lawyer and Cleveland loyalist to the Senate at the end of the summer, Hill, although with some difficulty, rallied his colleagues and Hornblower went down to defeat 24:30 four months later. Not one to capitulate readily, Cleveland, again ignoring Hill's admonitions, nominated another New Yorker of similar persuasions, Wheeler H. Peckham, that January. Following a month of debate, Hill's Senatorial-courtesy claims proved to be victorious again, this time by a nine-vote margin, 32:41. Angry and frustrated, the President, noting that he had no more "appropriate" New York names in reserve, determined to be satisfied with a draw: Hill's vetoes would stand, but there would be no more New Yorker nominations, at least not for the present vacancy. Instead, and to the nation's surprise, Cleveland turned to the South and to the Senate, selecting its respected and popular Democratic Majority Leader, Edward Douglass White of Louisiana, forty-eight years old. White was also a Roman Catholic, the first to be nominated since Mr. Chief Justice Taney. His surprised but delighted colleagues confirmed him unanimously on February 19, 1894, the same day his nomination came over from the White House.

The designation of Senator White was partly an effort by Cleveland to re-ingratiate himself with the Senate, but there were other sound reasons for it: White came from a state previously neglected in Court appointments; he had supported Cleveland both in and out of the Senate; his brand of conservative economics appealed to Cleveland; and the President had a warm personal regard for the kind, self-effacing bachelor. There have also been suggestions, recently increasingly disputed, that Cleveland wished to remove White from the Senate because as a rich sugar-plantation owner White had ardently opposed any relaxation in the protective tariff legislation the President was then endeavoring to see enacted.* White was advanced to the Chief Justiceship in 1910, but Cleveland did not live to see the promotion. He would have been pleased with the appointment for, although White did not come through on a number of issues, his record on the bench was close enough to the Cleveland philosophy to be "well within normal limits."

There had been yet another vacancy for Cleveland to fill, perhaps as unwelcome as it was unexpected: after having served for only two and a half years Mr. Justice Howell E. Jackson of Tennessee died in August 1895. Since Cleveland had given the New York seat to the Deep South in the last appointment round, he was determined to try to return to New York for his nominee. Stubborn when he chose to be, the President moved to re-nominate the already rejected William B. Hornblower; but the latter had had his fill of internecine combat and refused Cleveland's offer. Wisely, the President now swallowed his pride and resolved to placate Senator Hill. He wrote to him an exceedingly tactful letter of inquiry, concerning (of all people) the brother of the rejected Wheeler H. Peckham, the fifty-seven-year-old Rufus W. Peckham, in which he in effect asked Hill to approve the latter's candidacy. Cleveland closed his missive with the courteously stated hope that Hill might "find it consistent and agreeable to pave the way" [14] for the appointment. The placated New York Senator, although still vehemently opposed to Wheeler Peckham, voiced no objection to the nomination of brother Rufus, for Rufus had in no way been involved in the patronage squabbles between Hill and the President. His confirmation came promptly and easily.

---

* If White's opposition was a motive, the President's gesture was in vain: although Congress did pass a new tariff bill, it was but a slight improvement over the previous one.

Peckham, an able lawyer and public servant, had been in private practice for a quarter of a century; sixteen years a judge on the New York Supreme Court and the New York Court of Appeals, and District Attorney and corporation counsel for the state in Albany. His work had not received universal acclaim, but he was both shrewd and effective. Whatever his professional qualifications for the high bench, his avowed political philosophy was very much Clevelandesque Democratic: anti-Populist, anti-paternalistic in government, economically and socially conservative. In fact, Peckham embraced a Social Darwinist approach that went considerably beyond that of his nominator, fitting in comfortably with the kindred views of such established laissez-faire specialists as Fuller and Brewer. The confidant of tycoons such as James J. Hill, George F. Baker, Cornelius Vanderbilt, William Rockefeller, James Speyer, and Pierpont Morgan, he would not disappoint them during the fourteen years he served on the Supreme Court. Students of constitutional law and of the Fuller era remember Peckham best for his opinion for a bitterly split 5:4 Court in *Lochner* v. *New York* in 1905, where that bare majority declared unconstitutional New York's statute limiting hours of labor in bakeshops to sixty hours per week, or ten per day.[15] Invoking the age-old device of the *argumentum ad horrendum* Peckham declared that laws such as New York's fatally violated "freedom of contract," the freedom of the employer and the employee to enter into whatever contracts they wished to make, free from government interference—a freedom he saw guaranteed absolutely by the due process of law clauses of the Constitution. Over withering dissenting opinions by Justices Harlan and Holmes, with Holmes crying out "the Fourteenth Amendment does not enact Mr. Herbert Spencer's *Social Statics,*" Peckham conjured up horrid visions of the all-powerful, all-intrusive state if government were allowed thus to regulate contractual relationships. Vested property rights were indeed still secure.

William Henry Harrison's grandson, Benjamin, the filling of the "Cleveland Sandwich," a General in the Union Army, and an Indiana lawyer with service in Congress, is appropriately regarded as one of our lesser Presidents, but certainly not as a disastrous one—the historians having accorded him a "low average" ranking. An aloof and withdrawn aristocrat, an intellectual but generally devoid of much insight about government and politics, he was content to let the Republican party hierarchy dominate the affairs of state during his four years in office—although he was assuredly aware of what was going on. He was an economic conservative who, not without some misgivings, signed into law some potentially far-reaching regulatory legislation, such as the Sherman Anti-Trust Act of 1890. But he correctly guessed that the impact of such legislation lay in the future, notwithstanding the budding Populist movement. Honest about motives, reliable, conscientious, he made no secret of the kind of individual he wanted to send to the Court, and the four he appointed during his single term in office met his criteria readily: they were good Republicans (with the exception of Democratic family friend Howell E. Jackson); governmental and economic conservatives; experienced practicing lawyers and judges; and, if they were not from the same states as the jurists they replaced, they were at least from the same circuit or the same general geographic area. Like Cleveland, Harrison could be well pleased with the judicial performance of his nominees, although Henry B. Brown, his second nominee, occasionally proved more friendly to governmental regulation than his nominator might have wished. But as a group, both the Harrison and Cleveland Justices neatly followed Mr. Chief Justice Fuller's orchestration of freedom of contract, absence of governmental restraint on business activities, and the sanctity of property.

Harrison's first opportunity to make an appointment came with the death of Mr. Justice Stanley Matthews in March of 1889 after a remarkably capable career of less than eight years on the Court. It took the cautious President almost nine months to decide upon a replacement. He considered some two-score individuals, all of whom he had thoroughly investigated, ultimately narrowing his choice to two friends, David Josiah Brewer of Kansas and Henry Billings Brown of Michigan. They were conservative ideological kinsmen; they both had fine records as state and as federal lower court judges; they were both from the Midwest; they had been Yale classmates; they were both in their early fifties; they were both loyal Republicans; and they had both been recommended highly, not only by their political allies but by sitting Supreme Court Justices such as Miller and Jackson. It was truly an *embarras de richesse* in Harrison's eyes, and he evidently resolved that he would send both of these men to the high bench. But whom to name first? What apparently clinched the matter was a letter written by Brewer to Brown, conveniently brought to the President's attention by a mutual friend, in which Brewer, having become aware of Brown's candidacy as well as his own for the Matthews vacancy, self-effacingly expressed the hope that Brown rather than he would get the nod. Brewer expressed similar sentiments to a coterie of his friends who had begun to mount a letter-writing campaign in his behalf to Harrison. The President was so impressed with Brwer's apparent generosity that he opted for him (confirmation came speedily, 53:11), silently resolving to reserve any future vacancy for Brown. (Apparently, Brown, too, had written a letter of similar tone and sentiment to Brewer, but the President was unaware of it.)

Brewer was the nephew of the distinguished Mr. Justice Stephen J. Field, whom he now not only joined on the Court but whose policies he embraced and furthered eagerly. Indeed, the aging Field more or less relinquished his intellectual leadership to his nephew during the remaining eight years of their joint tenure on the bench. Born the son of a missionary in Izmir (Turkey), Brewer was jovial, witty, and intellectual. He had served fourteen years on the Supreme Court of Kansas and five on the U.S. Court of Appeals for the Eighth Circuit. Together with Mr. Justice Peckham, he became the leader of the ultra-conservative economic laissez-faire advocates on the Court, not only smoothly fitting into the Fuller Court's approach to public policy but going well beyond it in terms of judicial activism on behalf of vested property rights based on the "freedom of contract" doctrine. A diligent worker, Brewer wrote almost six hundred opinions during his twenty-one years on the bench, only one-tenth of these in dissent. His philosophy could be summarized in excerpts from a famed commencement address he delivered to the June 1891 graduating class at Yale:

> . . . The demands of absolute and eternal justice forbid that any private property, legally acquired and legally held, should be spoliated or destroyed in the interests of public health, morals, or welfare without just compensation [which, of course, he wanted the judiciary rather than the legislature to determine]. . . . From the time in earliest records, when Eve took loving possession of even the forbidden apple, the idea of property and sacredness of the right of its possession has never departed from the race . . . [for] human experience . . . declares that the love of acquirement, mingled with the joy of possession, is the real stimulus to human activity." [16]

Brewer's labors assuredly merited the "high average" rating granted him by the Court observers and President Harrison had every reason to be pleased with his nominee, even if he did not entirely agree with all of his ideas.

The President did not have to wait long to realize his hopes for Brown. After twenty-eight years of distinguished service, Mr. Justice Samuel F. Miller died on October 14, 1890, thus giving Harrison his second appointment in little more than a year. For two months he went through the motions of considering other worthy candidates; but there was never any doubt that he would nominate the prominent, conservative admiralty lawyer from Detroit, who at the time of his selection was a judge of he United States District Court for eastern Michigan. Earlier he had served as Federal Marshall and as Assistant U.S. Attorney in the same jurisdiction and as Judge of the Wayne County Circuit Court. He was confirmed without a record roll call in a matter of days. Blessed with a commendable judicial temperament, intelligent, expertly trained, hard-working, and pleasant, Brown became a worthy member of the Court. Deserving the just-below "near great" ranking accorded him, he demonstrated genuine independence while still generally adhering to the philosophy of economic conservatism of the day. Although he was on the Peckham-Brewer-Fuller majority side in the notorious 1905 *Lochner* decision striking down New York State's maximum-hour law for bakers,[17] he had been the author of the 1896 majority opinion—with Brewer and Peckham in dissent —upholding a maximum-hour law for miners in Utah.[18] Today he is best remembered for quite another opinion—*Plessy* v. *Ferguson*,[19] handed down in 1896, written for an 8:1 Court (with Harlan alone in dissent): it enshrined the "separate but equal" racial doctrine in constitutional law for the next six decades.

Mr. Justice Joseph P. Bradley, who had served so ably and influentially on the Court for twenty-two years, died in January 1892. Harrison, determined that the crucial Third Circuit (Pennsylvania, New Jersey, and Delaware) continue to be represented on the high bench, resolved to find a Pennsylvanian—especially since that state had not been so represented since Mr. Justice Strong's death in 1880. (Bradley, of course, was from New Jersey, but Harrison had convinced himself that New Jersey had no desirable candidate to offer.) The resolve may have appeared easy to carry out, but any Pennsylvanian of the President's choice would have to overcome the almost certain opposition of Matthew Quay, whose political machine was at bitter odds with Harrison. Quay also had his own candidate: J. H. Brown, an amiable, well-known attorney, eagerly backed by Pennsylvania's well-oiled political machine. Harrison, however, was not amused. Nor would he accept two other machine suggestions that would have received Quay's blessings: the aged Justice Edward Paxton and Justice Henry William, both of the State Supreme Court and both of whom enjoyed extensive support from the legal fraternity as well as from local, state, and national figures.

Instead, the President turned to a relatively unknown Pittsburgh lawyer, sixty-year-old George Shiras, Jr. Shiras came highly recommended by Harrison's Secretary of State, James G. Blaine, who also happened to be the candidate's cousin. Respected and well-liked by the Pennsylvania bar, Shiras was easy going and amiable, and he readily received non-Quay political support. Although he was not at all well known outside Pennsylvania, he had established an influential clientele of railroad, banking, oil, coal, and iron and steel interests—the natural constituents of a lawyer from western Pennsylvania. Among them was Andrew Carnegie, who personally urged Harrison not to be dissuaded by Senator Quay and promised his own support to the candidate. By now convinced that he had found the man he wanted, Harrison nominated the energetic Shiras, whose moderately conservative social, political, and economic persuasions dovetailed neatly with his own. Confirmation took a while, but aided by Senate Democrats, Shiras ultimately won confirmation on July 26, 1892. He was the first and to date the only appointee to reach the Supreme Court without holding public office or without actively participating in the political process. George Shiras's performance during eleven years on the bench was of average quality. He was workmanlike and predictably conservative, but not as inflexible as his colleagues Field, Fuller, Brewer, and Peckham on government regulatory questions. Yet he joined them far more often than not, and could normally be counted aboard the laissez-faire bandwagon of the times.

President Harrison's fourth opportunity for an appointment, his last, came when he was a lame duck, having been defeated by Grover Cleveland in 1892. But Mr. Justice L. Q. C. Lamar died in the following January with two months of the Harrison term still remaining. The President's choice was not only natural but far easier than might have been expected under the circumstances: the available candidates acceptable to him and the Senate were hardly numerous. But then serving on the U.S. Court of Appeals for the Sixth Circuit was Howell E. Jackson of Tennessee—not from Lamar's Mississippi, but close enough. A former colleague of Harrison's in the Senate, the sixty-year-old Jackson was a moderate Democrat and a close family friend. Associate Justice Brown urged Harrison to make the appointment—just as Jackson had done for Brown's candidacy three years earlier. Indeed, Brown insisted that it was he who had clinched matters by "inducing the President" [20] to nominate Jackson who, although opposing secession, had held office under the Confederacy. He was easily confirmed two weeks after the nomination reached the Senate early in February 1893. But what gave every indication of a promising ca-

reer on the Court was truncated by tuberculosis, which began to
plague Jackson soon after he took his seat. He carried on ably and
courageously, and close to the end attempted—unsuccessfully—to
save the federal income tax with his vote in the *Second Income
Tax Case* in May 1895.[21] Yet three months later he died—after
less than two and a half years of service on the bench.

The third President to be assassinated in office, William
McKinley of Canton, Ohio, had been comfortably re-elected for a
second term when he was fatally wounded on September 6, 1901,
at the Pan-American Exposition in Buffalo by Leon F. Czolgosz.
Before he became President he had been probably best known for
the protective tariff bill he had authored while a seven-term member of the House of Representatives. McKinley's Presidential re-
nown, however, is based largely upon his leading the country "into
the World," as he liked to put it, however reluctant he may have
been initially and however he may have disapproved of war.
Cheered on by his powerful political mentor, Marcus Alonzo
("Uncle Mark," or "Boss" Hanna), the business community, the
press, Congress, and his party, McKinley took the Stars and
Stripes to Cuba, Hawaii, Puerto Rico, the Philippines, and even
China. A skillful political organizer, and one of the ablest manip-
ulators of Congress ever to sit in the White House, McKinley
readily deserves the "high average" ranking bestowed upon him
by the historians of the Presidency. The dignified yet warm and
congenial McKinley was a truly popular figure, responsive to and
at home with the public at large, who trusted him and respected
his leadership even when it seemed to be vacillating.

McKinley had but a single opportunity to name a Supreme
Court Justice during his four and a half years in office; his two
predecessors had appointed eight members between 1887 and
1896! But his one selectee gave him, if not everyone else, particular pleasure: Joseph McKenna, fifty-five, a good friend and fellow
legislator. McKenna had first entered national politics as a member of the House of Representatives from California. He served
four consecutive terms; during the third term he became a member
of the potent tax-writing Ways and Means Committee, then

chaired by Congressman William McKinley. There McKenna faithfully supported the controversial McKinley Tariff and related social and economic measures. Generally regarded, and rightly so, as a distant and austere individual, McKenna nonetheless grew close to such prominent and influential Republican leaders as Theodore Roosevelt, Mark Hanna, William H. Taft, Speaker of the House Joseph G. "Czar" Cannon, and Senator Leland Stanford of California. It was on Stanford's recommendation in 1892 that Harrison had named McKenna to the Ninth U.S. Circuit Court of Appeals, where he served five undistinguished or even incompetent years.

McKinley and McKenna had become good friends, and there was widespread speculation that McKenna would get the first vacancy on the Court. A party faithful, he could boast of a staunchly conservative record in Congress as well as on the bench; the roster of his political associates was indeed impressive; and his philosophy of government and politics resembled McKinley's. The President had hoped that the aged Mr. Justice Stephen J. Field, in his thirty-fourth year, would gracefully retire with the Administration change, but Field made no such move and McKinley appointed McKenna as his Attorney General. Nine months later, however, Field, now in a state of marked physical and mental decline, was at last persuaded by his colleagues to step down—secure in the knowledge of a highly influential, distinguished tenure spanning almost three and a half decades (which stands next to Douglas's record) and nine Presidencies. McKinley quickly nominated McKenna—like Field a Californian—who had been a staunch Administration advocate of high tariffs, sound money, support of big business (without, however, being anti-labor per se), and economic laissez faire (but not totally averse to some governmental regulation). Another factor that weighed in the President's decision was his nominee's religion. McKenna was a devout Roman Catholic who had once considered the priesthood: his selection, McKinley hoped, would serve to allay the broadly held belief that he was partial to the American Protective Organization, a contemporary anti-Catholic organization. The nomination was delayed for five weeks, in part because of the vocal opposition of antitrust and anti-railroad interests; in part because of religious bigotry; and in part because of allegations by members of both bar and bench that McKenna's record on the lower federal court was mediocre, if not downright incompetent. But on January 21, 1898, he was confirmed without a formal roll call vote.

McKenna served for almost twenty-seven years; his record ran generally true to expectations both in terms of his jurisprudence and his average performance as a jurist. He proved, however, to be more flexible in the economic sector than might have been predicted—of which McKinley would very likely have approved. Although readily classifiable as politically conservative, neither McKinley nor Joseph McKenna was wedded to rigid doctrine. Nor was McKinley's Vice-President, T.R., whom fate thrust into the Presidency less than three years later.

7

Into the Twentieth Century:
From Theodore Roosevelt to Franklin Roosevelt
1901-1933

The youthful ex-Governor of New York who had reluctantly yielded to the entreaties of old-guard Republicans to accept the Vice-Presidency under McKinley in 1900 suddenly found himself President in 1901. Unlike those among his predecessors whom fate had unexpectedly advanced to that post, Theodore Roosevelt had little apprehension, let alone feelings of dismay or uncertainty. Supremely confident and a born leader, T.R. was a soldier-of-fortune and man-about-society who went on to become a true man of the people. His public literally adored him and were willing to forgive him almost anything. And there were some things to forgive!

Roosevelt threw himself into national leadership with a vengeance. Determined to give life and expression to the progressive movement, the "liberal nationalism" which he embraced, he pursued with the zeal of a crusader his vision of a better, more egalitarian nation. He coined the "stewardship theory" of the Presidency, which means that the President can do anything the Constitution or a Congressional act does not forbid him to do. In his words, it was the President's "duty to do anything that the needs of the nation demanded unless such action was forbidden by the Constitution or by the Laws. I acted for the public welfare, I acted for the common well-being of all our people." [1] The "All-American-Boy President" by no means succeeded in all he set out to do. But the over-all record of this courageous showman-activist earned him the second-highest "near great" ranking by the historians—just below Andrew Jackson, thus according him the number seven spot among the Presidents.

Theodore Roosevelt was determined to fill any vacancies on what he viewed as a "conservative and hidebound" Supreme Court only with individuals who would reflect his progressive political views—particularly in such areas as labor (pro), corporations and trusts (anti), improved race relations (pro), and regulatory power of the national government (pro). To share his philosophy of government and politics would thus become his single dominant criterion for nomination. As he wrote to fellow Republican leader and confidant Senator Henry Cabot Lodge of Massachusetts: "I should hold myself as guilty of an irreparable wrong to the nation if I should put [on the Court] any man who was not absolutely sane and sound on the great national policies for which we stand in public life." [2] Yet T.R. always insisted—at least publicly—that a jurist's "views on progressive social philosophies are entirely second in importance to his possession of a high and fine character." [3] In view of his emphasis on ideological kinship and character, it is hardly astonishing that he considered the geography principle of no moment. If his choice for a vacancy happened to reside in the "appropriate" state or circuit, fine; if not, fine, too: "I have grown to feel, most emphatically," he wrote to Lodge, "that the Supreme Court is a matter of too great importance to me to pay heed to where a man comes from." [4] Consequently Roosevelt sent two citizens of Massachusetts to the Court within four years, becoming the first President to go on public record with a policy of downgrading geography.

Roosevelt appointed three Justices to the Court, among them the judicial philosopher of the age, Oliver Wendell Holmes, Jr. In his choice of Holmes and the others—William H. Moody and William R. Day—the President faithfully adhered to his announced criteria of philosophical compatability, good character, and competence. Indeed, if Day clearly left the progressive reservation on many issues, Holmes and Moody would not. Yet Roosevelt was happy only with Moody, who was forced to resign less than four years after his appointment because of ill health. Holmes, especially during his early years on the Court, was "a bitter disappointment" to the President, "not because of any one decision but because of his general attitude." [5] Yet his antagonism actually stemmed chiefly from Holmes's "anti-antitrust" vote in the *Northern Securities Case* of 1904.[6]

President McKinley had been aware of Mr. Justice Horace Gray's failing health and for some time had pondered a replacement for the able and hard-working jurist from Massachusetts. But Gray held on to life and the bench until September 1902—one year after McKinley's murder. Roosevelt knew that his predecessor had intended to nominate Alfred Hameway, a leading Boston attorney, in Gray's place, but he did not feel found by McKinley's plans and had begun to scout about for other candidates even before Gray's death. Among those who caught T.R.'s eye was the renowned Oliver Wendell Holmes, Jr., Chief Justice of the Supreme Court of Massachusetts. A Boston Brahmin, author, editor, and Harvard faculty member, Holmes had served on the Massachusetts court for twenty years, three as Chief Justice. It was the same post Gray had held when President Arthur appointed him to the Supreme Court. That Holmes was from Gray's state and former judicial station meant little to Roosevelt; his concern lay in the real politics of registered Republican Holmes. As he did so often, T.R. turned for advice to Holmes's fellow Bostonian Henry Cabot Lodge, to whom he addressed a lengthy letter of inquiry. What were the candidate's views on antitrust legislation? On corporations? On labor? What of his philosophy on the evolving American scene of "liberal nationalism"? And what of a recent address given by Holmes on the centenary of John Marshall's appointment as Chief Justice in which Holmes had praised Marshall's role as "an independent political statesman" rather than that of "a great jurist"?

There were of course no doubts in T.R.'s mind concerning

Holmes's exceptional legal and intellectual qualifications for the post: his wit, articulateness, learning, and verve. The President, a physical-culture addict himself, admired the sixty-one-year-old, thrice seriously wounded Civil War veteran's energy, his amazing physical prowess, his sterling character, his judicial expertise. But he wanted to be reassured on Holmes's real as opposed to his nominal politics. Senator Lodge's response provided that reassurance: Holmes was universally considered "a constructive statesman," a "broad-minded constitutionalist," a man blessed with "broad humanity of feeling." In addition he possessed "sympathy for the class" from which he had drawn so many clients while practicing law in Boston. He seemed right on antitrust issues and right on race. T.R. was particularly pleased to note a Holmes dissent in a labor law case, *Plant* v. *Woods,* written while Holmes was Chief Justice of Massachusetts. It was entirely lawful, he wrote there, "for a body of workmen to try by combination to get more than they are now getting, although they do it at the expense of their fellows, and to that end strengthen their union by the boycott and the strike." [7] On December 2, 1902, Roosevelt sent Holmes's name to the Senate; two days later the appointment was unanimously confirmed.

Mr. Justice Holmes graced the Court for thirty exciting years, retiring at almost ninety-one. He will forever remain one of the intellectual giants of the high bench, a man who left a lasting mark not only on jurisprudence but on American society. He is one of the few in American constitutional history who can lay claim to undisputed greatness; sixty-one of the sixty-five Court observers rated him "great," with only John Marshall and Louis Brandeis ahead of him, Brandeis by but one vote. In many ways the supreme scholar and philosopher, Holmes insisted on objective examination of the facts and forces that explain the life of the law and its direction; far from blinding him to the vagaries of life, his philosophical bent prompted a healthy pragmatism in his view of democratic society. His consistent deference to the legislative process—unless it cut into the vitals of the Bill of Rights— demonstrated a commitment to the democratic process that has become legendary. For, essentially, Oliver Wendell Holmes was no democrat, he was a cynic and a skeptic who had little faith in reform movements (to him, "social reform worker types" were "the greatest bores in the world"). Though he fully respected the ideas and ideals of others, he was at heart an intellectual elitist who had no time for the unenlightened, let alone the foolish. But his questioning mind was thoroughly open and he believed in letting others have their say and their play.

Thus more than any other jurist to date Holmes bowed to legislative judgment—even if he may have disrespected the supporters of legislative judgment; even if, as he more than once put it with characteristic bluntness, it made him "vomit." For the great Yankee was fully persuaded that the people, speaking through their representatives, had a constitutional right to "make asses of themselves." As he once put it in an often-quoted statement to constitutional lawyer John W. Davis in connection with an interpretation of the Sherman Anti-Trust Act (which he regarded as one of the worst and certainly most poorly written pieces of federal legislation to be enacted during his lifetime): "Of course I know and every other sensible man knows, that the Sherman law is damned nonsense, but if my country wants to go to hell, I am here to help it." [8] Wisdom and constitutionality were not related: to Holmes and his many followers the Constitution required governmental obedience to its terms, not governmental wisdom.

Nor did Holmes confuse, in the words of one experienced Holmes observer, "his personal tastes and distastes with constitutional necessity." [9] One of his most frequently cited commentaries on that central point was made to his colleague Stone, who was then sixty-one years old: "Young man, about 75 years ago I learned that I was not God. And so, when the people . . . want to do something that I can't find anything in the Constitution expressly forbidding them to do, I say, whether I like it or not, 'Goddamit, let 'em to it.' " [10] He did find that the Constitution expressly forbade the invasion of fundamental civil liberties— especially freedom of expression. There he readily and resolutely invoked his power of judicial interposition.

To Holmes laws were made by men, not angels! And his abiding conviction—that the obligation to heed what he styled as "the felt necessities of the time" is eternal—was the most brilliant of the many facets that made him the intellectual leader of the Court. Even in dissent—which is where he found himself more often than not on key contemporary issues—Holmes led. Indeed, it is as "the great dissenter" that he is best known, especially since the post-1937 Court turned so many of his classic dissenting opinions into majority opinions. The following excerpts from dissenting opinions in milestone cases in constitutional law represent both literature and law:

> *the 1905 New York Bakeshop Case* (in which the Court struck down 5:4 the state's attempt to limit hours of work in bakeries): "The Fourteenth Amendment does not enact Mr. Herbert Spencer's *Social Statics*. . . . A constitution is not intended to embody a particular economic theory. . . . It is made for people of fundamentally differing views. . . ." [11]

> *the 1918 Child Labor Case* (in which the Court struck down 5:4 the federal government's attempt to regulate child labor): "If there is any matter upon which civilized countries have agreed it is the evil of premature and excessive child labor. I should have thought that if we were to introduce our own moral conceptions where in my opinion they do not belong, this was preeminently a case for upholding the exercise of all its powers by the United States." [12]

> *the 1919 Pro-Soviet Pamphleteer Case* (in which the Court upheld 7:2 the conviction of six self-styled "anarchist-Socialists" under the Espionage Act of 1917): "When men have realized that time has upset many fighting faiths, they may come to believe even more than they believe the very foundations of their own conduct that the ultimate good desired is better reached by free trade in ideas—that the best test of truth is the power of the thought to get itself accepted in the competition of the market, and that truth is the only ground upon which their wishes can be safely carried out. That at any rate is the theory of our Constitution. It is an experiment as all life is an experiment. Every year if not every day we have to wager our salvation upon some prophecy based upon imperfect knowledge. While that experiment is

part of our system I think that we should be eternally vigilant against attempts to check the expression of opinions that we loathe and believe to be fraught with death, unless they so imminently threaten immediate interference with the lawful and pressing purposes of the law that an immediate check is required to save the country.[13]

the 1925 New York Criminal Syndicalism Case (in which the Court 6:2 upheld one Benjamin Gitlow's conviction for violating the 1902 Criminal Anarchy Act by publishing a "Left Wing Manifesto"): "It is said that this manifesto was more than a theory, that it was an incitement. Every idea is an incitement. It offers itself for belief and if believed it is acted on unless some other belief outweighs it or some failure of energy stifles the movement at its birth. The only difference between the expression of opinion and an incitement in the narrower sense is the speaker's enthusiasm for the result. Eloquence may set fire to reason. . . . If in the long run the beliefs expressed in proletarian dictatorship are destined to be accepted by the dominant forces of the community, the only meaning of free speech is that they should be given their chance and have their way." [14]

and

the 1928 Wiretapping Case (in which the Court held 5:4 that wiretapping did not constitute a violation of the Fourth Amendment guarantees against unreasonable searches and seizures): "Wiretapping is dirty business. . . . The government ought not to use evidence obtained, and only obtainable, by a criminal act. . . . It is desirable that criminals should be detected and to that end all available evidence should be used. It is also desirable that the Government should not itself foster and pay for other crimes. . . . We have to choose, and for my part I think it a less evil that some criminals should escape than that the government should play an ignoble part." [15]

Theodore Roosevelt had every reason to praise Oliver Wendell Holmes; instead he peevishly carped about the work of this preeminent American jurist. Indeed, far from opposing him Holmes furthered and articulated Roosevelt's ideas through his presence on the Court—even if he did consider the President a "shallow intellect."

If Roosevelt had any reason to be disappointed or even to feel betrayed by an appointee, it was by virtue of the record established on the Court by his next choice, fifty-three-year-old William Rufus Day of Ohio. Initially, Day pleased T. R. mightily; he cast his vote in support of the Government's position in the aforementioned celebrated *Northern Securities Case*. But then he let the President down, opposing such vital federal programs as legislation designed to regulate hours and wages of labor. Thus he wrote the majority opinion, with Holmes in dissent, that struck down the Child Labor Law of 1916.[16] Moreover, he usually opposed assertive executive policy actions. Day was not Roosevelt's first choice (that was William Howard Taft) but his selection was entirely in line with the President's stated objectives and requirements.

In the summer of 1902 Mr. Justice George Shiras, Jr., of Pennsylvania told the President that he intended to retire early the next year. He had served ably but unspectacularly for a decade. T.R., meeting with two firm rebuffs from Taft, then Governor of the Philippine Islands, sought the latter's advice as well as that of other prominent Republican leaders such as Mark Hanna, Elihu Root, and Nelson Aldrich. Ohioan Hanna knew Day well from their association during the McKinley Administration when the latter had served as both Assistant Secretary of State and Secretary of State; and Taft had served with Day on the "Learned Sixth"—the U.S. Court of Appeals for the Sixth Circuit—to which McKinley had appointed him in 1899. Day had demonstrated his Republican fealty by working for Benjamin Harrison's election; ultimately he had become one of President McKinley's favorite legal, personal, and political advisers. As Assistant Secretary of the Navy, Roosevelt himself had worked closely with him. There had been ample opportunity to ascertain Day's real politics, and the President, if he could not have Taft, would be glad to have Day. He was confirmed quickly without a roll call on February 23, 1903.

Roosevelt's third and last opportunity to make a Supreme Court appointment came when Mr. Justice Henry B. Brown of Michigan announced that he would retire at the end of the 1905–6 term.

T. R. first focused upon the man Brown had recommended, former Attorney General Philander C. Knox, a U.S. Senator. But Knox declined, viewing the Court as a political dead end. The President, without any real hope, again offered the vacancy to Taft, now home from the Philippines and serving in his Cabinet as Secretary of War. But Taft was gunning for higher stakes. Roosevelt next offered the post to his trusted Secretary of State and political ally, Elihu H. Root, who declined, preferring to remain in active politics. Shortly thereafter Roosevelt called in Attorney General Moody, went over a list of possible candidates with him, then suddenly stopped, grinned, and asked him: "Is it possible that you do not know whom I am to appoint to this position? You, and you only, are the man." [17]

Massachusetts-born and educated at Andover and Harvard, William Henry Moody had entered upon the stage of national politics during the McKinley Administration, serving seven years in the U.S. House of Representatives. Previously he had established himself as a leading member of the Essex County bar, gaining national prominence in 1893 as one of the Commonwealth's prosecuting attorneys in the celebrated Lizzy Borden trial. Resembling Theodore Roosevelt in looks as well as actions, Moody became friendly with him during the President's stint as Assistant Secretary of the Navy under McKinley. In May 1902 Roosevelt had brought Moody into his Cabinet as Secretary of the Navy (the two men held identical views on the significance of naval power), an office in which Moody displayed exceptional administrative and organizational talents. When Philander Knox, the incumbent Attorney General, moved to the Senate in 1904, the President switched Moody to that position, one for which he was tailor-made. A trial lawyer par excellence, Moody launched assaults on the beef, sugar-refining, and oil trusts, although not always successfully. He also entered the thick of the railroad rate controversy with relish. In his early fifties, at the apex of his career, politically and socially close to Root, Taft, and Lodge as well as Roosevelt, here was a "natural" for the Court. T.R.—although he did anticipate serious criticism on the score—was not about to be stopped from selecting Moody, even though he would be the second Massachusetts appointee to the high bench in barely four years. He happily and eagerly forwarded the nomination, which was confirmed without delay *viva voce* in mid-December, 1906. Moody did not disappoint the President, who frequently voiced satisfaction with his friend's work on the bench—which has received high marks despite its brevity. Today Moody is probably best remembered for his learned and lucid (although overruled some six decades later) opinion for the Court in *Twining* v. *New Jersey* (1908), in which he held that the Fifth Amendment's privilege against self-incrimination was not as such binding on the states via the Fourteenth Amendment's due process of law clause.[18]

Although he was elected to and embarked upon the Presidency as Roosevelt's hand-picked protégé, William Howard Taft's conception of the office differed dramatically from his predecessor's in style as well as substance. Far from regarding it as a stewardcy, the portly Ohioan—the only man in American history to date to serve as both President and Chief Justice—viewed the role of President as a "passive" or "supervisory" one. As he made clear in *Our Chief Magistrate and His Powers,* a work based on lectures delivered at Columbia University in 1915, he was wholly dedicated to the proposition that the Chief Executive is bound by a literal interpretation of the Constitution; that there exists no "undefined residuum of power which he can exercise"; that not only respect but deference is due Congress.[19] Yet Taft, the executive humilitarian and literalist, was a driving judicial activist. He was happier and far more effective on the Court than in the White House. To him the Chief Justiceship was the realization of the dream of a lifetime; the Presidency, while an honor, was but a job to be done. Predictably, the President-watchers have ranked him just "average." Court observers, however, have ranked him "near great" for his work there.

In a number of ways Taft endeavored to continue the Roosevelt program of progressivism, of "liberal nationalism." Thus, although less sympathetic to conservation than Roosevelt, he successfully battled exploiters and speculators in coal and oil, and he instituted twice as many antitrust suits, winning more than his political mentor, the legendary "trust buster." Even so, Taft was far more conservative than T.R., cautious and at home with the G.O.P.'s conservative leadership. Often surprisingly indecisive, he found it easy to temporize and equivocate in a host of policy matters, although he stood firm against military involvement abroad. He was astonishingly inept politically—yet the burden of following the Roosevelt act would have weighed heavily on almost any successor.

In his single term Taft appointed six Justices to the Court, including one Chief Justice—at the time more than any President since George Washington. And in view of his often successful "pushing" for kindred souls during the years of his Chief Justiceship (1921–30) it might be claimed that he was responsible for even more. Taft chose his jurists with great care and with little concern for their nominal political affiliations (Lurton, White, and Lamar were Democrats, although all conservatives from the South) yet their performance on the bench was spotty in terms of his expectations. But he was philosophical about his choices: all were men of integrity; all were personally known to him; all except Hughes had had judicial experience. But most importantly he had carefully considered their real politics—he wanted no liberals of the stamp of Learned Hand, Louis Brandeis, or Benjamin Cardozo, potential candidates whom he regarded as "destroyers of the Constitution." [20] If some of his Justices were occasionally unpredictable, well, that was the price to be paid for achieving the separation of powers in which he so strongly believed.

Taft's first opportunity to nominate a member of the Court came with the death of Mr. Justice Rufus W. Peckham in October 1909. Peckham had been an apostle of laissez-faire capitalism and had served for fourteen years as a pillar of the Field-Brewer-Fuller approach to constitutional interpretation. Taft wanted someone in a rather different mold, and he knew exactly whom: his close friend, Professor Horace H. Lurton of the Vanderbilt University School of Law, for eight years his fellow judge on the "Learned Sixth." Earlier, in 1906, T.R. had wanted to appoint

Lurton but had been dissuaded by fellow Republican Henry Cabot Lodge because Lurton was a Tennessee Democrat. To Taft that was a non sequitur; he and Lurton were philosophical, political, and personal kinsmen. The President had long known and respected the legal talents of the Confederate Army veteran who had seen more than a quarter of a century of judicial service— sixteen years on the federal bench and ten on the state bench. Hence he resolved to appoint Lurton despite the latter's age (sixty-five) and despite Taft's avowal of a youth movement on the bench following a pronouncement that members of the Court who held on to their jobs in the face of advanced age were "near senility." "There was nothing," commented a jubilant Taft after Lurton's prompt, routine confirmation, "that I had so much at heart in my whole administration as Lurton's appointment." [21] Lurton died only four and a half years later. He had had little time to establish a record, let alone leave an imprint; what little of it there was pointed to a cautious, competent jurist steeped in judicial self-restraint.

In late March 1910, just a few months after Lurton's confirmation, Mr. Justice David J. Brewer died after more than twenty years of influential, doctrinaire service on the Court. It had earned Brewer the respect, if not the admiration, of students of constitutional law everywhere. If Brewer was not quite the equal of his uncle Stephen J. Field, he had carried the family ideological banner proudly and effectively. His departure from the scene enabled Taft to make his second and, as time would prove, his most important appointment: Charles Evans Hughes, Governor of New York, was then a youthful and vigorous forty-eight years and a bright new star in the Republican constellation. Taft had been afraid of him as a potential rival in 1908; now he frankly regarded Hughes as clear Presidential timber—stronger, indeed, than himself or Teddy Roosevelt. When he learned that Hughes seemed prepared, indeed eager, to leave the political scene, Taft quickly turned to him. Since he had some doubt as to Hughes's willingness to accept, Taft dangled the Chief Justiceship before him in a celebrated letter:

The Chief Justiceship is soon likely to be vacant and I should never regard the [until now] established practice of never promoting Associate Justices as one to be followed.[22]

But the President added an equally celebrated postscript:

Don't misunderstand me as to the Chief Justiceship. I mean if that office were now open, I should offer it to you and it is *probable* that if it were to become vacant during my term, I should promote you to it; *but, of course, conditions change,* so that it would not be right for me to say by way of promise what I would do in the future. Nor, on the other hand, would I have you think that your declination now would prevent my offering you the higher position, *should conditions remain as they are.*[23]

Hughes, fully conscious of the meaning of these ambiguities, acquiesced with grace and generosity. Those "conditions" would indeed "change" within a matter of months—with the coveted plum going to Edward D. White, not Hughes. And Hughes would resign from the bench in 1916 to run for the Presidency after all—only to return as Chief Justice in 1930 to succeed Taft, who had reached the post after White's death in 1921.

Only a few days after his designation Charles Evans Hughes sailed through the Senate with nary a ripple. He was a child prodigy who entered college at fourteen, earned a Phi Beta Kappa key, and was graduated at twenty-two from Columbia Law School, where he attained highest honors. As a youthful and brilliant lawyer he soon earned the universal respect of the profession; in addition to practicing law, he also taught it, and ultimately embarked upon a governmental career as a legislative counsel, culminating in the Governship of New York. But Hughes's ambitions for the highest office of all were initially blocked by Teddy Roosevelt, whose early plans had centered on Taft—not Hughes, whom he disliked. After his 1916 defeat Hughes ceased his quest for the Presidency and returned to the law and government service, ultimately becoming Secretary of State as well as a judge of the World Court.

Hughes's six years as Associate Justice were marked by carefully drafted, frequent opinions. A happy blend of conservatism and liberalism, he embraced a protective approach vis-à-vis both economic-proprietarian rights and civil rights and liberties. Thus he could say "no" to many pre-1937 attempts by the federal government to broaden the reach of the interstate commerce power, while championing political dissent in often beautiful and persuasive language:

> The greater the importance of safeguarding the community from incitements to the overthrow of our institutions by force and violence, the more imperative is the need to preserve inviolate the constitutional rights of free speech, free press, and free assembly in order to maintain the opportunity for free political discussion, to the end that government may be responsive to the will of the people and that changes, if desired, may be obtained by peaceful means. Therein lies the security of the Republic, the very foundation of constitutional government.[24]

During his brief Associate Justiceship Hughes wrote more opinions for the Court (151) than any other jurist, and in them he almost invariably spoke for an unanimous Court; in fact, in only nine of these cases were there dissents, and in only three of them by more than one Justice. (Hughes also wrote thirty-two dissenting opinions himself.) The days of his Chief Justiceship, however—to be discussed in Chapters 7 and 8—would prove to be dramatically different.

Hughes's confirmation came on May 2, 1910; on July 4, Mr. Chief Justice Fuller died, having been the faithful steward of economic laissez faire for twenty-two years—an era marked by a jurisprudence never again to return. The general expectation by insiders was that Taft would promote Hughes—his letter to Hughes being a well-known secret. Holmes, for example, wrote his friend Sir Frederick Pollock of his conviction that the post would go to Hughes rather than to himself.[25] The press also confidently predicted his elevation. But the President bided his time, during which a "boomlet" developed for Mr. Justice John Marshall Harlan. Taft, however, contemptuously dismissed such a possibility:

"I'll do no such damned thing. I won't make the position of Chief Justice a blue ribbon for the final years of any member of the Court. I want someone who will coordinate the activities of the Court and who has a reasonable expectation of serving ten or twenty years on the bench." [26] The President's confidential aides, such as Archie Butts, continued to urge him to appoint Hughes, but it now became evident that Taft was steering away from him. He asked Attorney General George W. Wickersham to poll the sitting members of the Court for their preference, which proved to be White. Teddy Roosevelt got into the act by informing Taft of his intense dislike of Hughes, that "upstart." And the more the President pondered Hughes's forty-eight years and excellent health the less convinced he became that he should promote him.

On December 12, 1910, having waited more than seven months to make up his mind, Free Mason, Unitarian Taft nominated devout Roman Catholic Edward Douglass White to the Chief Justiceship—the first sitting jurist to be promoted to that post in the history of the Court. "White, Not Hughes, for Chief Justice" proclaimed the headline in the *New York Times* [27] to what was popular acclaim, notwithstanding Speaker of the House "Uncle Joe" Cannon, who noted: "If Taft were Pope, he'd want to appoint some Protestants to the College of Cardinals." [28] The ascertainable reasons for the appointment were multiple: Taft considered White, then in his seventeenth year on the Court, to be the ablest administrator among his colleagues; he knew that White was popular among his colleagues; and White's real politics had proved eminently compatible with his own. Yet assuredly Taft was also motivated by his consuming ambition to attain the Chief Justiceship himself some day. He literally grieved aloud when he signed White's commission: "There is nothing I would have loved more than being Chief Justice of the United States. I cannot help seeing the irony in the fact that I, who desired that office so much, should now be signing the commission of another man." [29] Indeed! But White was now in his sixty-sixth year—hardly of the youthful strain Taft had promised but had produced to date only in the person of Hughes. Given the age of the new Chief Justice and some of the good fortune that had blessed the paths of the Taft family for some time, might not a future President on White's death, resignation, or retirement select a candidate so uniquely qualified and experienced—so "pregnant" a candidate—as William Howard Taft? It proved to be a superbly educated guess: White died in May of 1921, and President Harding selected his fellow Ohioan to fill the post. Had White succumbed during the Wilson era (1913–21) it is highly unlikely that Taft—who loathed Wilson and was not loved in return—would ever have realized his cherished dream.

During his decade on the Court as Chief Justice, Edward Douglass White continued the cautiously independent and evaluative approach to the law that had characterized his lengthy service as an Associate Justice. He had fully earned the respect and affection of his colleagues as well as Court experts who have ranked him, perhaps somewhat generously, as "near great." Although by background and persuasion an ideological conservative suspicious of the exercise of large-scale governmental power, he proved to be far from doctrinaire and, when he deemed it constitutionally justifiable, would back broad exercise of federal power, albeit selectively. Thus he authored opinions on the Adamson Act of 1916 which upheld the federal statute providing for an eight-hour day and railroad labor, and on the Importation of Impure Tea Act of 1897 which backed legislation sanctioning generous delegation of legislative power for the purpose of establishing standards to the Executive Branch. He also voted to uphold the federal income tax statute of 1894. On the other hand, he sided with Holmes in the *Northern Securities Case,* was the author of the Court's "rule of reason," which held that the Sherman Anti-Trust Act forbade only those combinations or contracts in restraint that were "unreasonable," and voted with those who struck down the federal child labor law of 1916.[30] Congenial and flexible, he proved himself to be a capable leader of the Court and sufficiently pleasing to his nominator. If he was not of the stature of the great Chief Justices such as Marshall, Taney, Hughes, Stone, and Warren, he deserves to be ranked with a second group including Taft and Waite.

White's promotion left his own Associate Justiceship to be filled. This time Taft turned to his own party, selecting the urbane Willis Van Devanter of Wyoming, a fifty-one-year-old Judge of the U.S. Court of Appeals for the Eighth Circuit. As a young man, the erstwhile Midwesterner had gone to Wyoming where he befriended the Republican Territorial Governor, Francis E. Warren, becoming his indispensable ally and helpmate. An able draftsman and administrator, he had supervised the revision of the territorial statutes and had served in various local and state legislative posts as well as Chief Justice of the Supreme Court of Wyoming. His reputation as a progressive during his stint in the U.S. Department of the Interior, where he served as an attorney specializing in matters involving public lands and Indian affairs, had been a real factor in his appointment to the Circuit Court by Roosevelt; but it soon became evident that his long-time association with powerful Western business combines had left him strongly conservative in terms of constitutional interpretation. Taft was well aware of that fact, yet he wanted to please restive elements in the Republican party. He was also seeking a candidate from the Midwest or the West, and he was generally comfortable with Van Devanter. The two men became close personal allies on the high bench—Taft regarded him as his favorite colleague—notwithstanding Van Devanter's far more pronounced intellectual conservatism. He is best known in his twenty-seven years on the Court for his senior membership in the Anti-New Deal group, the "Four Horsemen" (the other three were Justices James C. McReynolds, George Sutherland, and Pierce Butler); for being the tail to his colleague Sutherland's intellectual kite; and for writing fewer opinions than any other Justice who served with him— barely averaging three a year during his last decade on the Court, only one in two years, and none in one. Although he apparently made significant oral contributions in the Justices' Conferences, the dearth of his opinions and his doctrinaire rigidity prompted the experts to rate Mr. Justice Willis Van Devanter a "failure"—perhaps too harsh a judgment.

President Taft's fifth appointment (his fourth in little more than a year) also went to the Senate on December 12, 1910, and like Van Devanter was quickly confirmed by it without audible dissent. The vacancy, created by Mr. Justice William Henry Moody's widely regretted resignation after less than four years on the Court because of incapacitating acute rheumatism, went to another Southern Democrat, Joseph Rucker Lamar, a plantation-born Confederate Army veteran. Moody hailed from Massachusetts, but in Holmes that state and circuit had more than distinguished representation; in any event, geography did not figure large in Taft's appointment criteria. A member of the same family as ex-Supreme Court Justice L.Q.C. Lamar, the fifty-three-year-old renowned Georgia lawyer had served on his state's Supreme Court; had been a state legislator for two terms; and was being actively considered for an appointment to the United States Commerce Court when the President decided to send him to the top tribunal instead.

Although Taft was not so close personally to Lamar as he had been to Lurton, the former readily met the President's essential criteria. His judicial and legislative record had manifested the conservatism and ideological bent with which Taft was comfortable; his real politics was eminently acceptable. For example, the two men saw eye-to-eye on the protective tariff question, which was of great moment to the President. Moreover, Lamar's selection would strengthen Taft with such influential Southern political leaders as Democratic Senators Augustus O. Bacon of Georgia and Joseph W. Bailey of Texas, and close Presidential advisers such as Archie Butt and George W. Wickersham urged his choice insistently. His confirmation came within three days and without any audible dissent. Although he gave Taft no reason to regret his action, Lamar's record of barely five years on the Court was as insignificant as it was undistinguished.

Taft's sixth and last opportunity to people the Court came with the death of John Marshall Harlan on October 14, 1911. The Lincoln-appointed Kentuckian had served brilliantly for almost thirty-four years; his labors in behalf of a broad national interpretation and application of the Bill of Rights and the Civil War amendments laid the groundwork for many of the libertarian decisions of the mid-twentieth century. Mahlon Pitney of New Jersey —whom Taft would name to the Harlan seat after a hiatus of some four months—was cast in a different mold.

Initially the President had looked west of the Mississippi for Harlan's replacement, seriously considering Judge William Hook of Kansas (Eighth U.S. Circuit Court of Appeals) and his Secretary of Commerce and Labor, Charles Nagel of Missouri. But Hook had rendered himself persona non grata with the country's Negroes in a 1911 ruling upholding Oklahoma's "Jim Crow" statute,[31] and Nagel had become increasingly unpopular with labor, particularly because of his liberal stance on immigration. Taft now looked to the East and to New Jersey, from which no Justice had come since Joseph P. Bradley more than four decades earlier. But more important in Taft's mind as well as in those of his political strategists was that New Jersey could become a battleground between Taft's supporters and the supporters of Theodore Roosevelt, whose Presidential candidacy was now clearly emerging. Whether or not the selection of Pitney was decisive, New Jersey's Republican delegation did cast its votes for Taft in the National Convention of 1912.

But political implications of his nomination aside, Mahlon Pitney was appealing to Taft for other reasons: The "right" age at fifty-three, he had amassed eleven years of judicial experience (a key factor in Taft's eyes) while serving on various New Jersey courts; he had been a U.S. Congressman for two terms; and he had served as Republican Floor Leader and President of the New Jersey Senate. Pitney's record on the state bench showed a general commitment close to Taft's own, but Taft had nagging doubts about his approach to governmental regulation. Liberals and labor forces, however, had more than nagging doubts; they questioned Pitney's entire philosophy of government and politics and so mounted a major campaign against him. Although it succeeded in delaying confirmation for almost a month, the Senate finally approved him 50:26. Pitney's undistinguished decade on the Court, marked by increasingly reactionary votes—especially as the leader of the Court's anti-labor faction—soon began to displease his nominator. Later, as Chief Justice, Taft publicly pronounced Pitney to be a "weak member" of the Court to whom he could "not assign cases." [32]

Woodrow Wilson, according to the historical experts, is outranked among American Presidents only by George Washington, Abraham Lincoln, and Franklin Roosevelt. Wilson came to the office with strong intellectual as well as executive and administrative qualifications: a Ph.D. in political science and a former President of Princeton University and Governor of New Jersey, he had few peers in the Presidency in theoretical and practical knowledge of politics. Despite these high qualifications and his general success, Wilson experienced an unprecedented measure of pain and anguish in his country's rejection of the League of Nations and the Treaty of Versailles. For him it was the end of his life as well as his dream.

Victor in 1912 only because of the fatal Taft-Roosevelt split and but narrowly triumphant over Hughes in 1916, Wilson personified the New Freedom's quest for social and economic justice. In many ways he built upon the heritage of political reformers such as William Jennings Bryan and Theodore Roosevelt, and he eagerly sought the advice of practical idealists such as Louis Brandeis, whom he would send to the Court in 1916. Aristocratic, highly moral, Calvinistic, he preached rectitude—France's Georges Clemenceau once commented that "talking to Wilson is like talking to Jesus Christ"— [33] yet he understood and learned well the Presidential role. Until the tragedy of the League of Nations felled him, he was a powerful, driving political and intellectual leader. Indeed, he was a simply superb politician until he forgot or ignored the necessity to compromise.

Largely because of the avalanche of appointments that had fallen to Taft, Wilson had but three opportunities to appoint men to the Court during his eight years in office. One of those appointments went to Louis D. Brandeis, a giant among men on the Court; another to John H. Clarke, a noble and sensitive spirit; another, unfortunately, to James C. McReynolds, who was a total failure.

Woodrow Wilson's appointment criteria were neither novel nor precious. Like his two immediate predecessors he was more concerned with a candidate's real rather than nominal politics—hence Brandeis's registration as a Republican in Massachusetts was of no moment to him. Broadly, he required a liberal-progressive public policy and, especially, a dedication to trust-busting. Also like Taft and Roosevelt before him, he paid little attention to geography: if it was a factor at all it appeared only in McReynolds's appointment. Again like the two earlier Presidents, Wilson tended to favor individuals whom he knew personally or professionally. The one noticeable difference from the criteria of Taft and Roosevelt lay in his disregard for judicial experience. McReynolds and Brandeis thus had no judicial background, and Clarke had but four years. It is fair to conclude that the absence of such experience had no bearing on the collective performance of Wilson's nominees: they served as they did because of their makeup and their commitments—not because of presence or absence of judicial experience.

When in the summer of 1914 Horace H. Lurton died after little more than four years on the Court, Wilson moved rapidly to make his first nomination. James Clark McReynolds, his fifty-two-year-old Attorney General—like Lurton from Tennessee—had attended the Law School of the University of Virginia, ultimately entering government service. He evinced an early interest in trust-busting, receiving national attention in 1907 when as Assistant Attorney General he did yeoman duty in his handling of the tobacco trust. Later, when the Taft Administration took actions that McReynolds regarded as unduly compromising, he publicly resigned his post and broke with the Republican party. These events established his image as a fighter of trusts and big business. In due course McReynolds joined the Wilson forces and actively campaigned for Wilson's election. Ultimately he was appointed Attorney General.

As Attorney General, McReynolds continued his trust-busting activities, although with some aberrations. Still, Wilson was satisfied that his man would stand up to what he liked to refer to as the "Mr. Bigs," no matter what post they held and regardless of McReynolds's personal motivations—which, as has been suggested, were grounded in his fundamental agrarianism as well as in his dislike and distrust of "bigness" generally. So Wilson sent his Attorney General to the Court, perhaps with a tinge of doubt but with sufficient confidence in his progressivism. History would prove him utterly wrong—for McReynolds not only became a member of the anti-New Deal Four Horsemen, he became their loudest, most cantankerous, aggressive, intemperate, and reactionary representative. There have been suggestions, in increasing number of late, that Wilson was aware of McReynolds's inherent ultra-conservatism but that he was nonetheless willing to appoint him to the Court in order to get him out of the Cabinet. In the judgment of such a wise observer as Wilson's Secretary of the Navy, Josephus Daniels, the President, refusing to scuttle his faith in McReynolds and still convinced that he was a progressive at heart, resolved gracefully to "kick him upstairs." [34] If he was impossible to live with that did not mean that he was not politically progressive. And McReynolds, strongly backed by the Democratic party, was confirmed ten days after his nomination reached the Senate in mid-August 1914.

James Clark McReynolds's record and antics during his ensuing twenty-seven years on the Court are legion. Politically and jurisprudentially he came to embrace a philosophy of reaction to progress second to none, and in his personal demeanor on the bench was a disgrace to the Court. Manifesting blatant anti-Semitism, McReynolds refused to speak to Brandeis (the first Jew to sit on the Court) for three years following Brandeis's appointment and was only somewhat less obnoxious in his behavior to the gentle Benjamin Cardozo during whose swearing-in ceremony he pointedly read a newspaper. In 1922 McReynolds refused to accompany the Court to Philadelphia on a ceremonial occasion because, as he wrote to the exasperated Chief Justice Taft: "As you know, I am not always to be found when there is a Hebrew abroad. Therefore, my 'inability' to attend must not surprise you." [35] And because he would not sit next to Brandeis (where he belonged for seniority reasons) for the Court's annual picture-taking session in 1924, Taft decided that no Court picture would be taken at all that year.[36] Nor would McReynolds sign the customary dedicatory letter sent to all Court members on their retirement when that time came for Brandeis in 1939.

McReynolds also disliked Harlan Stone and his jurisprudence and carped about almost every opinion Stone wrote. Another of his targets was the sensitive John Hessin Clarke, whose voting record on the bench equally displeased him. While McReynolds's enmity was not decisive in Clark's resignation from the Court in 1922, it clearly contributed to his resolve to leave. "McReynolds," he wrote to Woodrow Wilson, "as you know, is the most reactionary judge on the Court. There were many other things which had better not be set down in black and white. . . ." [37] And ex-President Taft not only considered McReynolds weak, he regarded him as a selfish, prejudiced, bigoted person "and one who seems to delight in making others uncomfortable. . . ." [38]

Quite aside from Mr. Justice McReynolds's bigoted personality * was his performance on the Court—a bitter disappointment to Wilson. Not only did he shock the President almost at once by his vote against the constitutionality of a Kansas law outlawing "yellow dog" contracts,[39] he would *never* side with the President on any significant issue involving governmental regulatory activity. (Brandeis, on the other hand, rarely and Clarke never cast an anti-Wilson vote.) Unlike his colleagues Justices Sutherland and Van Devanter, he made no distinction between areas of public law such as Presidential authority in domestic and foreign policy decision-making or the Court's role in guarding civil rights and liberties. In the latter area even his colleague Pierce Butler would now and then join in a decision upholding a beleaguered individual.[40] Certainly McReynolds earned the all but unanimous con-

* He would not accept Jews, "smokers," or married or engaged individuals as law clerks.

demnation of the Court experts, who rated him at the top of their brief list of failures.

Wilson's next appointment, Louis Dembitz Brandeis, was designated "great" by all but three of the sixty-five experts. The Brandeis confirmation battle still ranks as the most bitter and most intensely fought in the history of the Court, and the delay of more than four months after Wilson submitted Brandeis's name to the Senate on January 28, 1916, is still a record.

The President's selection of the famed Boston attorney, "The People's Lawyer," had come on Mr. Justice Joseph R. Lamar's death earlier that January. Wilson had known and admired Brandeis for a good many years. As a youth of nineteen he had entered Harvard Law School directly from the Annen-Realschule in Dresden, Germany, graduating two years later at the head of his class. As a partner in the distinguished Boston law firm of Warren and Brandeis, he had amassed a fortune and toward the end of the century—with the encouragement of his partners—had begun to involve himself in public affairs, soon becoming a renowned legal champion of the redress of economic and political inequities. At the Supreme Court bar he was a familiar figure, always arguing eloquently and persuasively. His authorship of what became known as the "Brandeis Brief," which he first introduced in 1908 in *Muller* v. *Oregon,*[41] wrought a substantive and procedural revolution in the judicial process. In the *Muller* case, the Fuller Court —to universal surprise given its record on attempted governmental regulation of hours and working conditions—unanimously upheld Oregon's 1903 statute forbidding the employment of women in "mechanical establishments," factories, and laundries for more than ten hours per day. There is general agreement that had it not been for the "Brandeis Brief," the Oregon law would have been declared unconstitutional as a violation of due process of law. Brandeis's procedure was to submit a brief to the Court that disposed of the constitutional issues and precedents in two pages but devoted more than a hundred pages to statistical data on hours of labor, health, morals, and factory legislation abroad—all emphasizing the special status of women. (One cannot help but wonder whether such an emphasis would be sanctioned in the 1970s.)

But, as Wilson knew, Brandeis was far from a radical. He was deeply dedicated to his country and wanted to do all he could to attain a greater measure of democracy, of social justice, of egalitarianism. Yet notwithstanding his detractors in many segments of the business community, he was emphatically not "anti-business" or even "anti-big-business"; he was no enemy of capitalism, of free enterprise, of profits. Indeed, during his tenure of more than two decades, in which he wrote a myriad of opinions, Brandeis never authored an opinion in favor of the government in an antitrust case. But he was acutely conscious of maldistribution of power, reward, and opportunity, and he dedicated his life to a rectification of that condition—on as well as off the Court. Although Brandeis had been no stranger to President Wilson, the two men had not worked together until the Presidential campaign of 1912, when Brandeis's advice to the candidate was largely instrumental in shaping the Democratic position on social and economic matters. Brandeis became Wilson's close friend, adviser, and collaborator, and the President was determined to have him aboard during his Administration. When the Attorney Generalship, to which he had intended to appoint Brandeis, fell through because of the volatile opposition of the Boston bar, Wilson vowed to himself that another even more important spot would be found for Brandeis.

Recognizing the furor that a Brandeis nomination to the Court would cause, the President moved extremely cautiously when the time came. Fearing the consequences of early disclosure, he had consulted only one Senator before announcing the nomination: Robert M. LaFollette, the influential Wisconsin progressive whose small but vital band of supporters in the Senate were needed. LaFollette was delighted and assured the President of his backing, adding that it was about time that a progressive individual got on "that Court." When Wilson's gleeful announcement came in January 1916, all hell broke loose in the financial, legal, and political communities, where many powerful elements had long fought and feared him as a "radical." The opposition was directed largely at Brandeis's social and economic record and at his "sociological jurisprudence." But there is no question that much of the anti-Brandeis campaign was anti-Semitic in origin. Among the leaders of the large number of well-known members of the bar who led the professional opposition were its President Elihu Root, ex-Attorney General George W. Wickersham, and William Howard Taft.

Taft was no anti-Semite, but he loathed Brandeis for the nominee's role six years earlier in unearthing an embarrassing sleight-of-hand that he and Wickersham had executed in behalf of an accused Taft Cabinet member, Secretary of the Interior Richard A. Ballinger. But above all, Taft wanted the vacancy for himself! How he could have deluded himself into believing that Wilson would even consider him is difficult to comprehend; they had been outspoken enemies for some time. Suffice it to say that Taft craved the position so much that he was given to fantasies. In any event he was livid and wrote to one of his aides that the nomination represented "one of the deepest wounds" that he had sustained "as an American and a lover of the Constitution and a believer in progressive conservatism . . . [that] when you consider . . . that men were pressing me for the place, *es ist zum lachen*" [42] (it is ridiculous).

The confirmation battle raged against a background of some of the ugliest charges ever leveled against a distinguished public servant. It was finally terminated on June 1, 1916, by a 47:22 affirmative vote (the Judiciary Committee having reported the nomination favorably 10:8). Of those voting "aye," forty-four were cast by the forty-five Democratic Senators present and voting. The three lonely Republican votes in favor were those of Robert M. LaFollette, George W. Norris of Nebraska, and Miles Poindexter of Washington. The Wisconsin statesman had kept his promise to Wilson. Twenty-one of the twenty-two negative votes came from the other Republican Senators then present and voting, including such illustrious and influential men as Henry A. du Pont of Delaware, Henry Cabot Lodge of Massachusetts, George Sutherland of

Utah (soon to be a colleague of the appointee), Warren G. Harding of Ohio (the next President of the United States), and Albert B. Fall of New Mexico. The lone negative vote cast by a Democrat was that of Francis G. Newland of Nevada, who regarded Brandeis as lacking in "judicial temperament." Twenty-seven Senators, including the powerful William E. Borah of Idaho, did not vote: of them, twelve Republicans were paired against confirmation, and ten Democrats and two Republicans were paired in favor; three were absent. The President and his supporters were jubilant.

Until he retired at eighty-three in 1939, Mr. Justice Brandeis kept the Wilsonian faith, serving with diligence and conviction. He and Holmes, despite their different backgrounds and, indeed, political philosophy, became a veritable team—although frequently for different reasons. "Justices Holmes and Brandeis dissenting" became a hallmark for some of the most famous libertarian opinions of the fifteen years they served together.[43] It is a pity that Wilson did not live to hear Brandeis at his most eloquent: in a concurring opinion conerning civil liberties—joined by Holmes —he wrote: "Those who won our independence by revolution were not cowards. They did not fear political change. They did not exalt order at the cost of liberty. . . . Fear of serious injury cannot alone justify suppression of free speech and assembly. Men feared witches and burnt women. It is the function of free speech to free men from the bondage of irrational fears. . . ." [44]

Nine days after Brandeis had been confirmed, Associate Justice Charles Evans Hughes resigned to run for the Presidency, which gave Wilson his third and last opportunity to make a Supreme Court nomination. Six months later he proposed another liberal, a progressive of Wilsonian bent with a solid antitrust record, fifty-nine-year-old John Hessin Clarke of Ohio. Clarke, an old friend and associate of the new Secretary of War, Newton D. Baker, was then in his second year of service as a U.S. District Judge for Ohio, a post to which he had been appointed by Wilson on Baker's recommendation. Now Clarke's spokesman again interceded with the President on his friend's behalf; so did Brandeis. Wilson carefully studied Clarke's record off as well as on the bench. Not

entirely satisfied, he asked Baker to travel to Ohio to discuss matters with the Judge, especially the antitrust question. Baker's report pleased Wilson, who was now convinved that Clarke "could
be depended upon for a liberal and enlightened interpretation of
the law." [45] In July the President sent Clarke's name to the Senate, which confirmed the nomination unanimously ten days later
despite the opposition of ex-President Taft, a fellow Ohioan.

Clarke's brief tenure (six years) on the bench was solidly Wilsonian: progressive on social and economic matters and liberal on
civil rights and liberties. His votes did not stray from his nominator's reservation. Indeed, Clarke's philosophy was considerably to
the left of Wilson and Brandeis (and much closer to the position
of the man who ultimately succeeded Brandeis, William O. Douglas). Thus Clarke was the sole dissenter in the Court's veto of the
1922 child-labor tax law.[46] A committed and conscientious Justice, he nevertheless was unhappy on the Court. His resignation in
1922, purportedly to enable him to devote full time to the causes
of peace, was caused by at least two factors: first, he grew increasingly disillusioned with what he regarded as the Court's failure to
embrace a genuinely liberal approach to public policy; second, the
McReynolds antics and hostilities were anathema to gentle Clarke,
who was unwilling to ignore them and unable to cope with them.
Ironically, the vacancy he created by resigning would be filled by
the intellectual leader of the "Four Horsemen," George Sutherland, who utterly rejected Clarke's philosophy.

The election of 1920 brought to the Presidency the man who
has been universally regarded as the post's crassest failure to date,
Warren Gamaliel Harding of Marion, Ohio. There is no doubt
that he was patently unqualified to serve as President: his scan-
dal-ridden Administration was a disaster. Yet Harding was pathet-
ically conscious of his deficiencies. "My God," he told editor William Allen White, "This is a hell of a job. . . . My God-damn
friends, White, they're the ones that keep me walking the floors
nights. . . . This White House is a prison. I can't get away from
the men who dog my footsteps. I am in jail." [47] And in a moment
of introspection he admitted to President Nicholas Murray Butler

of Columbia University: "I am not fit for this office and should never have been here." [48] That Harding was not really "a bad man . . . [but] just a slob," [49] did not alter the fundamental truth of Harding's and history's conclusion: he was a man who should never have allowed himself to be chosen by the cynical "Ohio gang" and his Senate colleagues in that "smoke-filled room" in Chicago in mid-1920.

Yet Harding's public embrace of a "return to normalcy" had widespread popular support. Indeed, he was far from an unpopular figure in those brief two and a half years before his still somewhat clouded death in August 1923—but the accelerating evidence of financial and personal scandals penetrating his Administration could hardly be ignored. Although some of the worst, such as the Teapot Dome scandal (which involved his Departments of the Interior, Justice, and the Navy), did not break until after his demise, they could not fail to characterize his Presidency perpetually. True, he had some outstanding public servants in his Administration—such as Secretary of State Charles Evans Hughes, to whom he happily delegated the fullest authority—but such men were too few. Far too many betrayed Harding's rather childish faith and took advantage of his penchant for seeing and hearing no evil, which he extended to his own private behavior.

Harding appointed four men to the Supreme Court during his short tenure as President, two of whom, William Howard Taft and George Sutherland, have generally been accorded high ratings. Of the other two, Edward T. Sanford is generally rated mediocre, and Pierce Butler, a failure. Each of these men met Harding's general criteria for candidacy—which in fact were those of his designee for Chief Justice, William H. Taft. Thus their real politics were right, they were all experienced public figures, they were all conservative, property-minded, business-oriented attorneys. On the bench they ran true to form and with rare exceptions * voted together.

* One of the exceptions was Taft's and Sanford's recognition of governmental regulatory authority when together with Holmes they unsuccessfully attempted to sustain the 1918 District of Columbia minimum-wage law for women and children.[50]

Taft's influence over Harding in Court appointments is a unique illustration of a sitting jurist's weight-swinging. After virtually appointing himself Chief Justice in 1921, Taft made himself instantly available to Harding as an adviser on nominations—and not only judicial nominations. Taft's *modus operandi* was very simple: once a vacancy presented itself, he would literally bombard the President with firm recommendations and casual suggestions. True, he was not notably successful in winning his first choices, but he tellingly "used his influence to defeat selection of an 'off horse,' such as . . . Cardozo of New York. . . ." [51] Taft was determined to block the nomination of anyone who might side with that "dangerous twosome," Holmes and Brandeis. On the other hand, he enthusiastically backed the Sutherland and Butler candidacies and did nothing to stop Sanford's, for he was satisfied that all three were sound economic conservatives with proved antagonism toward contemporary "liberal progressive elements." To Taft, "[i]dentity of outlook was absolutely essential"; [52] everything else was secondary.

On June 29, William Howard Taft had finally become Chief Justice, affirmed with only four "no" votes on the same day the nomination reached the Senate. Yet the position that he regarded "next to my wife and children . . . the nearest thing to my heart in life," [53] did not fall into his lap without considerable maneuvering. Months before Harding's inauguration he had started to lobby. He had organized a campaign staff and, to dispel any notions Harding might have of appointing him to an Associate Justiceship, he had written the President-elect a note emphasizing that his interest "lay solely in the post of Chief Justice." [54] But now Taft had to bide his time: Mr. Chief Justice White had agreed to hold on until a Republican President succeeded Wilson, thus paving the way for Taft. And hold on he did—half blind and half deaf, White spurned the retirement pension for which he was eligible, serving until he died in harness on May 19, 1921. The country expected an instant announcement, *the* announcement, from President Harding. But the President procrastinated, hoping for the resignation of Associate Justice Clarke, rumored impending, in order to reward his intimate political adviser, ex-Senator George Sutherland. Almost beside himself with anxiety, the now sixty-four-year-old Taft pulled out all the stops and through intermediaries succeeded in convincing the President that no additional vacancy would occur—short of another death. Finally Harding concurred and acquiesced to Taft, who exulted: "I love judges and I love courts. They are my ideals on earth of what we shall meet afterward in Heaven under a just God." [55]

William Howard Taft served in his beloved center chair until he was afflicted with the acute circulatory ailments that necessitated his grief-stricken resignation in February and caused his death in March of 1930. His dedication to and affection for the Court were almost without parallel; few worked as hard as he did (during his membership, he wrote almost 20 per cent of the Court's opinions). Taft worshipped the institution and its functions; its personnel had become "his" even if Holmes, Brandeis, and Stone—all of whom respected and liked the "Big Chief"—would more often than not dissent from what had become a comfortable Taft majority. Chief Justice Taft provided administrative and technical leadership second to none at the time; his orchestration of consensus, of "massing" the Court into a majority, was often spectacular; he was a superb judicial leader and architect. And his sponsorship of and successful lobbying for the famous "Judges Bill" of 1925 [56] stands as a milestone in the Court's ability to function with discretion, dispatch, and efficiency. Yet the experts have not rated Taft "great"—and appropriately so. Neither his intellectual stance nor his applied jurisprudence was in a class with such "greats" as his predecessors John Marshall and Roger Taney and his successors Charles Evans Hughes, Harlan F. Stone, and Earl Warren. Instead, he has deservedly been placed at the head of the "near great" group, which also contains his predecessors Morrison R. Waite and Edward D. White.

On September 4, 1922, Mr. Justice John Hessin Clarke withdrew from the Court—bored, disenchanted, and disillusioned. On September 5 Harding nominated to the post sixty-year-old George Sutherland of Utah, and the Senate confirmed him the same day—

a speed record in the appointment process. Seldom in the history of the Court has a successor-candidate been so universally obvious: a close personal and political ally to the President, Sutherland was also enthusiastically backed by Taft, who had written to the nominee: "I look forward to having you on the bench with me. I know, as you do, that the President intends to put you there." [57] A devout Mormon, Sutherland was the first (and to date the only) Supreme Court Justice from Utah and one of the very few of foreign birth (England) to reach the high tribunal.

Sutherland came to the Court with a wealth of legal and governmental experience: a leading expert in constitutional law and an active member of the Utah bar and the Supreme Court bar for many years, he had served in the Utah Senate, the U.S. House of Representatives, and the U.S. Senate. His friendship with Harding began when the two served together in the upper house, the association culminating in the role of brain truster to the President. He could have had any position in the Harding Administration he desired, but he preferred to accept spot and trouble-shooting assignments for the President in Washington and abroad, in anticipation of a vacancy on the Court.

Once he attained the Court, George Sutherland demonstrated that the evaluation of his supporters had been entirely correct: he not only proved himself the conservative everyone knew him to be, but he soon became the lucid and articulate spokesman for the Court's solid Darwin-Spencer wing (also peopled by his colleagues Van Devanter, McReynolds, and Butler). The man whom his biographer characterized aptly as "A Man Against the State" [58] spent sixteen years on the Court as the personification of those against whom Holmes had railed in his anguished Lochner dissent: "The Fourteenth Amendment does not enact Mr. Herbert Spencer's *Social Statics.*" Yet to Sutherland—far more than to his fellow "Four Horsemen"—the Fourteenth Amendment meant "keep-your-hands-off-government" in the libertarian as well as the proprietarian sense. Thus it was he who in 1932 wrote the 7:2 majority opinion in the landmark "Scottsboro Case," *Powell* v. *Alabama,* [59] which became the bellwether in the gradually developing application of procedural safeguards in the Bill of Rights to the states by way of interpretation of the due process of law clause of the Fourteenth Amendment. His colleagues McReynolds and Butler dissented, of course.

As the intellectual leader of the Four Horsemen and their allies, Sutherland proved himself a worthy successor of the Field-Brewer-Peckham wing of the Fuller Court era. In the thirties he became the scourge of the New Deal, heading a majority that struck down more than a dozen pieces of domestic legislation fundamental to the New Deal in 1935–36.[60] Yet he was not blindly opposed to the exercise of governmental power, particularly in the realm of foreign relations. One of the most significant opinions in support of Presidential authority, *United States* v. *Curtiss-Wright Export Corporation*,[61] was from his pen. It is only just that no matter how many of them disapproved of his social Darwinism and Spencerian economics, the Court experts have rated him "near great." Sutherland, tired and out-voted after the Hughes-Roberts switch and Van Devanter's retirement in the spring of 1937, left the bench in 1938. He had more than fully lived up to Harding's and Taft's expectations.

So did Harding's next appointment, Pierce Butler, fifty-six and the least gifted and in many ways most doctrinaire of the Four Horsemen. The vacancy arose when Mr. Justice William Rufus Day, after almost two decades of vacillating performance on the Court, retired in October of 1922. It was the President's third opportunity in little more than a year to make an appointment. Taft, with Harding's blessing and the aid of his closest personal associate on the Bench, Willis Van Devanter, had already surveyed the field of prospective candidates. The Chief Justice readily persuaded the President that the Court had become "too Republican" in the public eye and that, consequently, the new appointee ought to be a "congenial" Democrat whose real politics would readily meet the Harding-Taft requirements.

Butler was one of nine children of a devout Roman Catholic immigrant family who had settled on a Minnesota farm after the mid-nineteenth-century potato famine in Ireland. He was a self-taught, self-made millionaire lawyer who had made his fortune as the able counsel for several Western and Midwestern railroads—whose interests he faithfully endeavored to serve after he reached the high bench. A life-long Cleveland Democrat, Butler preferred to practice politics behind the scene, usually as an adviser to Minnesota's Governors, but in the courtroom he was a skilled and devastating trial lawyer. In his personal codes he was sternly moralistic and inflexible and, although he affected a sense of humor and could be a convivial companion, he was neither charming nor tolerant. Suspicious and disdainful of what he styled "kooks," "wish-washy patriots," "Bolsheviks," and "Germany lovers," no friends of liberals or progressives, Butler gained national recognition as a meddlesome member of the Board of Regents of the University of Minnesota: Charging "unpatriotic behavior," "pro-Socialist attitudes," and "incompetence and insubordination," he was personally responsible for the cashiering of a political science professor, the non-contract renewal of a chemistry instructor and a rhetoric instructor, and the harassing of a senior economics professor.[62]

Taft did not approve of Butler's actions, but he did not consider them harmful either, and with Harding's backing he vigorously promoted his appointment. He even personally led the public and private campaign for Butler, mapping strategy before and during the hearings of the Senate Judiciary Committee. Harding, of course, readily concurred: he found Butler's ultra-conservatism entirely sympathetic; he deemed it prudent to appoint a "safe" Democrat and a member of a then "unrepresented" minority religion; and he found appealing the success story of the son of poor immigrant parents. Butler's candidacy ran into considerable opposition from the Senate, especially from the Progressives, led by Senator LaFollette, who in fact initially succeeded in blocking the nomination from being taken up in a special session of Congress. Like other liberals and moderates, the Progressives had been antagonized by Butler's inflexible stance on economic-proprietarian matters and by his intolerance and dogmatism while he was a University of Minnesota Regent. In the regular session of Congress (to which Harding had re-submitted the nomination) the Senate after a month's delay finally approved Butler by a vote of 61:8, with the unusually large number of twenty-seven abstentions. The margin of the confirming vote belied the bitter and deep-seated opposition to him.

The fears of the Progressives proved as justified as the hopes of Butler's backers: his record during seventeen years on the Court until his death in November 1939 was wholly and unswervingly in the Darwin-Spencer mold. Yet he was somewhat more sensitive than his companion-in-conservatism, James McReynolds, to claims of procedural due process violations, going so far as to join Holmes, Brandeis, and Stone in dissenting from Taft's opinion for a 5:4 majority in the *Olmstead Case* (1928),[63] which upheld the use of evidence by wiretapping. But he was consistently intolerant even to mild libertarian claims in such vital areas as freedom of speech and press, where his reactionary reading of the Constitution was second only to McReynolds's. Rated a "failure" by the experts, he hardly merits a kinder treatment than that historical evaluation has accorded him.

Harding's fourth and final opportunity to make an appointment to the Court resulted from the retirement of Mr. Justice Mahlon Pitney on the last day of 1922, after a decade of service characterized by vacillating judicial behavior and murkiness of style: one never quite knew what one's probings would uncover. Since the President had received considerable political support from the South, the designation of a Southerner (but a Republican, since Democrat McReynolds was a Tennessean) would make good political sense. Taft readily agreed with Harding and—like a wine steward, always prepared—suggested such Southern Republican stalwarts as Henry Anderson of Virginia (a Harding acquaintance) and his own ex-Solicitor General, William Marshall Bullitt. He also proposed Judge Charles M. Hough of the Second U.S. Circuit Court of Appeals. But Hough seemed old at sixty-four, and the other two appeared to have political liabilities. Attorney General Harry M. Daugherty, with Taft consenting, then suggested an oft-mentioned also-ran, U.S. Judge Edward T. Sanford of the Eastern

District of Tennessee. Taft was not wild about Sanford, but he was aware of the virtue of the candidate's lengthy judicial experience on lower federal courts, which both Sutherland and Butler entirely lacked. Harding was satisfied, given Sanford's general popularity with Republican leaders, his apparent conservatism on the bench, and his support among some labor leaders, to whom Pitney had been anathema. Nominated in late January 1923, the fifty-eight-year-old native of Kentucky, an honor graduate from the Harvard Law School, was easily confirmed within a few days.

By and large, the last Harding appointee fulfilled his and Taft's expectations during seven colorless years on the bench. Usually he could be found with the Chief and the Four Horsemen, but he was considerably more flexible than that group on some aspects of governmental regulation: when it came to the enforcement of the antitrust laws, which he supported even more faithfully than old trust-buster Taft himself, he left the Spencer-Darwin reservation. On civil libertarian matters, too, the Sanford record betrays some mercurial behavior: at times, such as in an important 1929 naturalization case,[64] he joined Holmes and Brandeis in dissent; at others, such as in the landmark *Gitlow Case* (1925) [65] he left the two and sided with the state against the individual on a crucial free expression issue. Nevertheless, it is for his majority opinion in *Gitlow* that Mr. Justice Sanford is best remembered. For while he held against Benjamin Gitlow's specific plea of constitutional protection under the First and Fourteenth amendments, he penned a famous dictum that marked the beginning of the long process of applying the provisions of the Bill of Rights to the several states: "We may and do assume," he wrote, "that freedom of speech and of the press . . . are among the fundamental personal rights and 'liberties' protected by the due process of law clause of the Fourteenth Amendment from impairment by the States [as well as by the Federal Government]." [66] It was a pronouncement that would prove of monumental significance as a judicial tool in the years to come. The next nominee to the Court, Harlan Fiske Stone, would avail himself of it with pioneering conviction and determination.

Although the political and philosophical outlook of Calvin

Coolidge was very much in line with that of the unfortunate man he succeeded, the one-time Massachusetts Governor was a total opposite in personal demeanor, habit, and commitment from Warren Harding. Stern, dour, no man of ideas, Coolidge presented a façade of granite ("How can they tell?" asked Dorothy Parker when informed that Coolidge had died); he seemed unaware of the world about him ("Calvin slept more than any other President," noted Alice Roosevelt Longworth). Yet Coolidge knew what he was doing and why, and he was fully dedicated to the philosophy behind his famous slogan: "The business of the United States is business." Shy and retiring yet stubborn and occasionally mercurial in temper, the hard-working, scrupulously honest, colorless, and moral President, known affectionately as "Silent Cal," was astonishingly popular. The times were tailor-made for his conservative businessman's approach to government. He was dedicated to running the country on a "sound, business-like, balanced-budget" basis; not only was he uninterested in foreign policy matters (he left these, like Wilson, to Charles Evans Hughes and later to Frank B. Kellogg), he was positively annoyed by them. Normalcy and prosperity were to be America's passwords during Coolidge's time—although normalcy and prosperity apparently did not embrace farmers or laborers, whom the President regarded as a collective nuisance, a thorn in the side of orderly, sound business practice. Yet the times obviously demanded more than the dedication to normalcy that Coolidge counseled. Social and economic turmoil was just over the horizon and, given Coolidge's lack of foresight, his lack of interest in the world of ideas, and his non-assertive executive leadership, it is not surprising that the observers of the Presidency have ranked him "below average," between two earlier undistinguished leaders, Millard Fillmore and Franklin Pierce.

Yet Coolidge was to give his country one of its most renowned Justices in the person of his Attorney General, Harlan Fiske Stone—his sole appointee to the Court. Little could the President realize that his New Hampshire friend Stone, the presumably safe ex-corporation lawyer with excellent Republican credentials, would

within a year join the Holmes-Brandeis dissenting duo, ultimately
becoming such a devoted defender of the constitutionality of New
Deal legislation—whatever he may have thought of its wisdom—
that Franklin Roosevelt would promote him to the Chief Justiceship! To Coolidge, whose death in 1933 spared him witness of the
last thirteen of his appointee's twenty-one years on the high bench,
Stone's performance was a disappointment of only slightly less
magnitude than such celebrated ones as Joseph Story's was to
Madison, Oliver Wendell Holmes's was to Teddy Roosevelt, and
James McReynolds's was to Wilson.

There is little doubt that the decision to send Stone to the Court
was Coolidge's alone, although a good many contemporary public figures would later claim credit for it. Among them was the
"Big Chief," who in a letter to his son Robert A. Taft pomp-
ously stated: "I rather forced the President into [Stone's] appointment"; [67] and Nicholas Murray Butler (like Taft enamored
of king-making) who insisted that he had been largely responsible.
Yet Stone later disputed both men, observing that he doubted that
"the responsibility for my appointment weighs very heavily on
either of them." [68] The record shows that although Coolidge did
receive Taft's and Butler's advice (along with that of many others
from Stone's legion of well-wishers), not only was the nomination
his own choice, but it was an entirely natural one, given Stone's
qualifications and the two men's long-standing association. [69]

Stone's career in private as well as public life had been a distinguished one. After attending Amherst College (where Calvin
Coolidge was a fellow student) and Columbia University Law
School, he taught and practiced law for a quarter of a century, attaining the Deanship at Columbia in 1910. The Teapot Dome
scandal became a national issue during his incumbency as Dean,
and when Attorney General Harry M. Daugherty at last resigned
in 1924, the President named Stone in his place. The appointment
was received with general public acclaim as well as relief. Stone
not only cleaned house in the Justice Department and in the Administration generally, he aided considerably in Coolidge's successful campaign for a full term of his own later that year. When

the octogenarian Mr. Justice Joseph McKenna (now practically senile) resigned in 1925 from the Court after twenty-seven years of at best mediocre performance, there were broad expectations that Coolidge would nominate another Californian, or at least a Westerner, to replace him. But the President was not concerned with geographic considerations: he wanted the man who had been his personal and political friend for three decades, who had been so helpful to him during the 1924 Presidential race, and who, above all, had proved himself to be a courageous, independent Attorney General. It was precisely because of these attributes that Stone was allegedly "kicked upstairs," somewhat as McReynolds had been. The press had a field day conjecturing that Coolidge's move would bail him out with his many big business supporters, a number of whose enterprises had felt the sting of Stone investigations and threatened litigation. Prominent among his targets was the powerful Aluminum Trust, in which the influential Secretary of the Treasury Andrew W. Mellon had pronounced professional and personal interests. Yet at best the "kicked upstairs" charge remains unproved; neither Stone himself nor Coolidge ever offered either comment or explanation.

Stone's nomination on January 5, 1925, met with all but universal approbation. But because he had incurred the enmity of the powerful Senator Burton K. Wheeler, a Montana Democrat of considerable influence, for refusing to drop a case brought against him [the Senator] by Attorney General Daugherty, his nomination ran into trouble when it reached the Senate floor. Representations were made to both Coolidge and Stone that the nomination be withdrawn; when the President promptly made it clear that he would not even consider doing so, the Senate moved unanimously to recommit the candidacy to its Judiciary Committee. This move was followed by a "first" in the history of Supreme Court nominations: the personal appearance of a candidate before the Committee. Hostile Senators cross-examined Stone mercilessly, yet he came through with flying colors in a performance marked by strength, dignity, and articulateness. The Committee recommended approval and the Senate concurred on February 5 by an overwhelming vote, 71:6. Senator Wheeler himself abstained, as did his Montana colleague Walsh, who had carried much of the burden of the anti-Stone case. Among the six who voted against approval was the redoubtable George W. Norris of Nebraska, who was convinced that Stone was a "tool of the House of Morgan." Sixteen years later, on the occasion of Stone's promotion to Chief Justice, Norris rose on the Senate floor, warmly applauded the elevation, and publicly confessed both error and regret for his earlier opposition.

Harlan Fiske Stone's sixteen years as Associate Justice and five years as Chief Justice earned him the nation's respect and gratitude and the accolade of "greatness" by the Court's observers. Because he was so frequently in dissent along with Holmes, Brandeis, and Cardozo, he is generally labeled as a liberal. But more than that, he was a fiercely independent, tolerant, courageous spirit whose creed combined a basic faith in the dignity and worth of the individual with a firm belief in the right and capacity of the people to govern themselves. His jurisprudential hallmark became a famed admonition and embrace of judicial self-restraint: his dissenting opinion in *United States* v. *Butler* (1936),[70] in which six members of the Court declared unconstitutional the New Deal's Agricultural Adjustment Act of 1933. Joined by Brandeis and Cardozo, Stone wrote: "The only check upon our own exercise of power is our own sense of self restraint. . . . Courts are not the only agency of government that must be assumed to have capacity to govern." He lived that creed until the end of his life, restating it dramatically from the bench on April 22, 1946—moments before he lapsed into unconsciousness, fatally stricken with a cerebral thrombosis: "It is not the function of this Court to disregard the will of Congress in the exercise of its constitutional power." [71]

Ironically, these last words were uttered by Stone in dissent from an opinion upholding an alien conscientious objector's right to qualify for citizenship—ironically, because it was Stone who had for so long fought for the very right he here disavowed. But he felt compelled to cast his vote as he did because Congress had earlier re-enacted the precise language of the naturalization laws here at issue, which Stone had opposed as "tortured constructions" and as unwise and undemocratic but not unconstitutional. To him this Congressional reaffirmation of legislative intent demanded judicial self-restraint, no matter what one's personal views. Yet it was in the realm of civil rights and liberties that Stone made his other, and possibly his most important, contribution: his commitment to the letter and spirit of the libertarian provisions of the Constitution demanded that there be a judicial posture recognizing a "preferred position" in America's constitutional structure for the cultural freedoms guaranteed in the First Amendment: speech, press, worship, and assembly, and all other crucial personal and political guarantees. Unlike enactments in the economic-proprietarian sphere, therefore, governmental action infringing upon those "preferred freedoms" would have to be presumed invalid. As he put it in 1938, members of the Court had a duty to subject to "more exacting judicial scrutiny" any and all legislation "which restricts the political processes which can ordinarily be expected to bring about repeal of undesirable legislation" and which reflect "prejudices against discrete and insular minorities." [72]

Yet Stone's happiest and most influential days on the Court were those as Associate Justice and not as Chief Justice. He was wholly dedicated, hard-working, and respected in both posts, but he lacked the executive capacity, the tactical decisiveness, and marshaling ability of a Taft or Hughes. Allowing himself to be drawn into too much petty detail and bickering, into too many endless Conference squabbles, he could hardly be regarded as an effective Chief. Nonetheless, his intellectual acumen, his perception of constitutional fundamentals, his eloquence and articulateness all combined to rank him among the great jurists.

Herbert Clark Hoover, the man who succeeded Coolidge in 1929, was a highly qualified, capable public servant. But despite every good intention, he was a failure as a President. If the experts have bestowed upon him a rating of "average" rather than "below average" or even "failure," it is very likely because they considered the "Great Engineer" abused, for the realities of his

record were grim indeed. From West Branch, Iowa, Hoover had
been a brilliant engineer and management expert, a masterful War
Food Administrator, and a highly successful Secretary of Commerce under Harding and Coolidge. Yet he was simply incapable
of coping with either the political process or, surprisingly, with
the social and economic problems of his day. An apostle of "rug-
ged individualism" and laissez-faire economics—a nineteenth-century man—he too was uncomfortable with the multiple demands
of multiple interest groups and was pathologically opposed to
strong federal action. After the stockmarket crash of October
1929, he had the inexorably bad luck to be saddled with the Great
Depression. His experience theoretically qualified him to deal with
the Depression, but sadly, his attempts to check it were belated,
ineffectual, and unconvincing. Moreover, he consistently made little of this catastrophe, bridled at criticism, and was practically incapable of admitting to error. And his few halting attempts at establishing viable public relations in a time of crisis were
disastrous. At the end, still pleading that "prosperity is just
around the corner," he had begun to stoop to name-calling, categorizing his political detractors in a manner that ill-befitted his position and character. In sum, Hoover provided little or no effective leadership; nonetheless, years later, he would re-emerge as a
respected *eminence grise* of the governmental process under Presidents Truman and Eisenhower.[73]

Hoover appointed three men to the Supreme Court: Charles
Evans Hughes, a Chief Justice with few peers; Benjamin N. Cardozo, one of the greatest men of the Court; and Owen J. Roberts,
an able and conscientious jurist. Even John J. Parker, his unfairly
rejected nominee, was a jurist of outstanding credentials who
unquestionably would have left a commendable record as a member of the Court. Indeed, other than an insistence on demonstrated
merit, Hoover's criteria for selection are more difficult to ascertain
than those of most other Presidents. He did favor prior judicial
experience, which all of his appointees save Roberts possessed in
considerable measure. He was, of course, concerned with real politics and, with the exception of Cardozo, the records of his candi-

dates represented the kind of Republican moderate-to-progressive, conservative business orientation with which he was comfortable. He respected their upper-middle- or upper-class educational and social backgrounds, and their public mindedness. Geography and religion became an issue only in the case of Cardozo.

Since Hoover lived to a ripe ninety years, he not only witnessed the performances of his three appointees, all of whom he survived by a wide margin of years, but he also watched the metamorphosis of the Court in 1937. It is not clear how Hoover really felt about the change, but it is known that he, having learned some of the bitter lessons of the realities of government and politics under stress, regarded it as inevitable and probably necessary. Cardozo, of course, had never been his kind of jurist, although he came to pronounce Cardozo's appointment as the proudest act of his career. Hughes and Roberts, however, had established a record before the 1937 switch with which Hoover certainly could live.

The President's initial opportunity came with the resignation of the fatally ill Chief Justice Taft on February 3, 1930. On Taft's bedside table lay a touching message from his eight colleagues, beginning: "We call you Chief Justice still, for we cannot quickly give up the title by which we have known you for all these later years and which you have made so dear to us." [74] Within five hours after having received Taft's resignation, President Hoover had named Charles Evans Hughes to replace him—with Taft's advance blessing and to the surprise of many observers, including the press, which had confidently expected the elevation of Stone. Actually, in late January, Attorney General William D. Mitchell had sought the assistance of Justices Van Devanter and Butler to ascertain that Hughes, who was somewhat hesitant, was available. On receiving their assurance, Hoover called in the still-reluctant Hughes, who at sixty-eight was quite content to remain in private life. There is considerable evidence that Stone himself (as well as the press) thought he was in the running for the Chief Justiceship. His failure to be named caused as much of a public eyebrow-raising as had Taft's own naming of Edward D. White rather than Hughes twenty years earlier. And it is entirely possible that Hoover would have been almost as comfortable with the naming of Stone as of Hughes. But while he never admitted it in so many words, it is fair to conclude that the President preferred Hughes's jurisprudential politics to Stone's and that the clamor of the Taft wing on behalf of Hughes probably proved to be decisive.[75]

Quite in contrast to his smooth confirmation as President Taft's nominee to the Associate Justiceship in 1910, Hughes now ran into considerable flak. His nominator, of course, was in deep trouble with Congress—where he would soon be faced with a Democratic majority—and some of the antagonism rubbed off on Hughes. But it was less a case of anti-nominator than anti-nominee: Charles Evans Hughes had, after all, voluntarily relinquished the Court for the active world of politics—why should he now be granted a return trip, and the top spot to boot? Moreover, Hughes had the misfortune of encountering opposition from both Republicans and Democrats in the Senate—albeit for different reasons. Conservative Southerners opposed him because they viewed him as too "city-bred," too record-prone to support national versus states' rights when the chips were down. The coalition of Republican-Progressive-Democratic liberals, centered on the Midwest and personified by such influential legislators as Idaho's Borah, Nebraska's Norris, Montana's Wheeler, and Wisconsin's LaFollette, were unhappy with Hughes because of his affinity for America's business and financial elite. In the end, however, supported by Democratic Senators Robert F. Wagner and Royal S. Copeland of New York (Hughes's home state), the bitterly contested nomination was approved by a vote of 52:26, eighteen Senators abstaining.

That Hughes, an impressive and stately figure, was superbly qualified to serve at the helm of the Court he knew so well was self-evident. Energetic, tough, and decisive, the near-septuagenarian firmly grasped the reins of leadership. An overwhelming choice as one of the great members of the Court, Hughes ranks at the pinnacle of achievement, perhaps second only to Marshall in administrative acumen and intellectual leadership, and in a class with Taney, Stone, and Warren in jurisprudential impact. As a presiding officer he was as impressive as John Marshall himself. And his ability to be realistic, to blend conservation of basic principles with a recognition of the need for change, enabled him to enhance consensus on fundamental issues. His beautifully articulated embrace of the essence of fundamental liberty was often crucial to its enhancement—perhaps even survival—in troubled moments. A leader and a doer, he was a realist at home in the world of ideas as well as in practical politics. In that role he consciously faced the need for the all-important change in direction of the Court over which he presided in 1937, stimulated by the *Realpolitik* of the times. Charles Evans Hughes was a giant among men.

In March 1930, barely one month after Hughes had replaced Taft, Mr. Justice Edward T. Sanford died unexpectedly, behind him seven years of average but not unimportant Court service. Although Hoover was not genuinely concerned with geography, he initially looked to the South for a replacement for the late Tennessee jurist. His choice devolved upon a well-known and well-liked North Carolina Republican, Judge John J. Parker of the U.S. Court of Appeals for the Fourth Circuit. His rejection by the narrow vote of 39:41 is now all but universally regarded not only as regrettable but as a blunder. It was the last Senatorial veto of a Supreme Court nominee until the Haynsworth and Carswell rejections four decades later.

The failure to win confirmation for Judge Parker resulted in President Hoover's selection of Owen J. Roberts, a fifty-five-year-old Pennsylvania Republican from a to-the-manner-born Philadelphia family. As the federal government's special prosecutor in the Teapot Dome oil scandals, he had achieved national recognition and praise; he had also served well as a Special U.S. Deputy Attorney General during World War I in connection with espionage and sabotage cases, and in the Justice Department of Pennsylvania. A judicious and modest person but an able and strong advocate, he was an eagerly sought out practitioner of the law, especially in the corporate field where he was close to the Pennsylvania Railroad, then very powerful. His nomination was broadly applauded—support came from all parts of the political spectrum. Conservatives looked to his long-standing business connections and liberals to his demonstrated humanitarian concerns: thus he commanded the vocal support of such key anti-Parker Republican Senators as Arthur Vandenberg (Michigan) and Charles L. McNary (Oregon), as well as of perpetual Republican mavericks Borah, LaFollette, and Norris. Roberts was confirmed by acclamation literally one minute after the Judiciary Committee, with its unanimous endorsement, sent the nomination to the floor of the Senate on May 21, 1930.

Yet Mr. Justice Roberts would lastingly please neither political wing. There was an almost terpsichorian quality about this benign, conscientious jurist who established a difficult-to-equal record of inconsistency in his voting on the bench. Beginning his Court career of fifteen years as a "centrist" or "neutralist" with certain articulated liberal policy notions, he soon rather steadfastly embraced the "Four Horsemen" approach to governmental functions and powers—with important exceptions.[76] Yet it was Roberts who, along with Hughes, executed the 1937 switch that changed the course of constitutional law in our time. The Chief Justice had probably been prepared to effect that switch considerably earlier, but for reasons of strategy and maximum unity preferred to wait until Roberts would join him. Yet having been so instrumental in the change, Roberts began to revert to his former posture once the last of the Four Horsemen, James McReynolds, had retired in 1941. In many ways a sympathetic and noble citizen, Roberts's tendencies to vacillate jurisprudentially have rendered evaluation difficult. Although he was considerably more able than "average," the rating usually accorded him by Court observers, Mr. Justice Roberts's performance makes any other categorization difficult to sustain. His resignation in 1945 was based largely on his disenchantment with what he regarded as wholesale deviations from established legal precedents by the Stone, or "Roosevelt," Court. If that was indeed the case, Roberts had had a hand in facilitating that policy.

On January 15, 1932, Oliver Wendell Holmes, Jr., now almost ninety-one but still alert and cheerful, bowed to old age and precarious health and resigned. More than three decades of an incredibly productive and towering judicial career thus came to an end. How to replace the "judicial philosopher of the age"? Hoover, striking out on his own, let it be known that he would like to see a "non-controversial western Republican" as the Old Yankee's successor. But almost at once the Chairman of the Senate's Judiciary Committee, George W. Norris, made it plain to the President that he and his fellow committeemen, largely Democrats and Progressive Republicans, would insist on a judicial liberal in the Holmes mold. Others were rather more specific: the entire faculty of the Law School of the University of Chicago urged Hoover to nominate Benjamin Nathan Cardozo, Chief Judge of the New York Court of Appeals—a man widely regarded as one of America's most brilliant jurists, one who might already have been on the U.S. Supreme Court had it not been for Taft's sustained opposition to him during the 1920s. The Deans of the prestigious schools of law of Harvard, Yale, and Columbia universities joined in a similar strongly worded plea. Labor as well as business leaders, liberals as well as conservatives, advocates of judicial self-restraint as well as judicial activists, all participated in a uniquely unified appeal on behalf of a candidate to the Court—so strong an impression had Cardozo made, so splendid a record had he achieved during his eighteen years as Associate Judge and Chief Judge on New York's highest tribunal, probably the country's busiest and most distinguished appellate state court.

The President could hardly have been unaware of the clamor for Cardozo's nomination. The now sixty-two-year-old Sephardic Jew from New York had not only made his mark as a jurist, but his stylistically beautiful and scholarly publications such as the still-seminal *The Nature of the Judicial Process* [77] had won him universal praise. His lucid, cogent opinions, his realistic approach to law and democratic society, his love of his land and its Constitution stamped him as Holmes's logical successor. But Hoover continued to demur; he really did not want to appoint a man, no matter how superbly and uniquely qualified he might be, from a state that already had two eminent "representatives" (Hughes—

whom he had sent there himself—and Stone) and whose religion (Jewish) was not only already represented on the Court (Brandeis), but which would assuredly cause McReynolds to act up again (it did). No, Herbert Hoover would look elsewhere, even though Stone had told him he would be willing to resign so that the nation might have Cardozo.[78]

Now, however, the powerful Chairman of the Senate Foreign Relations Committee, Republican William E. Borah of Idaho, whose support Hoover needed on other fronts, got into the act and loudly and repeatedly called for Cardozo's designation. No particular friend of Easterners, especially New Yorkers, Borah, like Norris and other wise legislators similarly placed, recognized Cardozo's rare merit. Twenty-four hours before Hoover had indicated he would announce his candidate publicly he called for Borah. In an often-told, dramatic confrontation between two proud men, the President, after discussing the vacancy generally, suddenly handed Borah a list on which he had ranked those individuals he was considering for the nomination in descending order of preference. The name at the bottom was that of Benjamin N. Cardozo. Borah glanced at it and replied: "Your list is all right, but you handed it to me upside down." Hoover protested that, first, there was the geographical question to be considered and, second, he had to take "religious or sectarian repercussions" into account. Senator Borah sharply retorted that "Cardozo belongs as much to Idaho as to New York" and that "geography should no more bar the judge than the presence of two Virginians—John Blair and Bushrod Washington—should have kept President Adams from naming John Marshall to be Chief Justice." And, he added sternly, "anyone who raises the question of race [sic] is unfit to advise you concerning so important a matter." [79] Hoover at last bowed to what he now regarded as the inevitable. His memoirs simply state: ". . . On February 15, 1932 . . . I nominated Chief Justice Benjamin N. Cardozo of the New York Court of Appeals, a Democrat. The appointment met with Senate approval." [80] Indeed it did, instantly and unanimously and without discussion or roll call when the nomination reached the floor of the Senate a few days later.

His brothers on the Court were delighted: "Hope you come soon," Stone wrote Cardozo on the very day of his official nomination. "We have been saving up some interesting cases for you." [81] Accurately, the *New York Times* commented that "seldom, if ever, in the history of the Court has an appointment been so universally commended." [82]

Whatever President Hoover might have thought of that statement, it did not of course surprise him that Cardozo would continue in the Holmes tradition. Thus unlike the other two later Hoover appointees, Hughes and Roberts, Cardozo at once joined the Brandeis and Stone wing of the Court, working with them in the minority for five years until the 1937 upheaval brought the other two Justices over. Although fate allowed him little more than six years on the high bench, he is eminently deserving of the recognition of greatness bestowed upon him. Those six years were among the most emotion-charged and contentious in the Court's history, and Cardozo more than did his part in recording the history of that period with opinions written with the pen of legal scholar and philosopher as well as poet and teacher. No Justice in the annals of constitutional law and history ever rendered a more enduring contribution in so brief a span of years: it was he who so lucidly and carefully spoke for the Court in 1937 in upholding the several key provisions of the landmark Social Security Act of 1935.[83] And it was he who authored the most significant basic decision ever pronounced by the Court on behalf of the application of the federal Bill of Rights to the several states, the celebrated "incorporation" case of *Palko* v. *Connecticut*.[84] There, for a unanimous Court save for the dissent (without opinion) by Mr. Justice Butler, Cardozo identified certain rights "so rooted in the traditions and conscience of our people as to be ranked as fundamental," so clearly constituting "the matrix, the indispensable condition, of nearly every other form of freedom" (such as freedom of speech, the press, worship, assembly, and petition) that, unlike certain others they were also protected against state infringement by virtue of the language of the Fourteenth Amendment.[85] The all but total application, absorption, or incorporation that has taken place since *Palko* is a tribute to Cardozo's jurisprudential pioneering in this fundamental aspect of democratic society.

Cardozo's friend and fellow judicial stylist and craftsman, Learned Hand, movingly eulogized the gentle spirit shortly after his death, concluding:

> In this America of ours when the passion for publicity is a disease, and where swarms of foolish, tawdry moths dash with rapture into its consuming fire, it was a rare good fortune that brought to such eminence a man so reserved, so unassuming, so retiring, so gracious to high and low, and so serene. He is gone, and while the west is still lighted with his radiance, it is well for us to pause and take count of our own coarser selves. He had a lesson to teach us if we care to stop and learn; a lesson at variance of most that we practice, and much that we profess.[86]

And Felix Frankfurter, who inherited the Cardozo seat, justly observed that the man whose opinions reflected not the "friction and passion of their day, but the abiding spirit of the Constitution," ranks "second only to Holmes in making of the judicial process a blend of continuity and creativeness." [87] Unlike Holmes, Cardozo lived to see, however briefly, the realization of at least some of his labors.

8
The Court Alters Course:
F.D.R. and Truman
1933 – 1953

In the depth of the worst economic and psychological depression
in the history of the United States, a remarkable man was swept
into office. Franklin Delano Roosevelt was the leader people
needed, not only because of his training, background, and understanding but also because of his optimism and his confident resolve to lead the nation out of a situation that might well have
doomed it. Far from turning the country over to the "Communists
and Socialists," as was so often charged, he orchestrated a New
Deal that in effect preserved the American system of enlightened
free enterprise.

The antithesis of his predecessor, Herbert Hoover, Roosevelt
was a man of action: tough, forceful, and decisive, he got things
done. And by and large his countrymen approved of his action,
electing him to the Presidency four times, despite sustained and
bitter attacks against him from powerful and influential critics, notable among them the press. Of course, as even his most ardent
admirers admit, F.D.R. was a fox as well as a lion. He was not
above deviousness, the dishonest rationale he advanced for the
Court-packing bill of 1937 being a case in point. Yet he was an
inspiring and successful leader; he gave to the American people
ideals, confidence, and hope. "The only thing we have to fear is

fear itself," he reassured them during the blackest days of the depression: 13 million were unemployed, 9100 banks were closed, the government was at a standstill. "This nation asks for action, and action now," he stated in setting forth a program of drastic action: The Congress had literally begged the President to lead, and he responded in full measure. In the ensuing "Hundred Days" F.D.R. swamped Congress with nearly a score of carefully spelled-out legislative messages—tough, basic recommendations designed to bring about economic recovery and, simultaneously, reform. The Legislative Branch concurred eagerly; desperate, it was ready to improvise and even to experiment. The recovery was gradual, but in the process one of the nation's most gifted leaders would forge a coalition of support that would carry him to an unprecedented re-election victory in 1936, with 60.8 per cent of the popular vote—a record until 1964 when Lyndon Baines Johnson (an early and ardent New Deal supporter) bested the master by three-tenths of one percentage point. By any count and any standard, Franklin Delano Roosevelt was a truly great leader, one who fully deserves his ranking of third on the scale of our Presidents, just below Lincoln and Washington.

Roosevelt was no radical, far from it. Yet he chafed under a governmental stand-off that, notwithstanding his overwhelming mandates in 1932 and 1936, saw the Supreme Court, now popularly dubbed the "Nine Old Men," say "no" to most New Deal legislation. The Court, usually by 6:3 or 5:4 votes, made mincemeat of the measures that the President and his Congress had so ardently desired and enacted. True, he could usually count on support from Justices Brandeis, Stone, and Cardozo who in addition to being personally sympathetic to most New Deal measures at hand practiced judicial restraint in the best tradition of the separation of powers. But the "Four Horsemen" (Justices Van Devanter, McReynolds, Sutherland, and Butler)—those direct descendants of Darwin and Spencer—were totally antagonistic to the New Deal, and they could usually count on support in their antagonism from Mr. Justice Roberts and Mr. Chief Justice Hughes.

When Roosevelt entered his second term he had made not a

single appointment to the Supreme Court! Little wonder he was convinced the fates were conspiring against him. Death and retirement seemed to have taken a holiday.

It was at this point that F.D.R., his patience thoroughly spent and his frustrations at their peak, resolved to effect radical Court reform, and on February 5, 1937, he sent to the Hill a sweeping piece of legislation designed to reorganize the federal judiciary in general and the Supreme Court in particular.[1] The measure would grant the President authority to appoint an additional jurist for each federal judge who, having served ten years or more, failed to retire within six months after reaching his seventieth birthday. The additional judge would be assigned to the same court on which the reluctant septuagenarian was serving. A ceiling of fifty such additional judges (for the entire federal judicial system) was provided for in the bill—with the maximum size of the Supreme Court pegged at fifteen. Had the bill become law, F.D.R. would have been able to appoint six "additional" Justices to the Court to serve with the "Nine Old Men." Their ages at that point ranged from Brandeis's eighty-one to Roberts's sixty-two, but each of the Four Horsemen and the Chief Justice was conveniently above seventy. Unfortunately, Roosevelt's message accompanying his scheme was devious and dishonest: as the main motivation for the bill it alleged that the Court was overburdened because of "insufficient personnel" and the physical disabilities of the jurists; it went on to charge that it was the conservatism bred of old age that caused so many of the Court's attitudinal difficulties. The real reason for the President's action was, of course, obvious to everyone: the Court's continuing vetoes over much-desired New Deal laws.

The President's message grievously offended Mr. Justice Brandeis, the Court's most liberal and most pro-New Deal member, who suggested to Mr. Chief Justice Hughes that he (Hughes) publicly deny the Presidential charge. Hughes promptly did so in a letter to the Chairman of the Senate Judiciary Committee. His statistics were irrefutable; the Court was readily in command of its docket. Whatever the weight of the Brandeis-Hughes refutation of F.D.R.'s charge, the ill-conceived plan for judicial reorganization hopelessly split the Democratic majority in the Senate; caused a storm of protest from bench and bar; and created an uproar among both constitutional conservatives and liberals. The bill was doomed: on June 14 the Senate Judiciary Committee reported it to the floor with an adverse vote of 8:10; on July 20 the Senate recommitted it to the Committee for burial. The vote was 70:20.

At least two interrelated crucial events had taken place between the bill's submittal in February and the Senate's actions in June and July. First, the Court made three key decisions that effected the "switch-in-time-that-saved-nine." The first took place on March 29, 1937, when Hughes and Roberts moved over to the Brandeis-Stone-Cardozo bloc in sustaining 5:4 Washington state's minimum-wage law for women in *West Coast Hotel* v. *Parrish*.[2] The second was the April 12 decision upholding, again in a 5:4 vote, one of the prize New Deal laws, the National Labor Relations Act of 1935 (the "Wagner Act").[3] The third "clincher," which came on May 24, upheld as constitutional the old-age tax and benefits and unemployment provisions of another major New Deal statute, the Social Security Act of 1935.[4] Well might F.D.R. and Congress be jubilant! No matter how insistently Hughes and Roberts might later deny that their switch to the liberal wing had been politically motivated, few students of the Court view their move as anything but a recognition of the handwriting on the wall.

The second major event followed closely on the heels of the Court's upholding the Social Security Act. The oldest of the Four Horsemen in both point of service (twenty-seven years) and age (seventy-eight), Mr. Justice Willis Van Devanter, announced on May 18—in what was scarcely accidental timing, the Court-packing bill being before the Judiciary Committee—that he would retire from the Court on June 1, 1937. At last, more than four and a half years after his election to the Presidency, Roosevelt had a Supreme Court vacancy to fill. The appointment went to loyal New Deal supporter Senator Hugo Lafayette Black of Alabama. And there would be eight other appointments, falling short of George Washington's record by only one: Stanley F. Reed, Felix Frankfurter, William O. Douglas, Frank Murphy, James F.

Byrnes, Harlan F. Stone (promoted to Chief Justice), Robert H. Jackson, and Wiley B. Rutledge. They were distinguished men by anyone's standards: of them, Black and Frankfurter have been ranked as "great," and Douglas, Jackson, and Rutledge as "near great"—a record attained by no other President.

No mystery attends Roosevelt's motivations in selecting his Supreme Court nominees. There were three major criteria: (1) absolute loyalty to the principles of the New Deal, particularly to governmental regulatory authority; (2) firm adherence to a libertarian and egalitarian philosophy of government under law; and (3) (once it had become clear that war clouds would cover the New World as well as the Old) full support of his war aims—which necessitated a generous interpretation of the extent of executive power. Of lesser importance were age and geography; nevertheless he considered such factors with great care. With occasional differences all of F.D.R.'s appointees lived up to his expectations during his lifetime: few Presidents had been rewarded with judicial performances so pleasing.

When Mr. Justice Van Devanter announced his retirement the leading candidate for the vacancy was Joseph T. Robinson of Arkansas, the Democratic Majority Leader of the Senate. A faithful New Dealer who had supported every New Deal measure that F.D.R. had sent to Congress, the popular, hard-working Robinson had also been an early and key backer of the President's Court-reorganization bill. Everything pointed to his designation. F.D.R. had evidently promised him a Supreme Court seat, although not necessarily the first available one. But according to the then still high-riding Postmaster-General and Democratic National Committee Chairman, James A. "Jim" Farley, Roosevelt had said that Robinson could count on being nominated.[5] And in an unusual move the Senate as a body endorsed the candidacy of its Democratic Leader. Yet F.D.R. had been forced to wait more than four years for that precious initial vacancy; now he would bide his time. He liked and was grateful to "Arkansas Joe"; still, there was just enough basic conservatism in Robinson's past to cast doubt on his reliability. Then fate intervened: on July 14, while leading the floor fight for the Court-packing bill, Senator Robinson suffered a fatal heart attack. Roosevelt at once instructed Homer S. Cummings, his Attorney General, to canvass the field of other "suitables," keeping in mind that the nominee had to be absolutely loyal to the New Deal program, and report back. By early August the search had narrowed to four loyal New Deal Democrats: U.S. Solicitor-General Stanley F. Reed of Kentucky, Senator Sherman Minton of Indiana, Senator Hugo L. Black of Alabama, and Assistant Attorney General Robert H. Jackson of New York. All four would become Supreme Court Justices eventually; it was Black's turn now. "Jesus Christ!" exclaimed White House Press Secretary Stephen Early when F.D.R. disclosed his choice to him on August 11.[6]

Steve Early's reaction was understandable. At first glance there was preciously little in the impoverished rural background of the fifty-one-year-old Senator to qualify him for the Supreme Court. True, he had had considerable experience as a lawyer among country sharecroppers, as a county solicitor, and as a police court judge and prosecutor in Birmingham; he had read widely; and he had a lucid, profound mind, but was he *really* the best F.D.R. could do? The President, of course, knew precisely what he was doing: Black, now in his second term in the Senate, had not only demonstrated enthusiastic and outspoken support of the New Deal, but he had staunchly supported the Court-packing bill. Those two factors were decisive—but F.D.R. also happily noted that Black had a long and effective record of siding with "little people" and "underdogs" and that he was from a part of the country that he, F.D.R., wanted to see represented on the Court. The nomination's announcement was met with approbation by most of Senator Black's colleagues and most New Deal spokesmen throughout the land. Yet it also evoked loud protests from both public and private sources. The intellectual and soft-spoken liberal was portrayed as being utterly unqualified by training, temperament, and constitutional dedication; as being blindly partisan; as being a radical rather than a liberal; as being, in fact, a phony liberal when it was revealed that he had been a member of the Ku

Klux Klan in the 1920s. The press—no more a friend of the Senator's than of his President—roasted Black for "combined lack of training on the one hand and extreme partisanship on the other." [7] But the Senate, although treated to the somewhat unaccustomed spectacle of a public debate on the merits of a sitting member, quickly confirmed its colleague (backed 13:4 in the Judiciary Committee) by a vote of 63:16 on August 17. [8]

When the verdict was in, Justice designate and Mrs. Black sailed for a European vacation. In their absence the *Pittsburgh Post-Gazette* published a six-day series of articles repeating the known facts of Black's erstwhile KKK membership, alleging as well that he not only was still a member of the hooded organization but that he had been secretly elected to life membership. Black was besieged abroad by reporters, but he characteristically disdained any comment until he stepped before radio microphones on October 1 to make the statement which was heard by the largest radio audience ever, save for those who listened to Edward VIII's abdication: [9]

> My words and acts are a matter of public record. I believe that my record as a Senator refutes every implication of racial or religious intolerance. It shows that I was of that group of liberal Senators who have consistently fought for civil, economic and religious rights of all Americans, without regard to race or creed. . . . I did join the Klan. I later resigned. I never rejoined. I have never considered and I do not now consider the unsolicited card given to me shortly after my nomination to the Senate as a membership of any kind in the Ku Klux Klan. I never used it. I did not even keep it. Before becoming a Senator I dropped the Klan. I have had nothing whatever to do with it since that time. I abandoned it. . . . [10]

The public was generally sympathetic and persuaded of his sincerity. Again characteristically, Mr. Justice Black said no more on the subject, refusing to discuss or re-open the matter during the remainder of his long life. "When this statement is ended," he had said, "my discussion of the question is closed." Three days after the broadcast he donned the robes of Associate Justice of the Su-

preme Court to begin a tenure of more than thirty-four years. It
was one marked by a distinction and an influence rare in the annals of the Court. How right the *Montgomery Advertiser* had
been when it observed: "What a joke it would be on Hugo's impassioned detractors if he should now turn out to be a very great
justice of the Supreme Court. Brandeis did it when every Substantial Citizen of the Republic felt that Wilson should have been impeached for appointing him. . . ." [11]

Few jurists have had the impact on law and society of Mr. Justice Hugo Lafayette Black. A constitutional literalist to whom
every work in the document represented a command, he nonetheless used the language of the Constitution to propound a jurisprudence that has had a lasting effect on the development of American constitutional law. His contributions were towering. They stand
as jurisprudential and intellectual landmarks in the evolving history of the land he loved so well. [12] He fully met F.D.R.'s expectations, of course. But that was in the short run; the New Deal as
such had run its course by the end of the 1930s. In the long run
Black's achievements encompass securing the central meaning of
the Constitution and of the Bill of Rights. At the pinnacle of his
legacy stands the now-all-but-complete nationalization of the Bill
of Rights, its application to all of the states through the due process clause of the Fourteenth Amendment. In what was probably
his most influential opinion in dissent, the *Adamson* case of
1947, [13] Hugo Black called for that nationalization, dramatically
expanding and elaborating the Cardozo position in the 1937 *Palko
Case.* [14] He lost by only one vote. But by constantly reiterating the
theme of constitutional intent as he perceived it in the Fourteenth
Amendment—"I cannot consider the Bill of Rights to be an out-
worn eighteenth-century 'strait jacket,' " he had thundered in
Adamson—he coaxed the Court step by step to his side. By the
late 1960s the Warren Court had, in effect, written into constitutional law its concurrence. [15]

It is generally agreed that the nationalization of the Bill of
Rights was Black's most visible achievement; yet it is but one of
many. Among those achievements were his leadership in pro-

pounding an "absolutist" theory of the First Amendment's freedom of expression guarantees, a theory that contributed heavily to the Warren Court's liberal definition of obscenity and to its striking down of much of the "subversive activities" legislation of the McCarthy era; his assertive majority opinions defining the line of separation between Church and State; his tenacious, literal interpretation of the protective provisions of the Constitution in the administration of justice, including the specific provisions against coerced confessions, compulsory self-incrimination, double jeopardy, and those defining the conditions of trial by jury and the availability of counsel; his victory over Justice Frankfurter in the arena of "political questions" that legalized the egalitarian representation ("one man, one vote") concept now broadly taken for granted. Probably Black's most moving opinion was written for a unanimous Court in the celebrated case of *Gideon* v. *Wainwright* (1963),[16] which overruled a decision of more than two decades earlier from which he had vigorously dissented: [17] *Gideon* enshrined the principle that any criminal defendant in a state as well as a federal proceeding who is too poor to pay for a lawyer has a constitutional right to be assigned one gratis by the government. For Black the opinion represented the affirmation of another moving plea written twenty-three years earlier in the famed case of *Chambers* v. *Florida*. Still viewed as one of his finest opinions, it held for a unanimous Court that the confessions obtained by Florida authorities to condemn four black defendants to death were patently coerced and therefore a clear violation of due process of law. In the most celebrated passage, at the close of his opinion, Black wrote:

Under our constitutional system courts stand against any winds that blow as havens of refuge for those who might otherwise suffer because they are helpless, weak, outnumbered, or because they are non-conforming victims of prejudice and public excitement. Due process of law, preserved for all by our Constitution, commands that no such practice as that disclosed by [the *Chambers* case record] shall send any accused to his death. No higher duty, no more solemn responsibility, rests upon this Court, than

that of translating into living law and maintaining this constitutional shield deliberately planned and inscribed for the benefit of
every human being to our Constitution—of whatever race, creed,
or persuasion.[18]

One week after ill health compelled his retirement in September
1971 at eighty-five, Mr. Justice Black died. "The law," as one of
those who knew him best wrote, "has lost a kindly giant." [19]
Friends who called at a funeral home in Washington before his
burial in Arlington National Cemetery received a poignant parting
gift—a copy of the Constitution. On a desk bearing a book for
visitors signatures was a pile of small paper-bound copies of the
document Black had so often referred to as "my legal bible"—a
copy of which he always carried in his pocket. He would have approved.

F.D.R.'s second appointment opportunity came within six
months of Black's when Mr. Justice George Sutherland, second of
the Four Horsemen to retire, stepped down in January 1938.
F.D.R.'s choice was no surprise: Stanley F. Reed, the Solicitor
General, had been high on the list when F.D.R. nominated Black.
He was approved without objection on January 25. Reed had
studied law at Columbia and Virginia, later practicing law in his
native Kentucky. In the late 1920s he had entered government service in response to President Hoover's successive invitations to
serve as general counsel to the Federal Loan Board and the Reconstruction Finance Corporation. He then moved to the Attorney
General's office as a special assistant, serving there until F.D.R.,
conscious of Reed's faithful New Deal adherence, named him Solicitor General in 1935. It was a crucial period for the New Deal
and its legislation, and the President needed an individual in the
post who could be trusted to back the Administration fully. Given
the composition of the Court, Reed won few cases before the
Court until the 1937 switch occurred, but he always ardently supported New Deal principles.

In terms of his fundamental commitment to F.D.R.'s governmental philosophy, Reed was a logical choice. But he also was an
attractive candidate because of his age (fifty-three); his state (the

Border states were then not "represented" on the Court); his impressive legal reputation; his solid character and personal popularity; and his non-controversial image.

Reed, whose authorship of more than three hundred opinions during almost two decades of service stamped him as one of the workhorses of the Court, was the least glamorous and least mercurial of the Roosevelt Justices. He faithfully backed the President's program, but observers generally label him as a conservative on the bench—probably because he moved more slowly and cautiously than his colleagues and because he was reluctant to side with his more liberal associates in their rulings favoring individuals vis-à-vis government. This was especially true in national security and criminal justice cases, in which Reed usually fit into the "law and order" mold. But he solidly backed the Court's developing position on racial segregation; thus, in 1946, he wrote the opinion in *Morgan* v. *Virginia* invalidating racial segregation in interstate buses [20] and, in 1944, the opinion in *Smith* v. *Allwright* [21] striking down for an 8:1 court the "White Primary" of the Texas Democratic party as an unconstitutional violation of the Fifteenth Amendment. Ironically, Mr. Chief Justice Stone had initially assigned the case to Mr. Justice Frankfurter but, given the emotional nature of the controversy, had yielded to Mr. Justice Jackson's plea that it be given to someone else—someone more amenable to the South than a foreign-born Jew and a Harvard educated, none-too-loyal Democrat. [22]

Felix Frankfurter was the next man to be appointed to the Court. This, Roosevelt's third opportunity to appoint a Supreme Court Justice, came with the untimely death of the jurist and man Frankfurter revered, Benjamin N. Cardozo (whose seat had been formerly occupied by Frankfurter's greatest hero, Oliver Wendell Holmes). For almost a quarter of a century Frankfurter would serve with brilliance, dedication, and persuasiveness, almost equaling the performance of Hugo L. Black in lasting impact and influence. Black and Frankfurter were often in fundamental jurisprudential disagreement, but unfailingly with respect and appreciation. These two men towered over a Court with probably more talent than any other in the tribunal's history. Their impact on American jurisprudence was not only profound, it was seminal.

F.D.R., who had known Frankfurter since his days as Assistant Secretary of the Navy, had fully intended to send him to the Court, and told him so. Yet on Cardozo's death he informed his friend and adviser that he could not do so now; that he hoped to appoint him when and if Brandeis resigned; that he felt a genuine need to choose someone from west of the Mississippi to counterbalance a bench now entirely made up of Easterners. He then asked Frankfurter to prepare dossiers on prospective candidates from the desired area.[23] Roosevelt made no secret of his intentions which, in turn, set into motion a veritable ground swell for Frankfurter, reminiscent of the events surrounding Hoover's nomination of Cardozo. Fifty-six years old, Frankfurter was a brilliant scholar and teacher (he had taught for twenty-five years at the Harvard Law School); a superb lawyer; an effective, shrewd administrator; a connoisseur of personnel; and a highly effective public servant with considerable experience in federal and state government. He had become a close Presidential adviser and confidant in the evolving New Deal; he had aided in the drafting of legislation; and he had recommended many able young appointees to the Roosevelt Administration—often derisively referred to as "Felix's Happy Hotdogs" because of their alleged political coloration.

The pressure on F.D.R. to designate Professor Frankfurter became intense: his closest personal and political advisers, such as his Solicitor General, Robert H. Jackson; his Secretary of the Interior, Harold L. Ickes; his Man Friday, Harry Hopkins; his friend and political ally, Senator George Norris; and, most persuasively, Mr. Justice Stone, all implored the President to place excellence over geography. Jackson scored points by urging F.D.R. to choose the man if for no other reason than naming "someone who can interpret [the Constitution] with scholarship and with sufficient assurance to face Chief Justice Hughes in conference and hold his own in discussion." [24] The President yielded, announcing to his entourage that "there isn't anybody in the West . . . who is of sufficient stature." [25] Frankfurter himself recorded that at 7:00 p.m. on January 4, 1939, while he was in his B.V.D.s, late to receive a dinner guest, the phone rang in his study, "and there was the ebullient, the exuberant, resilient warmth-enveloping voice of the President of the United States, 'Hello. How are You?' " Then, after asking about Frankfurter's wife, Marion, F.D.R. told him not once, but several times: "You know, I told you I don't want to appoint you to the Supreme Court of the United States. . . . I mean it. . . . I mean this. I mean this. I don't want to appoint you. . . . I just don't want to appoint you. . . . I told you I can't name you." Underwear-clad, and eager to go down to dinner, Frankfurter agreed again and again with his caller, becoming more and more exasperated. He was hardly prepared for the President's next words: "But wherever I turn, wherever I turn and to whomever I talk that matters to me, I am made to realize that you are the only person fit to succeed Holmes and Cardozo." Adding: "Unless you give me an insurmountable objection I'm going to send your name in for the Court tomorrow at twelve o'clock." The overwhelmed Frankfurter replied softly, "All I can say is that I wish my mother were alive." [26] Senate confirmation, by unanimous voice vote, came twelve days later, after some protracted opposition by Senator Pat McCarran (D.-Nev.), who tried to link the nominee with Communism.

Senator McCarran need not have worried. Frankfurter was a native of Vienna, but he loved his adopted country and its institutions as few men did. This long-time champion of the poor, the oppressed, the underdog, the persecuted had but one aim: to make America an even better place to live for an even greater number of people. A passionate believer in the democratic process with an abiding regard for the British concept of legislative supremacy, he had dedicated his twenty-three years on the Court to the proposition that the people should govern, but that it was up to their representatives in the legislature, not the judiciary, to make laws. Thus Frankfurter became increasingly known as an articulate and persuasive advocate of judicial abnegation in favor of legislative action. "When in doubt, don't," became the Frankfurter maxim.

So dedicated was he to the principle of judicial restraint that Fred Rodell referred to him as "the Supreme Court's Emily Post." [27] Walton Hamilton characterized him as "weaving crochet patches of legalism on the fingers of the case." [28] Frankfurter's jurisprudential philosophy, of course, enabled him to back the New Deal's program to the fullest—enacted as it was by the people's duly chosen representatives. F.D.R. was pleased, indeed. In social and economic legislation Frankfurter could be found with the other Justices appointed by Roosevelt. But when it came to the interpretation of the Bill of Rights, he and Black and the other "liberatarian activists" (especially Douglas, Murphy, and Rutledge) would often part company—for Frankfurter brought the same sense of judicial restraint to legislation concerning human rights as he did to legislation concerning economic issues. He could be a powerful spokesman on behalf of due process of law: as the author for a unanimous Court in *Rochin* v. *California* (1952),[29] he delivered a magnificent lecture to Los Angeles County police authorities on the requirements of procedural due process. He accorded the Fourth Amendment's safeguards against unreasonable searches and seizures a place second to none in the Bill of Rights. Yet this champion of human freedom who had fought so hard to save Sacco and Vanzetti stood like Canute against his personal convictions when it came to his role as a jurist. Thus, notwithstanding his abhorrence of capital punishment, he could not bring himself to provide the necessary fifth vote to save Willie Francis, a teen-age Louisiana Negro, from a second trip to the electric chair (the malfunctioning instrument had failed to do its grim job the first time).[30] Frankfurter felt bound by what he viewed as the commands of the Federalist division of powers—in spite of his outcry to Mr. Justice Burton, whose dissenting opinion he had seen: "I have to hold on to myself not to reach your result." [31] Yet he had used all of his considerable influence—unsuccessfully—in trying through powerful friends to persuade the Governor to commute Willie's sentence.

Frankfurter's scrupulous adherence to his duty as a judge despite his personal commitments is perhaps even better illustrated by his most famous dissenting opinion in a civil liberties case. It came in 1943 when a 6:3 Court, overruling an earlier Frankfurter opinion,[32] declared unconstitutional a West Virginia statute that compelled school children to salute the flag as a daily exercise.[33] Frankfurter, of course, would not have voted for such a law had he been a legislator, since it compelled saluting even by those, like the Jehovah's Witnesses, who regarded the act as paying homage to a graven image. But as a jurist he could not bring himself to join the majority opinion that the compulsory salute constituted an unconstitutional invasion of the free exercise of religion and freedom of expression guaranteed by Amendments One and Fourteen:

> One who belongs to the most vilified and persecuted minority in history is not likely to be insensible to the freedoms guaranteed by our Constitution. Were my purely personal attitude relevant I should whole-heartedly associate myself with the general libertarian view in the Court's opinion, representing as they do the thought and action of a lifetime. But as judges we are neither Jew, nor Gentile, neither Catholic nor agnostic. We owe equal attachment to the Constitution and are equally bound by our judicial obligations whether we derive our citizenship from the earliest or the latest immigrants to these shores. As a member of this Court I am not justified in writing my private notions of policy into the Constitution, no matter how deeply I may cherish them or how mischievous I may deem their disregard. . . .[34]

Frankfurter's conception of the judical function is also illustrated by his continuing battle, successful until the momentous 1962 *Baker* v. *Carr* [35] reapportionment-redistricting decision, against the Court's dealing with "political questions." In an impassioned sixty-eight-page dissenting opinion joined by his disciple John Marshall Harlan, he warned the Court that it was about to enter a "mathematical quagmire," that it must stay out of such "a political thicket." He further admonished the majority of six: "There is not under our Constitution a judicial remedy for every political mischief. In a democratic society like ours, relief must come through an aroused popular conscience that sears the conscience of the people's representatives." [36] But, asked his opponents tellingly, what happens when there are no electoral channels open to "sear" that conscience?

Felix Frankfurter died on February 22, 1965. A great jurist in defeat as well as victory, he left a major imprint on the American scene. In a memorial editorial the *New York Times* summed up eloquently: "As a philosopher and scholar of the law, a judicial craftsman, a master of prose style and a formative influence on a generation of American lawyers and public officials, Felix Frankfurter was a major shaper of the history of his age." [37] And dozens of newspapers ended their obituaries with the above-quoted sentences from his *Baker* v. *Carr* dissenting opinion.

Four weeks after President Roosevelt had nominated Frankfurter, Mr. Justice Louis D. Brandeis retired after twenty-three years. F.D.R. thus had his fourth vacancy in little more than three and a half years. How matters had changed since those first frustrating years! The President still wanted a Westerner, and his youthful Chairman of the Securities and Exchange Commission, William O. Douglas, born in Ottertail County, Minnesota, and raised in Yakima, Washington, was a likely candidate. But Douglas had spent half of his forty-one years in New York (Columbia Law School), in New Haven, Connecticut (Yale Law School Faculty), and in Washington, D.C. (government service), and Roosevelt viewed him as two-thirds Easterner. He had promised a "true Westerner" and, besides, the Court *was* in his corner, though perhaps not by a comfortable margin. Thus he took no immediate action. Yet pressure began to build from his close advisers. After all, Douglas was personally as well as philosophically close to Brandeis on social, economic, political, and constitutional policy; he was an ardent and articulate New Dealer; he believed that the law had to be alive to the demands of the times; he had an outstanding legal mind; he was a proved expert in the intricacies of public finance and corporation problems. Further persuasion came with a press conference dramatically called by Senator William Borah of Idaho, now ranking member of the Senate Judiciary Committee. In that conference he "claimed" Douglas as "one of the West's finest and brightest sons." [38] F.D.R., now convinced, telephoned Douglas on a golf course to inform him of his decision and then sent Douglas's name to the Senate on March 20. He was confirmed promptly by a vote of 62:4—the youngest appointee since Mr. Justice Joseph Story in 1811. Ironically, the four "no" votes (cast by Republican Senators) categorized Douglas as a "reactionary tool of Wall Street!" [39]

Mr. Justice William O. Douglas remains very much a member of the Court more than thirty-five years after his appointment. Beyond seventy-five, he is still incredibly vigorous both physically and intellectually, despite a pace-maker in his chest and a fourth wife almost fifty years his junior. Although all of F.D.R.'s appointees came through for him and the New Deal, no one did more so, with more consistency and with more concern for the results of decisions, than Douglas. And, ultimately, Douglas has compiled a civil liberties record on the bench second to none: in close to 95 per cent of all cases involving line-drawing between the rights of the individual and those of society, he has sided with the former. The Douglas human-rights posture thus would not be checked by the verbiage of the Constitution: if that document and its Bill of Rights did not provide the kind of protection for the individual Douglas deemed necessary to bring about justice under law, well, he would find it—as he did in his famed and controversial opinion in the *Connecticut Birth Control Case* of 1965, in *"penumbras, formed by emanations from those guarantees of the Bill of Rights that help give them life and substance."* [40] Often embattled off as well as on the Court, this colorful and brilliant scholar has eloquently articulated his posture again and again—in cases at law as well as from the lecture podium, in books as well as journals, including *Playboy* magazine. As he put it on one occasion: "The American Government is premised on the theory that if the mind of man is to be free, his ideas, his beliefs, his ideology, his philosophy must be placed beyond the reach of government." [41] While unquestionably doctrinaire and result-oriented, Douglas deserves the "near great" rating of the Court historians just as did his jurisprudential opposites Field and Sutherland.

No hesitation whatever attended F.D.R.'s filling of his fifth va-

cancy. On November 16, 1939, Pierce Butler, one of the two remaining Four Horsemen, died after seventeen years on the Court.
On the same morning, the President informed Frank Murphy, his
forty-six-year-old Attorney General, that he was his choice to succeed the New Deal's nemesis. Murphy at first demurred, feeling
"utterly inadequate," [42] but he ultimately accepted and was officially nominated on January 4, 1940. The Senate confirmed him a
few days later. The tall, gaunt Murphy was in many ways a "natural" for the position. Like Butler he was a Midwesterner and a
good Irish Catholic of middle-class origin. Widely known as a crusading New Deal liberal, he had served in the 1920s as a U.S. Assistant Attorney and as a Detroit judge—a post he held until,
successfully courting the support of the numerous Irish and black
citizens, he was elected Mayor of Detroit in 1929. During the Depression, which affected the Motor City severely, Murphy became
a strong and articulate advocate of federal aid. After Roosevelt's
election in 1932, for which he worked tirelessly, Murphy was
chosen President of the Conference of Mayors and later was appointed Governor of the Philippines by F.D.R. In 1936 Murphy
gave up that post not only to aid in the Presidential campaign but
to run (successfully) for the Governorship of Michigan, and thus
to aid the national ticket in securing that key industrial state.

Two years later Murphy lost his bid for re-election, and Roosevelt appointed him his Attorney General. The repeated suggestions that Murphy was later "kicked upstairs" to the Court from
the Justice Department may hold some truth, but F.D.R. might
very well have appointed Murphy anyway, if perhaps not quite so
soon. Murphy, not an interested or conscientious administrator,
paid little heed to the modus operandi of his department; he
placed heavy emphasis in antitrust litigation, neglecting such crucial areas as internal revenue; and, like many Attorneys General
before and after him, he did not get along well with the powerful
head of the F.B.I., J. Edgar Hoover. In view of Murphy's other
qualifications, F.D.R. quite conceivably decided to expedite his
promotion and to give the Attorney Generalship to the man who
was supposed to get it in the first place, Solicitor General Robert

H. Jackson. "Bob, I suppose you know that you're to come into this office," Murphy had told Jackson, "that I am here only temporarily." [43]

Frank Murphy was cut down by a fatal heart attack little more than nine years later. During that time he established himself as not only 100 per cent loyal to the New Deal but as the Court's most advanced civil libertarian, outscoring all others in his generous support of individual rights and claims. He alone among the libertarian block of Black, Douglas, and Rutledge dissented (together with Justices Roberts and Jackson) from the 1944 landmark decision of *Korematsu* v. *United States* written by Black,[44] which upheld the war-time evacuation from the West Coast of more than 100,000 Japanese-Americans, of whom three-quarters were American-born citizens. In his emotion-charged opinion,[45] Murphy assailed the evacuation program as one that "goes over the 'very brink of constitutional power' and falls into the ugly abyss of racism." Pronouncing it a flagrant violation of due process of law, he angrily and sarcastically characterized the military order, now sanctioned by the Court, as "based upon an erroneous assumption of racial guilt" and justified upon "questionable racial and sociological grounds not ordinarily within the realm of expert military judgment. . . ." And once again it was Murphy who, with Rutledge by his side, wanted to strike down as unconstitutional the military trial and conviction of Japanese General Yamashita, Commanding General of the Japanese army group that had wrought such havoc in the Philippines. Black and Douglas were with the majority opinion by Mr. Chief Justice Stone in that 1946 decision,[46] but Murphy argued in defeat that the Court's failure to extend the guarantees of the Fifth and Sixth amendments to General Yamashita was crassly unconstitutional and would hinder the "reconcilation necessary to a peaceful world." [47]

Murphy would all but inevitably side with the underdog—were he an enemy alien, a rank offender at the bar of criminal justice, or a member of a beleaguered religious sect. In *Adamson* v. *California* (1947),[48] with Rutledge concurring, he articulated the doctrine that if the specific provisions of the Bill of Rights did not provide sufficient safeguard against abusive governmental action, "constitutional condemnation in terms of a lack of due process despite the absence of a specific provision in the Bill of Rights" would be warranted. To Black, who also dissented in that landmark case (but for different reasons) the Murphy-Rutledge posture was an obvious invocation of natural law, which he regarded as an "incongruous excrescence on our Constitution." [49] Very likely because his concerns and productivity on the Court were essentially one-dimensional, no matter how noble and hortatory, Murphy was accorded, with considerable justice, only an "average" rating. Yet he was a major influence in the spectrum that concerned him most—man's freedom and dignity.

The last of the Four Horsemen, and probably the most tenacious and reactionary member, announced his retirement early in 1941. James McReynolds had been on the Court for twenty-seven years, was nearing eighty, and simply decided that there was no point in staying on. F.D.R. heartily agreed! Most Court observers believed that the President would now turn to his Attorney General, but Bob Jackson had been in office scarcely a year, and Roosevelt felt he could not now spare him. Moreover, many of his most influential party leaders, including Senators Alben W. Barkley of Kentucky, Pat Harrison of Mississippi, and Carter Glass of Virginia, were pushing hard for F.D.R.'s political and personal ally Senator James F. Byrnes of South Carolina, who had often and prominently been mentioned as a possible candidate and who held a barrelful of I.O.U.s for loyal Democratic party service. The President himself had mentioned the Court to Byrnes on sundry occasions but, because of Byrnes's role as an influential, articulate, and shrewd Administration stalwart in the Senate, he hesitated to move him—especially since he no longer had to worry about the Court's posture on his programs. Byrnes was unquestionably more conservative than any of the other members of the Court F.D.R. had appointed, but the President was not genuinely concerned on that score—the Court was now safely "pro-New Deal" and "pro-libertarian." What finally determined Byrnes's selection was his failure to receive the Vice-Presidential nomination in the Democratic Convention of 1940. Byrnes, who himself had harbored Presidential ambitions but had staunchly supported F.D.R. for a third term, was grievously disappointed. The President was eager to please his loyal lieutenant, and he responded to Senator Glass's entreaties: "Of course, I will appoint him. . . . He is just as much my friend as yours—I wanted him to be my running mate in 1940. . . . My only regret in appointing him is that I need him so much in the Senate." [50] And appoint him he did—but only after delaying for close to five months because of crucial pending legislation in the Senate. On June 12, 1941, Byrnes's colleagues proudly confirmed him unanimously and without reference to the Judiciary Committee. Wesley McCune, a chronicler of the Roosevelt Court, reported that F.D.R. remarked during Byrnes's swearing-in ceremony:

> . . . He wished he were Solomon and could halve Jimmy Byrnes, keeping one half in the Senate and the other half on the Court. At that moment, he was losing the smoothest, most effective worker he had ever had in the Senate, at the same time acquiring an unknown quantity for his Court.[51]

The sixty-two-year-old Byrnes—who would live on for another three decades, most of it in a variety of federal and state governmental posts—had a remarkable record of governmental experience. After brief executive and judicial service in his native South Carolina, he served seven terms in the U.S. House of Representatives and two in the Senate. He had first met F.D.R. when the latter was Governor-elect of New York; the two men had formed a lasting political and personal alliance. Byrnes gave important support to Roosevelt in the 1932 Presidential election, and he went on to become one of his most trusted advisers. An invaluable leader in the Senate, he even backed the Court-packing bill. And the President could count on him fully in such vital legislation as selective service and lend-lease.

Jimmy Byrnes lasted for little more than a year on the Court: a man of action, a doer and a planner, he was not comfortable as a jurist. Thus in the fall of 1942, when Roosevelt asked him to step down to assume the post of "Assistant President for Economic Affairs," he reasily assented—he was delighted to be able to return to the active political arena. With the possible exception of his authorship of a case propounding the right of free interstate travel,[52] he left no mark on the Court, whose observers have rated him a failure—a grossly unfair judgment in view of the brevity of his membership.

On June 2, 1941, ten days before the Byrnes confirmation, the great Charles Evans Hughes, in his eightieth year, advised F.D.R. of his intention to retire on July 1. He had served brilliantly for eleven difficult years. His declining health dictated an earlier withdrawal, but he wanted to see a replacement for the McReynolds vacancy before creating a new one. Roosevelt, with five of his appointees on the high bench and the sixth one certain to be approved by the Senate, felt no pressure to nominate a successor quickly, especially since the Court was about to adjourn until October. But Hughes and his colleagues strongly implored F.D.R. not to delay, and the President acquiesced. For some time he had been pondering a successor to Hughes, and it was widely assumed that his choice lay between two eminent lawyers: Mr. Justice Harlan F. Stone and Attorney General Robert H. Jackson.

F.D.R.'s heart was clearly with Jackson, a New Deal loyalist of long standing who had fought with him all the way. Moreover, he had more than once mentioned the Chief Justiceship to Jackson, who had made clear to his President that he wanted the position very much. Yet F.D.R. hesitated—being acutely aware that a professional ground swell was about to arise for Stone. He called Hughes to the White House to discuss his successor; the retiring Chief immediately volunteered that "Stone's record gave him first claim on the honor." [53] Hughes also approved Jackson's candidacy but stuck to his preference, based on judicial performance. Roosevelt later conferred with Mr. Justice Frankfurter and asked him point-blank which of the two men he would prefer as Chief Justice. Wishing F.D.R. had not asked that question, Frankfurter replied:

On personal grounds I'd prefer Bob. While I've known Stone longer and our relations are excellent and happy, I feel closer friendship with Bob. But from the national interest I am bound to say that there is no reason for preferring Bob to Stone—quite the contrary. Stone is senior and qualified professionally to be C.J. But for me the decisive consideration, considering the fact that Stone is qualified, is that Bob is of your personal and political family, as it were, while Stone is a Republican. . . . when war does come, the country should feel you are a national, the Nation's President, and not a partisan President. Few things would contribute as much to confidence in you as a national and not a partisan President than for you to name a Republican, who has the profession's confidence, as Chief Justice.[54]

The President did not commit himself, but Frankfurter was fairly confident that the choice would be Stone, and he so informed his fellow Associate Justice. A few days later F.D.R. discussed the matter with Jackson, explained the persuasiveness of Frankfurter's logic, and again assured his Attorney General that he would send him to the Court. Jackson concurred fully with Frankfurter and received the President's permission to advise Stone himself. Not many years later, after he had become a member of the Court, Jackson would write that the need for judicial leadership and the "desirability for a symbol of stability as well as progress" were evidently the reasons for Stone's elevation "in the interest of [the fostering of the] judiciary as an institution." [55]

A nation-wide chorus of praise and acclaim greeted Stone's nomination on June 12, 1941. The press was ecstatic, the judiciary delighted, the intellectual community reassured, Congress happy. When the nomination officially reached the floor of the Senate on June 27, he was confirmed viva voce without a single objection.

Harlan Fiske Stone was almost sixty-nine when he succeeded Hughes. He would live for less than five years, but—although those years proved far less satisfactory, less happy than his sixteen as Associate Justice—they did not deter the experts from ranking him as one of the great jurists to grace the bench. Yet he was clearly more comfortable in being a member of the team than in leading it. Not a first-rate administrator like Taft, not a skillful and disciplinary Court-master like Hughes, not a ruthless crafts-man like Marshall, not so persuasive as Taney, not so innovative as Warren, his reluctance to crack down and his aversion to do battle with warring factions contributed to a marked divisiveness on the Court during his Chief Justiceship, led by the prolonged and nasty feud between Black and Jackson. Moreover, he really disdained the routine of administrative detail that he now found incumbent upon him. Yet there were precious few who understood and followed the commands and restraints of the Constitution, who supported the essence of limited government, who enhanced the concept of popular government under law, who furthered respect for the Bill of Rights as fully as Stone did.

Since he could not be groom Robert H. Jackson would be best man. To no one's surprise the forty-nine-year-old Attorney General was selected to fill the vacancy created by the Stone promotion. His appointment took a while longer to be approved than had been anticipated, chiefly because of the opposition of Senator Millard E. Tydings (D.-Md.), who was unhappy with Jackson ever since he had refused to prosecute columnist Drew Pearson for publishing a libel against him (Tydings). But the Judiciary Committee unanimously approved Jackson after but a few minutes' deliberation, and the Senate confirmed him on July 11 with only Tydings dissenting.

Jackson was eminently qualified to serve on the Court. Although he had not had a single day of judicial experience, and although his formal legal training had been meager indeed (he passed the New York bar exams without having graduated from law school), he achieved a reputation as a brilliant private and public lawyer in upstate New York, where he had built a lucrative practice and become active in Democratic politics. He achieved early national exposure as a close ally of Roosevelt when the latter was Governor of New York, and as an effective campaigner for him at the Democratic National Convention as well as during the election of 1932. Initially he refused to follow his friend and idol to Washington, but ultimately he yielded, accepting Roosevelt's appointment as General Counsel of the Bureau of Internal Revenue. A vigorous defender of and spokesman for the New Deal programs (including the Court-packing scheme) Jackson began a rapid climb through sundry posts, notably in the Department of Justice. Beginning as an Assistant Attorney General in the Anti-Trust Division, he succeeded to the Solicitor Generalship (where he did so well in his role as the "Government's Lawyer" that Mr. Justice Brandeis was moved to comment that "Jackson should be Solicitor General for life") [56] and then to the Attorney Generalship. In each of his posts he combined hard work and expertise with persuasiveness, charm, and a superb command of English.

The Court historians have recognized Jackson's achievements as "near great." But his tenure was not an entirely happy one. He had really wanted to be Chief Justice; tragically his path was blocked by a doctrinal and personal feud with Hugo Black. Largely because of Jackson's strong feelings, some of their controversy was carried on in public—harming Jackson far more than Black and exacerbating Mr. Chief Justice Stone's difficulties in maintaining a harmonious Court. Jackson's acceptance of President Truman's request in 1945 to become the United States Chief Prosecutor at the Nürnberg Nazi War Crimes Trials and his subsequent absence from the Court for an entire term compounded his difficulties with his colleagues—not to mention the business of the Court, which had to operate with eight Justices and the all-too-present danger of 4:4 tie votes. Jackson was brilliant at Nürnberg, yet he returned from the trials a different man: the once libertarian judicial activist [57] who had so often sided with Black, Douglas, Murphy, and Rutledge had become profoundly cautious, a markedly conservative interpreter of the Bill of Rights. He now more often than not sided with the Frankfurter wing of the Court, which took a generally restrictive stand in matters affecting national security and state criminal justice procedures.[58] This intriguing metamorphosis may well have resulted from his Nürnberg experiences and his first-hand perception of the melancholy events resulting in the destruction of the Weimar Republic and the rise of Nazism. It was his conclusive judgment that one of the major contributory factors was the failure of the Weimar Government to crack down on radical dissenters and groups.

Yet he remained an apostle of judicial restraint in the economic-proprietarian sphere, supporting governmental authority to regulate and thus remaining true to his basic New Deal commitments. And even if there were no other justification for holding Jackson in high esteem as a jurist, his magnificent prose—second in beauty and clarity perhaps only to that of Cardozo—has earned him a high regard. Who could ever forget the haunting beauty of his phrases, such as those in his memorable opinion striking down the West Virginia flag salute in 1943?: "Those who begin coercive elimination of dissent," he warned his countrymen, "soon find themselves exterminating dissenters. Compulsory unification of opinion achieves only the unanimity of the graveyard." And elaborating:

> If there is any fixed star in our constitutional constellation, it is that no official, high or petty, can prescribe what shall be orthodox in politics, nationalism, religion, or other matters of opinion or force citizens to confess by word or act their faith therein. . . . The very purpose of a Bill of Rights was to withdraw certain subjects from the vicissitudes of political controversy, to place them beyond the reach of majorities and officials and to establish them as legal principles to be applied by the Courts. One's right to life, liberty, and property, to free speech, a free press, freedom of worship and assembly, and other fundamental rights may not be submitted to vote; they depend on the outcome of no elections.[59]

On October 9, 1954, Jackson died—having participated that May in the Court's unanimously decided, momentous *Public School Desegregation Cases*.[60] In some ways he died a bitter and disappointed man—never having attained the coveted Court leadership—but he left a legacy as "America's Advocate." [61]

Roosevelt had now appointed eight Justices in less than four years. Barring unforeseeable illnesses or resignations, that certainly would be the end of the line. Yet in October 1942 came

Mr. Justice Byrnes's resignation from the Court and the ninth vacancy! This time there was no obvious successor, no obvious political debt to be paid. Such major New Deal supporters as Messrs. Black, Reed, Frankfurter, Douglas, Murphy, Jackson, and Byrnes had been sent to the Court; others, such as Francis Biddle, the able Attorney General, were not interested. At last F.D.R. might indulge his desire to nominate someone from west of the Mississippi. There was no rush as far as he was concerned, and he asked Biddle to look around carefully for a likely candidate. The ultimate nominee, pressed on the Administration by Biddle as well as by such allies as Senator Norris, Justices Murphy and Douglas, and particularly by the distinguished *Des Moines Register* and *Chicago Sun* journalist Irving Brant, was a rather "marginal" Westerner, but with more claims to that region than Douglas: Judge Wiley Rutledge of the United States Court of Appeals for the District of Columbia. Rutledge was the only Roosevelt appointee with federal judicial experience (four years) and one of only three with *any* judicial background—the other two being Black and Murphy. F.D.R. was not personally acquainted with Rutledge, but after chatting with him at the White House and being assured by Biddle that the candidate was a bona fide libertarian, an early and solid New Dealer who had ardently championed the Court-packing plan, and a judge whose opinions demonstrated a solid commitment to the Presidential philosophy, he nominated him in February 1943. Confirmation came readily without a formal roll call.

Born in Kentucky, brought up there and in North Carolina and Tennessee, schooled in Tennessee and Wisconsin, Rutledge had taught and worked in the public school systems of Colorado, Indiana, and New Mexico before becoming Professor of Law at the University of Colorado, Professor of Law and Dean at Washington University in St. Louis, and Dean at the University of Iowa's School of Law. In 1939 he was appointed to the federal bench. He had figured in Court speculation for the Cardozo seat, and particularly for the Brandeis seat. Once he attained the bench, Rutledge—who genuinely loved people of all walks of life—showed his libertarian colors. Indeed, his score in behalf of individual claims against alleged violations by government was higher than any of his colleagues (followed closely by Murphy's). Thus it was Rutledge who joined Murphy's generous extensions of civil liberty safeguards beyond the Constitution's verbiage when he concurred in the latter's famed dissenting opinion in *Adamson* v. *California* in 1947:

> I agree that the specific guarantees of the Bill of Rights should be carried over intact into the first section of the Fourteenth Amendment. But I am not prepared to say that the latter is entirely and necessarily limited by the Bill of Rights. *Occasions may arise where a proceeding falls so far short of conforming to fundamental standards of procedure as to warrant constitutional condemnation in terms of lack of due process despite the absence of specific provisions in the Bill of Rights.*[62]

During his scant six and a half years on the bench Rutledge's scholarship, his mastery of the law, his articulate explication of difficult issues, and his prodigious workmanship combined to establish him as a jurist who well earned the "near great" rating that the experts bestowed upon him. The years of Rutledge's tenure saw the Court at its libertarian apogee; after his death it would not return to a similar posture until the heyday of the Warren Court.

Rutledge left a proud record, highlighted by some celebrated dissenting opinions, such as those for In re *Yamashita,* and *Everson* v. *Board of Education of Ewing Township.* The former decision upheld 7:2 Japanese General Tomoyuki's summary military commision conviction for violating the rules of war. The latter sanctioned 5:4 state-subsidized transportation of parochial as well as public school students. Rutledge regarded these opinions as his best. Thus he admonished the Stone-led majority in *Yamashita* that it "is not in our tradition for anyone to be charged with crime which is defined after his conduct, alleged to be criminal, has taken place; or in language not sufficient to inform him of the nature of the offense or to enable him to make defense. Mass guilt we do not impute to individuals. . . ." [63] And, in *Everson,* before appending Madison's "Memorial and Remonstrance Against Religious Assessment," Rutledge warned the Black-led majority: "Like St. Paul's freedom, religious liberty with a great price must be bought. And for those who exercise it most fully, by insisting upon religious education for their children mixed with secular, by the terms of our Constitution the price is greater than for others." [64] When he succumbed to a cerebral hemmorhage at the age of fifty-seven while vacationing in Maine in September 1949, an era came to an end. Wiley Rutledge had been the last Roosevelt appointee: the three (Burton, Vinson, and Clark) whom President Truman would send to the Court between F.D.R.'s and Rutledge's death were of a different philosophical and jurisprudential stripe indeed; so would be Rutledge's replacement (Minton).

When asked how he had felt when Mrs. Roosevelt informed him that afternoon of April 12, 1945, in her White House study that he was now the President, Harry S Truman responded, "Did you ever have a load of hay fall on you?" [65] Defying all predictions, he went on to become an assertive, powerful, and successful leader—at least in foreign affairs. He played a significant part in forging post-World War II American foreign policy, notably with regard to the initial combat use of the atomic bomb, the Marshall Plan, "Point Four," the Greece-Turkey Truman Doctrine, the North Atlantic Treaty Organization, the Berlin Airlift, the Korean War. To the surprise of many observers, the President-watchers have accorded him a "near great" rating, just below Jackson, Theodore Roosevelt, and Polk and just above John Adams and Cleveland.

Given his miserable relations with Congress—and they were just that, whether it was controlled by his own or by the Republican party—and his generally low public image, that rating is rather on the generous side. Yet the plain, although hardly plainspoken, forthright man from Missouri gradually won the grudging admiration and even affection of many of his countrymen. By 1948 he had won enough support to capture the election—an astounding victory in the face of insurmountable odds and in defiance of all major pollsters—over the urbane and experienced Thomas E. Dewey. Truman's warmth, folksiness, and simplicity atoned for much of his public coarseness and the all-but-impossible task of following in the footsteps of Franklin D. Roosevelt. Yet he showed a keen awareness of his country's needs and a toughness about first constitutional principles—as evinced by his summary sacking of that ideal of the American Center and Right, General of the Army Douglas MacArthur, when the latter began to assume too much civilian and military authority. Harry Truman knew how to make the big decisions.

Unfortunately, he was also given to extravagant notions of loyalty that prompted him to make many a "crony" appointment— not excluding those he was enabled to make to the Supreme Court. There were four, and all were old buddies: Harold H. Burton, a fellow U.S. Senator (R.-Ohio) and member of the highly effective Truman War Investigating Committee; Fred M. Vinson, long-time legislative and executive ally; Tom C. Clark, the President's Attorney General and confidant; and Sherman Minton, another former Senatorial colleague (D.-Ind.) and friend. With the possible exception of Clark, whose seventeen years of service on the Court have often been underestimated, it was a mediocre group. The Court experts, in fact, have rated Burton, Vinson, and Minton among the eight "failures" to sit on the Court (Clark they rated as average). No serious Court observer or student has challenged that assessment in Minton's case, but a good many have challenged the ratings of Burton and Vinson. No one familiar with the record, however, has ever regarded either of the latter as being entitled to anything higher than "below average" or at best "average." Truman's appointments may have been undistinguished, but they assuredly did not represent a departure from his criteria for the post: they had all held public office; they were his political, professional, and personal friends; he knew them; he liked them; he liked their politics. Loyal to a fault, he wanted to reward them and he did. That he was given a public roasting in almost every instance bothered him not one whit. He had done what he deemed appropriate, and so, as he wondrously always managed to do where others fretted and worried, he slept the peace of the confident! Occasionally they failed to support him: in the famed *Steel Seizure Case* of 1952 [66] Truman lost Burton's and Clark's votes and thus the decision. His appointees however, generally sided with his views of government and Constitution, views that were strongly weighted in favor of governmental regulatory authority and internal security.

The first Truman appointment was fifty-seven-year-old Republican Senator from Ohio Harold Hitz Burton, who succeeded to the seat vacated in July 1945 by Mr. Justice Owen J. Roberts. Burton's selection, which was unanimously approved by his Senatorial colleagues, was undoubtedly strongly motivated by personal and political kinship, but it would be unjust to label it only that. True, Burton and Truman had often championed similar causes in the Senate, and Burton had served well and closely with Truman when the latter headed the highly successful Special Committee to Investigate the National Defense Program ("Truman War Operations Committee") in the early 1940s. But there were other reasons and motivations: the persuasive advice given to the President that in the interest of national unity he designate a Republican to replace Roberts, a G. O. P. member from neighboring Pennsylvania; Mr. Chief Justice Stone's advance approval of Burton because of his legislative experience (which Stone judged would prove helpful in cases of statutory construction); Burton's judicious and judicial temperament; the assumption that Democratic Governor Frank Lausche of Ohio would name a Democrat to Burton's Senate seat (he did); and the faithful support Senator Burton had given the Democratic party on foreign policy and even on some domestic programs, such as T.V.A. and agricultural subsidies, during his four years in the upper house.

Popular among his colleagues and a hard worker, although only occasionally eloquent of pen, Mr. Justice Burton's thirteen years on the Court were characterized by a combination of uncertainty, deliberate caution, independence, and unpredictability. He was most comfortable with the views and approaches to public law of his colleagues Vinson, Jackson, Frankfurter, Reed, Minton, and

Clark—rarely could he be found in the libertarian Black-Doug-las-Murphy-Rutledge wing. Nonetheless, there were times when he would cross over, especially when he believed the state or federal government to be taking impermissible shortcuts with constitutionally guaranteed basic liberties,[67] and he demonstrated a generally tough view on the question of separation of Church and State.[68] But he was essentially a devotee of the self-restraint, "when-in-doubt-don't" school of jurisprudence, and he was far happier in the role of follower than leader.

When Harlan Fiske Stone's distinguished career on the bench suddenly came to an end on April 22, 1946, President Truman was confronted with the awesome responsibility of naming a new Chief Justice of the United States. It was a particularly difficult task at the time because of the personality clashes that had recently developed—especially the increasingly unpleasant feud between Justices Black and Jackson, with the latter publicly accusing the former of blocking his ascendancy to the top spot on the Court, and because of a serious conflict of interest involving a former law partner. Although Black remained silent, he was obviously both hurt and angry about the unwarranted attack on his judgment, integrity, and honor.[69] Truman quickly perceived that he could not promote any of the Court's sitting members, although he was fully alive to Jackson's strong claims to the Chief Justiceship. Moreover, he had consulted with former Chief Justice Hughes and former Associate Justice Roberts, both of whom strongly urged the President to select someone not then on the Court in order to maximize a successful restoration of peace and harmony.[70] Harry Truman did not hesitate long: he turned to one of the nation's most versatile and most experienced public servants, his good friend and Secretary of the Treasury Fred Moore Vinson, then fifty-six years of age, whom both Hughes and Roberts had specifically suggested as an excellent candidate.[71] Vinson seemed ideal for the position—given his demonstrated administrative and legislative leadership—but he did not succeed on the Court and his tenure was an unhappy one.

In 1924, after three years as Commonwealth Attorney in Kentucky, Fred Vinson had come to Washington as a young Congressman and soon began yeoman service in behalf of the New Deal. As an expert member of the tax-writing House Committee on Ways and Means during much of his fourteen years in the House of Representatives, he had helped to forge some of the most significant parts of the Roosevelt program—including the T.V.A., the Agricultural Adjustment Act, the Coal Act, and the National Industrial Recovery Act—and he was one of the principal architects of the Social Security Act of 1935. In late 1937 he accepted F.D.R.'s reward of a judgeship on the U.S. Circuit Court of Appeals for the District of Columbia, where he served for five years. But in the spring of 1943 he resigned to become Director of the Office of Economic Stabilization. After two years in that hot spot he served briefly as Federal Loan Administrator and Director of the Office of War Mobilization and Reconversion before moving to the Treasury under Truman. Vinson had been of invaluable aid and a trusted adviser to the new President during his difficult first year in office; Truman not only shared Vinson's political philosophy but admired his popularity, his relaxed friendliness, his delightful sense of humor, and his ability to listen to all sides of a question and to effect compromise. To the President, Vinson was *the* person "capable of unifying the . . . Court and thereby improving its public image," [72] and he eagerly nominated his friend to be the thirteenth Chief Justice on June 7, 1946. Confirmation by the Senate was uncontested and came two weeks later.

Fred M. Vinson served as Chief Justice for little more than seven years, just two years longer than the brief Chief Justiceship of Harlan Stone. His tenure was not a fortunate one, either in his role as presiding officer or as jurist. It is unfair and inaccurate, however, to categorize him as a "failure" on the bench—as the Court's historians have done. True, he did not succeed in eradicating the in-fighting on his Court; but he at least managed to confine it to the tribunal's inner sanctum, with even the Jackson-Black feud disappearing from the public stage. True, he was an indifferent, even poor, opinion-writer; but on his side he usually had such master craftsmen of style and intellect as Frankfurter and Jackson.

True, the percentage of the work output of his Court was exceptionally low; but it did wrestle with trouble areas such as inherent Presidential power (the *Steel Seizure Case* of 1952); [73] national security (*The Dennis Top Eleven Communists Case* of 1951); [74] segregation in schools (*The Texas and Oklahoma Segregation Cases* of 1950); [75] and segregation in housing (*The Restrictive Covenant Cases* of 1948). [76] The Chief Justice wrote the controlling opinions in all except the *Steel Seizure Case,* where he authored the dissenting opinion (pro-seizure) for himself, Reed, and Minton. Yet over-all, Vinson demonstrated an astonishing lack of leadership: the role of Chief Justice was simply beyond his ken. The Court's jurisprudential split was, if anything, exacerbated during his tenure—with more 5:4 opinions than in any other comparable period. Vinson died in September 1953, a disappointed and dissatisfied occupant of the center chair.

Mr. Justice Murphy's sudden death in July 1949 created the third Court vacancy during the Truman Administration. To no one's surprise the President once more turned to a trusted friend and political ally, this time his Attorney General for the past four years, Tom C. Clark of Texas—the first Lone Star State denizen to sit on the Court. Then only forty-nine, Clark was known as a favorite protégé of the powerful Democratic Senator from Texas, Tom Connally. He had spent fifteen years as a prosecuting attorney on both the state and federal levels of government, including five years in a Dallas County District Attorney's office; two years as head of the federal Justice Department's Anti-Trust Division; several months in a ticklish assignment in 1942 of overseeing the removal of Japanese-Americans from the Pacific Coast to inland relocation centers; and two years as Assistant Attorney General in charge of the Criminal Division, before succeeding Francis Biddle as Attorney General. Clark, an assertive, resourceful, and courageous Attorney General, became one of Truman's closest advisers on key domestic issues. Their association had its genesis in Clark's cooperation with the "Truman Committee," which found a powerful working ally in him. Moreover, in 1944 Clark and Truman, who was at that time a Senator, collaborated in an abortive attempt to substitute Speaker Sam Rayburn for Henry Wallace as F.D.R.'s running mate. (Ultimately the Vice-Presidential candidate was Harry Truman himself.) Clark continued as a Truman loyalist throughout the mid- and late 1940s and was an important campaigner for Truman in 1948. His selection represented recognition and reward for proved loyalty to President and party.

But it was far from a popular one, and the fifty-year-old Clark's confirmation by a vote of 73:8 does not indicate some of the sustained opposition to his selection from the press, members of the legal profession, Congressmen, and other influential public figures. The opposition was based in part upon what was considered blatant cronydom and cashing-in of political I.O.U.s; in part upon what was viewed as an anti-libertarian posture, especially in procedural safeguards in criminal justice and toward minority groups; in part because of what some regarded as a marginal and authoritarian performance in the Justice Department. The outspoken Harold L. Ickes, for one, made no secret of his outrage: in a *New Republic* article entitled "Tom Clark Should Say 'No Thanks,' " he contended that the President had shifted Clark to the Court to get rid of the weakest member of his Cabinet; that Truman was under no obligation whatsoever to this "second-rate political hack who has known what backs to slap and when"; concluding that "perhaps it was in keeping that the least able of Attorneys General of the United States should, as a result of raw political favoritism, become the least able of the members of the Supreme Court." [77] Clark's initial performance on the Court appeared to bear out, if not Ickes's worst fears, a good many of the doubts of his detractors. He seemed ill at ease on the high bench; he was more concerned with "going along" than with independence or innovation; he seemed to be overly concerned with Truman's expectations of his role; and he betrayed a tough stance on the rights of defendants in internal security cases. Yet before long this much-maligned appointee began to demonstrate a cautious, innovative streak in the authorship of major opinions in the separation of powers and civil libertarian sectors, evincing a sophisticated command of constitutional construction.

Thus Clark's concurring opinion in the *Steel Seizure Case* of
1952,[78] in which he voted to deny Truman's seizure of the struck
steel mills, came closer than any of the other six opinions to the
heart of the matter: he objected to executive usurpation of legislative authority in the presence of ascertainable Congressional intent.* His declarations of unconstitutionality for unanimous Courts,
also in 1952, of the Oklahoma loyalty oath for teachers and state
officials,[79] and New York's censorship of the film "The Miracle," [80]
demonstrated a genuine attachment to the principles of the First
Amendment; and a host of Clark-authored landmark decisions in
the 1960s, such as the application of the exclusionary rule to state
criminal procedure in the famed case of *Mapp* v. *Ohio*,[81] proved
that a security-conscious "law and order" devotee, too, knew how
to uphold fundamental rights even in the contentious realm of accused criminals. His eighteen years on the Court cast him into a
role of a determined, if cautious, craftsman of the law who frequently became a "swing man" between the liberal and conservative blocs on the bench. While he remained essentially true to his
assertive strong government position, he was fully aware of the
basic lines and limits inherent in constitutionalism and the nature
of the judicial function. With the passing of the years many of his
critics had second thoughts about Tom Clark and gladly acknowledged that here was not only the ablest of the four Truman appointees but a jurist of far above average capability and performance. The country deeply regretted his self-imposed resignation at
the close of the 1966–67 term when his son Ramsey Clark became
Attorney General of the United States.

If Mr. Justice Clark's record on the Court is proof of man's inherent ability to grow remarkably in a position of high responsibility and authority, President Truman's fourth and last appointee
pointed to the converse. Sherman Minton was never an intellectual
giant, and despite the genuine affection of his colleagues he was
essentially uncomfortable among high-powered judicial individual-

---

* For which Truman called him "that damn fool from Texas" and "my big-
gest mistake" (quoted in *The Washington Post,* Nov. 22, 1973, p. 1).

ists. His seven-year stint on the Court has been universally and justly regarded as a failure. He had had eight years of experience on the United States Court of Appeals for the Seventh Circuit, but that body was devoid of such judicial powers as Black, Frankfurter, Douglas, Jackson, and Warren. Minton, who succeeded to the seat vacated by Mr. Justice Rutledge's untimely death in the early fall of 1949, was essentially happiest as a practitioner of practical politics. It was in that role that he had first met Harry Truman in a historical accident of seating in the United States Senate following the Democratic landslide victory in the Congressional elections of 1934: a new row of seats had to be installed for the Democrats in the rear of the chamber, and freshmen Senators Minton of Indiana and Truman of Missouri found themselves seated next to one another. They soon became fast friends. Minton quickly rose to the post of Democratic Whip but lost his bid for re-election six years later when Wendell Willkie swept Minton's home state of Indiana into the G.O.P. column. F.D.R. thereupon appointed Minton, who had been a loyal New Dealer, to a White House post as Administrative Assistant, a role Minton enjoyed enormously. But he readily moved into the Court of Appeals opening that Roosevelt offered him just a few months later. It was while he was serving there that, eight years later, he received a now well-known telephone call from President Truman: "Shay," the President said, "I'm naming you to the Supreme Court. What do you think of that?" Minton's reply was quick: "I think it's fine." [82] Loyal political and personal dedication was once again rewarded.

Some of Minton's ex-colleagues in the Senate did not think it was so "fine," however, and Republican Senators Homer Ferguson of Michigan and Forrest C. Donnell of Missouri requested that Judge Minton appear before the Senate Judiciary Committee to respond to questions. He declined the "invitation," noting that he would stand on his record as a Judge and Senator. The Senate subsequently proceeded to vote on his confirmation, approving him 48:16. The ardent New Dealer continued to support strong governmental action during his few years on the Court, and Truman had no cause to regret his appointment on that score. But he left the President and many old colleagues of his New Deal Senate days on the civil libertarian front, where he immediately joined the so-called "conservative" wing of the Court, then consisting of Mr. Chief Justice Vinson and Associate Justices Reed, Burton, and, for a time, Clark. The likeable, witty, and popular Minton did his share of work on the bench but wrote no opinions of lasting significance. It is characteristic of the essentially humble Minton that he regarded his most important vote on the bench to be a silent one: the one he cast with the unanimous Justices in May 1954 joining Mr. Chief Justice Earl Warren's historic opinion which, free from any either dissenting or concurring opinions, declared compulsory segregation of public schools unconstitutional.[83]

9

The Almost Immediate Past:
From Ike Through L.B.J.
1953—1969

General of the Army Dwight David Eisenhower was elected to the White House as a Republican, but he could just as easily have been elected on the Democratic ticket. After two decades of Democratic rule, "Had enough?" was the key slogan of Eisenhower's campaign in 1952. He was elected by a wide margin and following one popular term in office, he was re-elected by an even wider margin—although the Democrats recaptured both houses of Congress. "Ike," the Nation's foremost war hero, the victorious Commander of the Allied Expeditionary Forces in Europe, could do almost no wrong in the public's eyes. Enormously likeable and even modest despite his towering successes, he was accorded a father-like image, which enabled him, for example, to settle the Korean War on terms for which the Democrats undoubtedly would have been roasted. To his eternal credit, he cast off any accouterments of militarism, and when in doubt about engaging the military, as in Indo-China, he opted for non-involvement. On the one occasion on which he was persuaded to resort to military force in order to uphold the Constitution, the Little Rock desegregation crisis in the fall of 1958, he sent troops with the utmost reluctance. That action, according to his principal adviser-assistant, Sherman Adams, represented "a Constitutional duty which was the most repugnant to him of all his acts in his eight years in the White House." [1]

It is conceivable that Eisenhower's reluctance to be tagged "military" or "strong" caused him to step into the background, to provide little leadership. In effect, he wanted Congress to do the leading. Ike's attitude was one of pointed deference to the legislative process, often totally out of proportion to need. Moreover, this capable, even superb war-time leader frequently failed to lead at all, even when he could have done so readily and with much support. When Senator Joseph R. McCarthy sent out divisive and dangerous attacks on not only individuals but on the very fiber of constitutional government, Ike failed to engage in much-needed public battle, thus disdaining to "get into the gutter with that man." And when the President had the opportunity to lend the prestige of his person and office to the 1954–55 Supreme Court decisions concerning desegregation of the public schools, he demurred. It was not until the last two years of his Presidency, after the dismissal of Sherman Adams and the death of John Foster Dulles, that Dwight Eisenhower would abandon his policy of "reign" in order to "rule"—within carefully defined limits, of course.

There is little doubt that because of unfulfilled expectations, wasted potential, a "when-in-doubt, don't" approach to government and politics, the presidential historians have ranked Eisenhower a very low "average," barely above "below average." When he was informed that he had been rated twenty-second and Truman ninth, the walls of his study in his Gettysburg farm reverberated with some old-fashioned purple outbursts. Ike's rating is, of course, much too low in terms of the over-all services he performed for his country, but the experts simply concluded that he merited no more for his Presidency, given his failure to provide leadership.

Yet Eisenhower deserves a hearty "well done," for all save one of the five Supreme Court appointments he was enabled to make between 1953 and 1958. For he sent to the Court a great Chief Justice (Earl Warren); a truly distinguished "jurists' jurist" (John Marshall Harlan); a sensitive humanist (William J. Brennan, Jr.);

and an able, independent legal craftsman (Potter Stewart). His one failure was the selection of Charles E. Whittaker, whom history has placed near the bottom in terms of Court performance, and who has the rare distinction of being the only modern Supreme Court Justice publicly to criticize not only the Court's sitting members but the institution itself. He stepped down from the bench after only five years. Ike's self-recorded set of criteria for nomination comprised, first, character and ability that could command the "respect, pride, and confidence of the populace"; [2] second, a basic philosophy of moderate progressivism, common sense, high ideals, the "absence of extreme views"; [3] third (after the Warren appointment, which would become Ike's most acute disappointment) prior judicial service, in the belief that such service would "provide an inkling of his philosophy"; [4] fourth, geographic balance; fifth, religious balance; sixth, an upper age limit of sixty-two, unless, as he put it, "other qualifications were unusually impressive"; [5] and finally, a thorough F.B.I. check of the candidate and the approval of the American Bar Association. [6]

On September 8, 1953, only eight months after Eisenhower had assumed office, Mr. Chief Justice Vinson died. It was Ike's first opportunity to act on a vacancy and the appointment he made would revolutionize American constitutional law (which is not precisely what he had in mind). As he chronicled it himself in his autobiography, initially he gave "serious thought" to appointing John Foster Dulles; but his Secretary of State declined, stating that as long as the President was happy with his performance in that post, he had no interest in any other. [7] Although Ike never expressly said so, it is now clear that there were other front-runners. Thomas E. Dewey of New York probably could have had the post, but he took himself out of the running; the evidence is inconclusive whether it was actually offered to him. The distinguished Chief Justice of New Jersey, Arthur T. Vanderbilt, a Republican in the Eisenhower-Dewey mold, and probably the nation's foremost judicial administrator, was also a frequently mentioned candidate. Indeed, there is some evidence that he thought he had the President's verbal promise of an appointment.

His health was not good, however, and, in any event, Ike agreed with Attorney General Herbert Brownell that the political verities clearly mandated a preference for Governor Earl Warren of California, another strong contender. Perhaps there would be more than one vacancy to fill; Vanderbilt would be given every consideration. In the President's own words:

> A few months prior to the death of Chief Justice Vinson, I had talked to Gov. Earl Warren of California about his basic philosophy and been quite pleased that his views seemed to reflect high ideals and a great deal of common sense. During this conversation I told the Governor that I was considering the possibility of appointing him to the Supreme Court and I was definitely inclined to do so if, in the future, a vacancy should occur. However, neither he nor I was thinking of the special post of Chief Justice nor was I definitely committed to any appointment.[8]

Now, on Vinson's death, Ike's attention centered increasingly on Warren. But recognizing that his own contacts with the Californian had been sketchy, he asked Brownell to fly out to the Coast to find out more about the Governor's "record of attainments as a lawyer, as district attorney and as Attorney General of California." Ike wanted "the conclusions of a qualified lawyer on the matter." [9] Herbert Brownell was indeed that; he was also a shrewd political practitioner who had been Dewey's campaign manager on numerous occasions and had served as Chairman of the Republican National Committee. Thus Brownell was well aware of a political debt to be paid. For it had been Warren—whether or not he realized that his own candidacy for the Presidency in 1952 was probably doomed—who was primarily responsible for swinging all but eight of California's seventy-member delegation at the Nominating Convention to Eisenhower rather than to Senator Robert A. Taft at a particularly crucial stage in the jockeying involving certain contested Southern delegations.

Ike and his advisers were also agreed that Warren's experience, leadership qualities, and administrative expertise constituted precisely the kind of medicine the badly faction-rent Vinson Court needed. Moreover, Ike was pleased to note that Warren had fought the 1937 Court-packing bill; favored state jurisdiction over offshore oil lands; and had backed the Court's anti-steel seizure decision in 1952. There may have been one other factor involved: Warren, the unprecedented three-term Governor of California, although a loyal Republican, had long been a thorn in the side of the partisan California Republican leadership (which included Vice-President Richard M. Nixon and Senate Majority Leader William F. Knowland) because of his confirmed progressivism, his independence, and his link to the Democrats, many of whom had consistently supported him. Ambitious and influential political figures (such as Nixon and Knowland) would be delighted to see Warren removed from California politics, for they realized that his position at the home polls was well-nigh impregnable. Initially Ike had offered Warren a Cabinet post, but he declined, indicating that he would, however, be honored to be considered for "that other post" the President had discussed with him some time earlier. If there was no other way of removing Warren from the California scene, well, the state's Republican orthodoxy was willing even to pay the price of his elevation to the Chief Justiceship of the United States.

Earl Warren was eminently qualified on all counts to serve as Chief Justice of the Supreme Court. Born in 1891 of Norwegian immigrant parents, he had capped his undergraduate days at the University of California at Berkeley with a bachelor of law and a doctor of jurisprudence degree. After practicing law for a brief time, he joined the infantry during World War I, ultimately attaining the rank of captain. On his return from the army he clerked for the California legislature, became Deputy City Attorney of Sacramento for a year; Deputy District Attorney of Alameda County for five years; and then, for fourteen years its District Attorney. His superb record in a difficult post enabled him to cross-file on the Republican, Democratic, and Progressive party tickets for Attorney General of California in 1938, and portending the future, he won all three! Warren logically progressed to the Governorship, first being elected in 1942, then re-elected in 1946 and

1950, inevitably with bipartisan and multi-partisan support. He was Dewey's running mate in the Presidential elections of 1948, and had it not been for Eisenhower's overwhelming national popularity, Earl Warren might have moved into the White House in 1952.

Instead he found himself nominated for the Chief Justiceship on September 30, 1953, amid wide-spread acclaim and approval. Since Congress was not in session, Eisenhower gave Warren a recess appointment, fully anticipating more or less automatic confirmation on Congress's return in January 1954. Yet he had not reckoned with the die-hard, perverse opposition of Republican Senator William Langer of North Dakota, a senior member of the Senate's Judiciary Committee, who had then begun his prolonged six-year campaign of opposing any and all nominees to the Court until someone from his home state (which had never been so-honored) would receive an appointment. (He went to his grave in 1959, his hopes still unrealized—as they are to this day.) For two months Langer and a few conservative Southern Democrats, who joined in an attack on what they called Warren's "left wing," "ultra-liberal" views, prevented a vote on the confirmation. It came on March 1, unanimously.

Had the Senate been able to predict the ultimate course of the "Warren Court"—indeed, by his own assertions, had the President been able to look into the future—the confirmation might have been denied then and there. But Warren's record as a prosecutor showed some tough law-and-order crusading; what is more, he was the man who had so strongly and successfully urged evacuation of Japanese-Americans from their homes and land in 1942. Those were hardly the marks of a "muddleheaded liberal"! But though the bombshell of *Brown* v. *Board of Education of Topeka* [10] lay just two months in the future, the new Chief Justice moved cautiously at first, demonstrating the kind of gradualism and deliberateness that had characterized his approach to every new position he had held. Thus, notwithstanding *Brown* and his decisive leadership therein, the new Chief did not immediately manifest the libertarian activism that would eventually result in all-out assaults on the Court, accompanied by the distribution of "Impeach Earl Warren" bumper stickers and Warren Impeachment Kits.

As of mid-1956 it became clear that Earl Warren was in the process of providing leadership for a libertarian approach to public law and personal rights that went far beyond the Eisenhower brand of progressive Republicanism. To Eisenhower the new Warren represented all but a betrayal of older beliefs and understandings, and his recognition of the man's judicial independence, which he regarded as judicial "legislating," was bitter and frustrating. But the Chief Justice, usually with Justices Black and Douglas (and later Brennan) by his side, wrought a constitutional revolution in the application of the Bill of Rights to the states; in the generous interpretation of specific provisions of safeguards for the individual; in the application and interpretation of the Civil War amendments; in rendering any executive or legislative classification by race and by sex "suspect"; in the liberalization of the right to vote, the right to run for office, and the right to fair representation; and in many other sectors of the freedom of the individual. Of course, Earl Warren did not do this alone; the seeds were already there. But it was he who provided the leadership on the Court; he whose assertive views of the judicial role and vision of constitutional fulfillment made the judicial revolution possible; he whose knowledge of men and administrative savoir faire succeeded in "massing" the Court for the "big decisions" with results second only to those achieved in different constitutional areas by John Marshall; he whose dedication to the ideals of equal justice under law gave hope to the downtrodden; he who insisted that for democratic society to succeed its people must have ready access to their government.

Earl Warren was not a great lawyer in the mold of a Taney or a Hughes; not a great legal scholar in the tradition of a Brandeis or a Frankfurter; not a supreme stylist like Cardozo or Jackson; not a judicial philosopher like Holmes or Black. But he was the Chief Justice par excellence—second in greatness only to John Marshall himself in the eyes of most impartial students of the Court as well as the Court's critics. Like Marshall he understood and utilized the tools of leadership available to him and he knew how to bring men together, how to set a tone and fashion a mood. He was a wise man and a warm, kind human being. He was the Court.

It is a pity that some of the momentous opinions Earl Warren wrote were not delivered with more clarity and explicitness, with more close legal reasoning, more historical proof—a pity because the public he loved and whom he served so conscientiously would have been better able to understand him. Yet his leadership left more milestones in constitutional adjudication and interpretation than any other Chief Justiceship save Marshall's. Among the many decisions Warren himself wrote, five were outstanding: (1) *Brown* v. *Board of Education of Topeka* (1954) was probably his supreme achievement. His unanimous Court declared compulsory segregation by race in the public schools to be an unconstitutional violation of the equal protection of the laws.[11] Of this decision John P. Frank, a close Court observer and once clerk to Mr. Justice Black, wrote: "Of his individual contributions, history will have enough to say; but it will never need to say more than that he wrote the school-segregation opinion." [12] (2) *Watkins* v. *United States* (1957), in which the Court held 6:1 that "the vice of vagueness" so prevalent in the conduct of congressional investigating committees (particularly the House Committee on Un-American Activities) was a derogation of the due process of law clause of the Fifth Amendment.[13] The Chief Justice's rambling opinion was virtually a lecture to Congress on constitutional law. (3) *Reynolds* v. *Sims* (1964), where the Court ruled 6:3 that both houses of a state legislature must be apportioned on a "one-man, one-vote" basis, with the Chief Justice holding that "legislators represent people, not trees or acres. Legislators are elected by voters, not farms or cities or economic interest." [14] Warren regarded his Court's work in redistricting and reapportionment of even greater importance than that of desegregation. (4) *Miranda* v. *Arizona* (1966), in which the Court held 5:4 that the confession of a person in custody cannot be used against him unless he has been provided with a series of six specific and protective rules against self-incrimination.[15] The highly prescriptive nature of this opinion brought down the wrath of many an objective legal scholar as well as that of law-enforcement officers and laymen. And (5) *Powell* v. *McCormack* (1969), Mr. Chief Justice Warren's valedictory opinion before turning over the center seat to Judge Warren Earl Burger, whom the out-going Chief reversed in this case, ruling for his 8:1 Court that the U.S. House of Representatives had improperly excluded the errant Adam Clayton Powell as a member in 1967 since—whatever else he might have done—he did meet the requirements of the Constitution as to age, citizenship, and residence.[16] It was characteristic and fitting that Warren's last opinion before his retirement was another lecture on constitutional law to Congress; that it was for an almost unanimous Court; and that it dealt with an issue most earlier Courts would have declined to hear on the ground that the issue constituted a "political question," into which "thicket" judicial bodies should not venture.

Other key decisions rendered by the Court under Earl Warren's sixteen years at its helm were, for example, such far-reaching and contentious rulings as that of *Engel* v. *Vitale*, written by Hugo L. Black for a 6:1 Court in 1962, ruling unconstitutional on grounds of separation of Church and State the daily recitation of state-prescribed prayers in public schools; [17] and that of *New York Times Co.* v. *Sullivan*, written by William J. Brennan for a unanimous Court, vastly extending freedom of the press by holding that a public official could not collect on a defamatory falsehood relating to his official conduct unless he or she could prove that it was made with "actual malice." [18] With Warren's departure an era had truly ended. But he left, in the words of the poet Archibald MacLeish, having "restored the future," having "enabled us to raise our heads and to begin." [19]

On October 9, 1954, Mr. Justice Robert H. Jackson, who had served brilliantly and controversially for thirteen years, suffered a fatal heart attack while en route to the Court. He had been initially stricken in March but had left the hospital on May 17,

1954, in order to join his colleagues in the announcement of the unanimously decided *Brown* v. *Board of Education of Topeka.*[20] President Eisenhower moved at once to fill the vacancy. His close advisers Dewey and Brownell could have had the nomination, but as before neither was interested; thus he turned to a "Dewey-Brownell man," a distinguished New York attorney and judge, John Marshall Harlan. Named for his grandfather, who had himself been named for John Marshall, the second Harlan ideally fitted the Eisenhower criteria for Supreme Court service: He was a life-long, solid Republican, but he had always kept a low political profile and was widely regarded as nonpartisan, he was well-known, well-established, and of unquestioned integrity; he was of proved legal acumen. Eisenhower had appointed Harlan to the U.S. Circuit Court of Appeals earlier that year; at fifty-five he was of the right age; and although a native of Chicago, he had long lived in New York, Jackson's state. Moreover, the reserved but engaging legal scholar, who had practiced law versatilely for twenty-five years with one of New York City's most prestigious firms, was widely regarded as a progressive conservative in the Eisenhower mold. Ike thus happily nominated him to the Court early that November, fully expecting swift confirmation, especially since he had received the enthusiastic support of the American Bar Association's Committee on Judiciary.

Yet the nomination ran into trouble. It had first gone to the Senate as a recess-appointment early in November, but in a special session of Congress later that month the Senate refused to take action. When the legislators returned for the regular session in January 1955, not only Senator Langer, who continued his now-predictable opposition of all non-North Dakotan nominees to the Court, but a bevy of largely Southern Democrats attacked the Harlan nomination, contending that he was "ultra-liberal," hostile to the South, dedicated to reforming the Constitution by "judicial fiat." Nothing, of course, could have been further from fact, especially in the light of Harlan's subsequent record of judicial restraint and cautious judicial craftsmanship, which must later have given some of his critics considerable pause. His detractors, however, managed to prevent confirmation until March 16, when it came 71:11.

If Warren fell far short of reaching Ike's expectations, Harlan's record on the Court more than amply fulfilled them. Harlan probably gave his nominator some anxious moments during his first two years, when he more often than not joined the Court's libertarian wing in national security cases—even writing the Court's opinion in *Yates* v. *United States*,[21] which backed the right to advocate the theoretical overthrow of the government by force and violence as opposed to advocating direct action. But as of 1957 Harlan left that wing to find his niche with Frankfurter, Clark, and the other incoming Eisenhower appointees in a generally conservative judicial approach. Indeed, it was Frankfurter who became Harlan's mentor and idol on the bench, and it was Harlan who assumed the role of Court leader and spokesman of judicial restraint after Frankfurter's retirement in 1962. In stark contrast to the judicial posture of his grandfather, the second Harlan thus spent the balance of his total of sixteen years on the bench in arguing for a limited judicial role in political and social issues and for the strict separation of state and federal responsibilities. Like the first Harlan often finding himself in the role of dissenter (he cast an average of more than sixty dissents annually between 1963 and 1967), his lucid, precedent-invoking opinions, which explained and exhorted his philosophy of the judicial role in the governmental process, earned him wide recognition as an intellectual leader of the Court.

John Marshall Harlan's grandfather had earned his recognition as a great Justice largely because of his tenacious libertarian activism on an ultra-conservative Court. The grandson was accorded the well-earned rank of "near great" for consistently, and often persuasively, resisting the use of the judicial function as the innovator and prescriber of social and political reform. He never tired of exhorting his colleagues as well as his fellow citizens that the only viable role for the Court is a limited one; that it should stay out of the "political thicket" at all costs; that it should eschew the dismantling of federalism; that, as he put it so memorably in dissenting from the contentious *Reynolds* v. *Sims* (1964) 6:3 Warren opinion extending the "one man, one vote" rule to both houses of state legislatures:

> *The Constitution is not a panacea for every blot upon the public welfare; nor should this Court, ordained as a judicial body, be thought of as a general haven for reform movements.* This Constitution is an instrument of government, fundamental to which is the premise that in a diffusion of governmental authority lies the greatest promise that this Nation will realize for all its citizens. This Court, limited in function in accordance with that premise, does not serve its high purpose when it exceeds its authority, even to satisfy justified impatience with the slow workings of the political process.[22]

Yet while Harlan's philosophy of judicial restraint caused him often to disagree with the majority of the activist Warren Court, notably on issues such as reapportionment-redistricting, criminal justice, and the range of Congressional authority over state elections, he would not stand for governmental short cuts in the name of law and order. Thus practices such as wiretapping and eavesdropping, illegal invasions of human privacy, incursions on freedom of expression, and racial segregation met his determined opposition. How intensely proud he was of his grandfather's lone dissenting opinion in *Plessy* v. *Ferguson* (1896)![23] On his death in 1971 one of his former law clerks, Paul M. Bator of the Harvard School of Law, exhorted Harlan's abiding faithfulness to law "in the largest sense—the sense that makes democracy possible." He was, recalled Professor Bator: "one of those rare public men" for whom the democratic faith meant "fidelity to the whole law, every day and not every other day, fidelity not only to those rules which define other people's power but also those which limited his own."[24]

In October 1956 Mr. Justice Sherman Minton resigned after only seven years on the Court. Ike moved quickly to fill the third vacancy—it was close to the presidential elections, and an able nominee would hardly hurt his chances for re-election. The President publicly insisted that his candidate would have to have at

least three specific qualifications: relative youth; judicial experience; and excellent standing with his state bar as well as the
American Bar Association. The candidate advanced by the influential Chief Justice of New Jersey, Arthur T. Vanderbilt (long a
potential nominee himself but now no longer in good health) appeared to possess these qualifications and more. He was Vanderbilt's long-time protégé and friend and colleague on the New Jersey Supreme Court, William J. Brennan, Jr.—then but fifty years
of age. Mr. Justice Vanderbilt had pushed Brennan's candidacy
for some time, but he was not alone in voicing support for the
able and vigorous New Jersey jurist, who had won admiration for
his clear, thoughtful, and moderately liberal opinions on the
bench. While Vanderbilt's statement to Ike that Brennan "possessed the finest 'judicial mind' that he had known" [25] may well
have been overly enthusiastic, there was no doubt of Brennan's
outstanding qualifications. The American and New Jersey Bar as-
sociations, the American Judicature Society, and numerous prominent individuals and private groups, including the Holy Name Society and other Roman Catholic organizations, rallied around him.
The President easily concurred in the encomiums and in the
political wisdom of designating, especially in an election year, a
Democrat who also happened to be a Roman Catholic. It might
well avoid a "return home" by the Eisenhower Democrats of
1952, buttressing the non-political or bipartisan atmosphere in
which Ike felt most comfortable. Moreover, there had been no
one of Brennan's religious faith on the bench since Mr. Justice
Murphy's death in 1949; why not "restore" the time-honored
Roman Catholic seat on the Court? The metropolitan East would
be pleased, indeed! In fine, here was a still youthful, highly qualified, experienced jurist with broad political appeal and nationwide
backing. Ike gave Justice-designate Brennan a recess appointment
that October, which he formalized on Congress's return in January
1957. Brennan's confirmation, like Harlan's, was delayed. Predictably, there was the Langer opposition, but there was also that of
Senator Joseph R. McCarthy—of whom the nominee had been
openly critical in the past. McCarthy, however, now long beyond

his days of heady power and influence, was able to do no more than to cast the lone "no" when the informal voice vote came in March.

Professor Frankfurter had always admonished his students not to be unduly swayed by professorial advocacy, that their guiding motto should be "think for yourself." Years later, when he served with one of those students—William Brennan—Frankfurter asked whimsically whether it was really necessary for Brennan to have taken his former teacher's admonition so literally? Indeed, Mr. Justice Brennan struck out on his own, with a creativity and diligence that won him a "near great" rating by the Court's observers. But the President who sent him to the Court was only slightly less irked by and disenchanted with Brennan's evolving record than with Earl Warren's (whose opinions Brennan joined in most instances). When Eisenhower was asked later if he had made any mistakes while he had been President, he replied: "Yes, two, and they are both sitting on the Supreme Court."

By inclination less of a judicial activist than Warren at the outset, and given to more careful expression, Brennan became a member of the Court's libertarian wing. His abiding dedication to the freedoms of the First Amendment, notably those of speech and press, soon saw him assigned some of the leading libertarian opinions of the Warren Court era. Thus he authored the tribunal's significant and unanimous judgment in the *New York Times Libel Case of 1964*,[26] which established that a public official, in order to recover damages for a publication criticizing his official conduct, would have to show "actual malice" on the part of its publisher. Extolling the "uninhibited, robust, and wide-open" nature of debate on public issues, Brennan held that "libel can claim no talismanic immunity from constitutional limitations," that it must be "measured by standards that satisfy the First Amendment."

Mr. Justice Brennan, now in his eighteenth year on the Court, has continued to champion a generous interpretation of the Bill of Rights and the later civil-rights amendments, notably the Fourteenth and Fifteenth amendments. He has also become the Court's leading expert on that vexatious line between freedom of artistic

expression and proscribable obscenity [27] (though he found himself in
the minority of four who dissented from the contentious 1973 decisions that accorded generous leeway to the states in judging obscenity).[28] Perhaps, however, he will be best remembered for his
precedent-shattering opinion for a 6:2 Court in *Baker* v. *Carr* in
1962.[29] There, over lengthy, bitter dissenting opinions by Frankfurter and Harlan, Brennan, joined by Warren, Black, Douglas,
Clark, and Stewart, held that aggrieved individuals had a constitutionally guaranteed right to come to the judicial branch in order to
scrutinize alleged unjust apportionment by the states. The decision, which set into motion a revolution in legislative districting
and apportionment, was a fitting tribute to the judicial resourceful-
ness and perseverance of its self-effacing author—who time and
again warned that "the interest of the government is not that it
shall win a case, but that Justice shall be done!" [30]

In February 1957 Mr. Justice Stanley F. Reed retired after
more than nineteen years on the Court. Ike's fourth appointment
went to a "rags-to-riches" figure who, on the basis of background
and experience, gave every promise of becoming an outstanding
Justice. But he did not: Charles Evans Whittaker was a major disappointment on the bench, deservedly rated as a "failure" by the
Court experts. He found the pressures of the high tribunal's
docket overwhelming; he was uncomfortable with the jurisprudence and personality of some of his colleagues (Douglas in particular); and in the face of his general distaste for and anguish in
his new role, his health began to deteriorate. In April 1962 he retired, five years after he had become a member of the Court.

That the President had selected him, however, was entirely
comprehensible, for he met all of Eisenhower's criteria: like Kentucky's Reed he came from a mid-central state (Missouri); his age
(fifty-six) was appropriate; he had made a record as one of the
outstanding corporate trial lawyers of the region; he was a conservative Republican, yet he had made a genuine effort to appear
non-partisan in his private and public legal career; he had the enthusiastic backing of bench and bar as well as of the GOP's political leadership; and he had previous judicial experience on lower

federal benches. Moreover, both Ike and Attorney General Brownell were impressed with the success story of the President's fellow Kansan who, while going to law school in the evenings, had worked as an office boy in one of Kansas City's most prestigious corporate law firms, a firm in which he ultimately had become a senior partner. He had first come to the Administration's attention in 1954 when a vacancy occurred on the United States District Court for Kansas. Ike's brother Arthur, a Kansas City banker, was a close friend of Whittaker's; and Roy Roberts, influential Republican publisher of the *Kansas City Star,* and Kansas's two Republican Senators, Harry Darby and Frank Carlson, had all pushed hard for Whittaker, who was given the Judgeship forthwith. Two years later he was promoted to the U.S. Court of Appeals for the Eighth Circuit, whence, after less than a year, and on Arthur Eisenhower's [31] and Brownell's strong recommendations, he was promoted to the Supreme Court. He was readily confirmed without a formal roll call in March 1957.

Whittaker's posture on the Court was conservative and fully in line with the President's expectations. But he never found satisfaction, let alone enjoyment, in his brief tenure and he wrote no opinions of genuine consequence. In fact, he managed to average little more than one a year. Three years after his "disabled" retirement in 1962 he requested to be relieved from that status and resigned in order to return to the world of private enterprise with General Motors. Only then were his health, spirit, and joie de vivre restored.

Ike's fifth and last Court appointment was cut from an entirely different cloth in terms of his posture vis-à-vis the judicial function. Potter Stewart, however, had not only been brought up in comfortable circumstances but his father, James Garfield Stewart, had served as Mayor of Cincinnati and Chief Justice of the Supreme Court of Ohio. The Stewarts had long been prominently active in Ohio Republican politics as part of the political retinue of Senator Robert A. Taft—for whose Presidential aspirations young Potter campaigned assiduously in the late 1940s. In mid-1952, however, he transferred his allegiance to Eisenhower, for he was convinced that Ike could win, and he was in fact more comfortable with Eisenhower's political stance than he was with Taft's. Still, he kept his ties with Ohio's conservative Republican organization, in which the state's junior U.S. Senator John Bricker, played a key role. It was Bricker who first brought the likeable and well-educated (Yale University, Cambridge University, and Yale Law School) Stewart to Ike's attention by suggesting him for a vacancy on the United States Court of Appeals for the Fifth Circuit in 1954. Impressed with his background and credentials, which included service as a naval officer during World War II and a partnership in one of New York City's best law firms, the President appointed the then only thirty-nine-year-old attorney to that court. Four years later came the call to the Supreme Court.

During his brief tenure on the Court of Appeals, Potter Stewart quickly came to the attention of the legal fraternity through his carefully crafted, lucid opinions, his engaging style, and his independent jurisprudence. He demonstrated a healthy respect for judicial restraint but also indicated strong attachment to such libertarian commitments as freedom of expression and desegregation. His colleagues valued his understanding of the judicial role; and not surprisingly his name was prominently mentioned for promotion to the Supreme Court as early as the Reed vacancy in 1957. But he had to wait for another year and a half until his fellow Ohioan, Mr. Justice Harold H. Burton, retired from the Court early in October 1958. Ike then gave the brilliant young jurist a recess appointment to the Supreme Court.

Not everyone, however, was enchanted. Not at all enchanted was the Southern Democratic establishment in the Senate that, quite correctly, assumed that Stewart would become a "sure vote" on behalf of claims of racial amelioration. His record on the lower bench had given every indication of such behavior. A confirmation battle on Congress's return in January was assured. Spearheading it was the distinguished and powerful leader of the Southern bloc, Senator Richard B. Russell of Georgia, who charged that the Stewart nomination was "a part of a deliberate policy by the Department of Justice to perpetuate some recent decisions of the

Court in segregation rulings, which decisions were partly based on *amicus curiae* briefs submitted by the Department of Justice." [32] He and his colleagues made clear that the opposition was not against the nominee himself; that, as Senator James O. Eastland of Mississippi put it, he was "an able lawyer . . . a man of integrity . . . very conscientious . . . an improvement over what we now have on the supreme bench"; [33] but that his stance on civil rights was objectionable, that it was symbolic of what Eastland viewed as the "fundamentally wrong" trend on the Court.[34] Stewart had made no secret of his commitment to the 1954 *Desegregation Cases* decision when, during his confirmation hearings before the Senate Judiciary Committee, he noted: "I would not like you to vote for me on the assumption . . . that I am dedicated to the cause of overturning that decision. Because, I am not." [35] The Committee subsequently approved him 12:3, Democratic Senators Eastland, Olin D. Johnston of South Carolina, and John L. McClellan of Arkansas the nays. Two of their Southern colleagues, Estes Kefauver of Tennessee and Sam J. Ervin, Jr., of North Carolina had voted to report the nomination to the Senate floor; the latter, however, would ultimately oppose confirmation itself. For four months and one day opponents then delayed the Stewart confirmation vote! When at last it came on May 5, 1959, the tally was 70:17, with the entire senatorial delegations from Alabama, Arkansas, Georgia, Louisiana, Mississippi, North Carolina, South Carolina, and Virginia, and Senator Spessard L. Holland of Florida voting "no." [36]

Mr. Justice Stewart lived up fully to the expectations of President Eisenhower and the Southern Senators. Now in his fifteenth year on the Court, he has charted a generally progressive-conservative or moderately liberal course, depending upon one's perception. During the heyday of the Warren Court, he was more often than not found on the cautious, conservative side, especially in matters concerning law and order and reapportionment and redistricting. But his stance on racial and sexual discrimination, and on the First and Fourteenth amendments' guarantees of freedom of expression, have found him only slightly less pro-individual or pro-group than the Court's most advanced libertarian activists, such as Douglas and Brennan. Thus, although yielding to no one in his devotion to the tenets of federalism, Stewart brooks no equivocation with egalitarian constitutional guarantees and commands. And some of his well-known opinions in the constitutional "disaster area" of obscenity testify to his generous approach to freedom of speech and press as well as privacy. Hence, his exasperated, concurring observation in *Jacobellis* v. *Ohio* (1964) (involving the movie *Les Amants*) that, under the First and Fourteenth amendments, criminal laws in this area are limited to hard-core pornography—which, he went on to say, he could characterize only with "I know it when I see it." [37] He had hardly assumed his seat on the bench in 1959 when he gave notice of his opposition to censorship of any kind by writing the Court's unanimous opinion that struck down the New York Board of Regents' proscription of the film version of D. H. Lawrence's *Lady Chatterley's Lover,* warning that the advocacy of ideas was not subject to censorship; that by doing so the state had "struck at the very heart of constitutionally protected liberty." [38] At the same time, however, Stewart was not about to be a party to a policy that, in his view, rendered the Bill of Rights "into a suicide pact"—a commitment to law enforcement that might well mean giving the benefit of the doubt to government rather than individual. Consequently, it was natural for Stewart to line up with like-minded Justices Clark, Harlan, and White in the realm of criminal procedure in dissenting from such celebrated and contentious 5:4 rulings as those in *Escobedo* v. *Illinois* [39] and *Miranda* v. *Arizona.*[40]

Stewart, high in President Nixon's esteem, was being seriously considered for promotion to Chief Justice on Earl Warren's ultimate retirement in 1969—and he might very well have been nominated. But he asked Nixon to remove him from the list of possibilities, believing strongly that the interests of the tribunal warranted an appointment from outside its membership. After Warren's and Fortas's departure from the bench, followed two years later by those of Black and Harlan, Stewart and Byron R. White became the "swing men" on what had by then become the

"Burger Court." It is a role admirably suited for the cautious, judicious, fair-minded student of judicial power, whom the Court historians have adjudged to merit a "high average" ranking. He is still young and his current role of occupying the fluid center may well portend an ultimately more notable achievement.

Murdered on November 22, 1963, less than three years after he had assumed office at forty-three, John Fitzgerald Kennedy, the first Roman Catholic to be elected President, was not allowed sufficient time to establish a ratable record in office. Handsome, urbane, and cultured, surrounded by a glamorous family, he set an elegant new tone and style for the country. His ringing phrases captured the imagination and the attention of the young; his cautious willingness to experiment and pioneer, at least on paper, roused the intellectual community to his side; his frequent, open press conferences, replete with good-natured give-and-take, rendered him highly popular with the media. He was a master in the art of communicating, among modern Presidents probably second only to F.D.R. His Administration sparkled with ideas for a better and more constructive life for more people everywhere. Yet in most instances—the Peace Corps being a notable exception—their realization had to await the advent of his successor, who knew how to translate the Kennedy ideals and ideas into legislative reality—something which Kennedy had not generally mastered. Had he lived and been granted another term in office, chances are that he would have recouped a good many of his defeats at the hand of Congress—even as he had overcome those in foreign policy after the Bay of Pigs debacle in 1961. His courageously principled confrontation with Chairman Nikita S. Khrushchev of the U.S.S.R. over Soviet missile deployment in Cuba one year later was proof of his mettle, as was the establishment of the "hot line" to Moscow and the negotiation and ratification of the Nuclear Test Ban Treaty of 1963. On the other side of the developing ledger, however, was the emerging involvement in Vietnam, for which the Kennedy Administration must share a very real measure of blame.

John Kennedy was able to make two appointments to the Court, both going to members of his election and governmental team: Deputy Attorney General Byron R. White and Secretary of Labor Arthur J. Goldberg. He chose them pre-eminently because he knew them both well; because he was comfortable with them personally, professionally, and philosophically; because he trusted their dedication to the country and to the Constitution; because, in his brother Bobby's characterization, they were "his kind of people." It is conceivable that the President raised an eyebrow or two, given White's fairly prompt turn-to-the-right on the bench, but he had little more than one term of Court to observe the two men. Goldberg, of course, allowed himself to be coaxed off the high bench by Lyndon Johnson less than two years after Kennedy's death. It is tempting to muse how the shape of constitutional law might now be different had he lived and had Goldberg, as would almost surely have been the case, remained on the Court!

President Kennedy's first opportunity to fill a Court vacancy came with Mr. Justice Charles E. Whittaker's eager withdrawal, effective April 1, 1962. Primary responsibility for the search for a successor fell naturally to the Attorney General, Robert F. Kennedy. There was no dearth of excellent candidates—essentially there never is if the will to find them exists—and, in fact, the two brothers had already compiled a list of distinguished possibilities for contingency purposes. It consisted of six outstanding figures in governmental and legal circles: two were high-ranking members of the Kennedy Cabinet (Secretary of Labor Arthur J. Goldberg and Deputy Attorney General, Byron R. White); two were *the* probably most highly regarded state supreme court Chief Justices (Walter B. Schaefer of California and Roger J. Traynor of Illinois); one was an able and effective member of the United States Court of Appeals for the Third Circuit (William H. Hastie); and one was one of the country's most renowned professors of constitutional law (Paul A. Freund of Harvard).

Since all of the individuals on the list more than amply met the Kennedy requirements of professional qualification, personal integrity, public visibility, and experience; since all had evinced real politics more or less sympathetic to that of the Administration, the two brothers could afford to let other considerations govern. They were not especially concerned with age and geography (although they dealt with those factors collaterally) or with the presence or absence of judicial experience, and they were thus able to indulge in the luxury of selecting someone with whom they would be truly comfortable, both professionally and personally. Ultimately their choices narrowed to Goldberg and White, and J.F.K. would send both to the Court in due course. There was strong pressure for the two outstanding state Chief Justices, but neither brother knew either one directly. Professor Freund, whom they did know well, was a strong candidate—in fact some deemed him more in the running than Goldberg.[41] But Freund had some strong detractors in the legal fraternity and, more important, he was very much a "Frankfurter man" jurisprudentially (and, like Frankfurter, Jewish). There is considerable speculation that had Mr. Justice Frankfurter stepped down from the Court then rather than some five months later, Paul Freund would very likely have replaced him. Judge Hastie, the first black person to sit on a U.S. Court of Appeals, was an attractive candidate, indeed. But the President had just encountered rough-going in Congress with his embarrassingly unsuccessful attempt to create a Cabinet-level Department of Housing and Urban Development, with Robert C. Weaver, an able and experienced black public servant, as its Secretary; and he shied away from another potentially dangerous political confrontation. Thus it came down to Goldberg or White. Some time later, Robert Kennedy related the events of the ultimate decision to a reporter:

> The Attorney General tilted back in his chair and said "You wanted someone who generally agreed with you on what role government should play in American life, what role the individual in society should have. You didn't think how he would vote in an apportionment case or in a criminal case. You wanted someone who, in the long run, you could believe would be best. You wanted someone who agreed generally with your views of the country." Both he and the President believed that White and Arthur Goldberg met that test. They could not be as sure of the others on the list.[42]

Byron White seemed perfectly suited and J.F.K. was even closer to him than to Goldberg. A youthful and vigorous forty-five, White was born in Fort Collins, Colorado and grew up in Wellington, a tiny town in a sugar-beet growing area near the Wyoming border. He knew poverty and hard work early, and while still a young boy, worked in the fields and on the railroad. Yet success was not long in coming. In 1938 he was graduated at the top of his class from the University of Colorado. He had been President of the Student Body, had earned an early Phi Beta Kappa key and had been a popular All-American in football ("Whizzer White"). He won a Rhodes Scholarship to Oxford, but decided to delay enrollment for one term to accept a lucrative contract to play professional football for the Pittsburgh Steelers. At the end of the season he was off to Oxford; in London he met and became a close friend of John Kennedy, whose father was then Ambassador to the Court of St. James. When war broke out late in 1939, all Rhodes scholars were sent home and White entered the Yale School of Law (also concurrently playing outstanding football with the Detroit Lions). He enlisted in the Navy in 1942, serving in the Solomon Islands as PT-boat squadron skipper and intelligence officer; one of his fellow PT-boat officers was Jack Kennedy. It was White who wrote the official account of the battle events that were later portrayed in the movie *PT 109*. After the war, White returned to Yale where he was graduated *magna cum laude;* served as law clerk to Mr. Chief Justice Vinson; and then began thirteen years of private practice in a prestigious Denver law firm. When in the late 1950s Jack Kennedy entered the Presidential race seriously, White became an effective and staunch supporter and organized the nationwide Citizens for Kennedy–Johnson in 1960. After the victorious election White was awarded with an appointment as Deputy United States Attorney General, a post in which he served with élan and distinction, especially in his personal command of the 600 federal marshals whom he sent to help quell racial disturbances in Montgomery, Alabama, in May 1961. A smiling President was observed pointing with obvious pleasure and satisfaction to the front-page head-

line of the *New York Herald Tribune:* WHIZZER WHITE TO
SUPREME COURT—LAWYER, NAVAL OFFICER, FOOT-
BALL STAR." The subtitle read "Kennedy Picks Friend, An
Aid in Justice Dept." [43]

Almost at once it became clear that Mr. Justice White would
embark upon an independent, utterly non-doctrinaire career. It is
one that defies categorization other than to note that it has been
considerably more conservative in some areas of civil liberty than
might have been anticipated by his nominator. Thus during the remaining years of the Warren era, White could normally be found
with Stewart, Harlan, and Clark on the side of governmental authority in many of the famed criminal justice decisions, such as
Escobedo v. *Illinois* (1964) [44] and *Miranda* v. *Arizona* (1966).[45]
On the other hand, in First Amendment free-expression cases
(where the libertarians could usually count on Stewart) White was
more often on the other side, as he proved to be in certain symbolic speech [46] and, especially, in obscenity decisions: in the landmark 1973 obscenity cases he provided the decisive fifth vote by
joining the four Nixon appointees in adopting a tough regulatory
posture.[47] Conversely, his posture on the race issue was consistently more activist or liberal than Stewart's.[48] White's general
stance and his centrist alliance with Stewart both became more
pronounced when the Warren Court became the Burger Court. On
the latter, the two Justices clearly held the key or swing votes between the two generally predictable blocks as of 1971–72. This
became particularly evident in such significant, emotion-charged
issues as abortion (1973),[49] capital punishment (1972),[50] the 1971
Pentagon Papers Cases [51] (involving the government's right to
classify documents in the interest of national security versus the
right of the press to publish them once they had fallen into its
hands) as well as the *Texas Property Tax Case* (1973) [52] (where
the two were on opposite sides), and in the *Richmond / Suburban
Counties School Consolidation Case* (1973) [53] (where they were,
in all likelihood, again on opposite sides in an unidentified tie-
decision). It represents a deliberate and deliberative role, clothed
with often decisive power, that Mr. Justice White, now in his

thirteenth year on the Court, evidently relishes. Perhaps somewhat less sophisticated and more blunt than Stewart, White has been accorded a rating among the "average" Justices. Future events may well dictate a reassessment; in the meantime Mr. Justice White will in all probability continue along the not easily predictable, centrist course he has charted for himself.

On August 28, 1962, Felix Frankfurter, the brilliant jurist whom Judge Learned Hand once styled as "the most important single figure in our whole judicial system," [54] bowed to the effects of a stroke suffered during the preceding April and, in a touching letter to President Kennedy, announced his retirement from "the institution whose concerns have been the absorbing interest of my life." [55] On the twenty-ninth the President acceded to the request in a warm and sensitive reply. That afternoon he called a news conference in which he made the event public and announced that he had chosen Secretary of Labor Arthur J. Goldberg to fill the Holmes-Cardozo-Frankfurter seat. It did not come as a surprise to many. The fifty-four-year-old renowned labor expert had been more or less next in line after White for the post he very much wanted. Kennedy's regard and enthusiasm for Goldberg's ability and his warm personal feelings toward him were a matter of record. If there was any momentary hesitation in naming him to the Court at all, it was because of the President's reluctance to lose so close a personal and political adviser, and so skillful a Cabinet member, one who had long been one of the country's most successful and most respected labor-management conciliators. But after momentarily pondering the possibility of nominating Abraham A. Ribicoff, his recently designated Secretary of Health, Education, and Welfare and long-time supporter, he reasoned it was more important to have an individual of Goldberg's qualities on the Court than in the Executive Branch. Kennedy had discussed his intentions with both Mr. Chief Justice Warren and Frankfurter himself, and found wholehearted backing of his choice. The nation's reaction was universally favorable and, after receiving the ready approval of the Senate Judiciary Committee, Arthur Goldberg was confirmed at the end of September. Only Senator Strom

Thurmond of South Carolina recorded his opposition—albeit without giving a reason. Thus the new Justice could take his seat in time for the October 1962 term of Court.

Like the man he succeeded, a Jew and of immigrant stock, Goldberg's rise to the top was in the best American tradition of *per aspera ad astra.* "America Sings in Goldberg Story," Ralph McGill headlined his column of September 8 in *The Washington Evening Star,* pointing to the appointee's passion for books and education that aided his rise to the top. Goldberg was born on Chicago's West Side, one of eleven children of Russian-born parents, and worked his way through Northwestern University Law School, graduating at the top of his class in 1929. For a time he worked for a firm that had him headed toward becoming a specialist on mortgage foreclosures. Goldberg loathed that task and ultimately opened his own law office, soon beginning to specialize in labor law. It became the center of his professional career that led him into a supremely successful thirteen-year role as general counsel of the United Steel Workers, the Congress of Industrial Organizations, and the American Federation of Labor, whence he entered the Kennedy Administration. Cultured and scholarly, he was a man of action as well as ideas, and indeed a worthy successor to Felix Frankfurter.

But Arthur Goldberg, as had been widely expected, pursued an entirely different jurisprudence than that practiced so tenaciously by Felix Frankfurter for almost a quarter of a century. The new Justice lost little time in demonstrating his attachment to the kind of judicial activism in the realms of civil rights and liberties that henceforth gave the Warren Court a usually solid "libertarian" wing. Thus he was more frequently on the opposite side of the Court's line-up than White, although, in his own perception of the judicial function, the President was pleased by the roles played by both men. During less than three years on the Court Mr. Justice Goldberg showed a zest for innovation in the law that left an imprint far out of proportion to the brief period he served—so brief that the Court's observers believed that an "average" ranking would be the only equitable one to bestow. But his energy and ability and his pioneering in the world of new policy decisions helped to change American constitutional law. Thus, although he was no longer on the Court to see the ideas adopted by a majority, it was he who first raised the specter of the unconstitutionality of the death penalty on the basis of the cruel and unusual punishment and due process of law clauses; [56] it was he who gave an expansive interpretation to the "additional fundamental rights" that he found in the Ninth Amendment; [57] it was he who spoke for the 6:3 Court that ruled the denial of passports to members of the Communist Party and its fronts "unconstitutional on its face"; [58] and it was he who authored the Court's landmark 5:4 decision in the coerced confession case of *Escobedo* v. *Illinois* (1964).[59] Why did he leave the job he cherished so much? Surely the President had no particular leverage on him. Numerous highly speculative reasons have been advanced ever since, a good many of them contrived and silly. According to L.B.J. himself, he had heard from economist John Kenneth Galbraith, among others, that Goldberg "would step down from his position to take a job that would be more challenging to him." [60] Arthur Goldberg, from his vantage point, candidly asserted that he had agreed to leave the Court for two reasons: first, his deep conviction that he might be able to negotiate an end to the nightmare in Vietnam; and, second, his profound commitment to public service. He also was influenced by a clearly implied understanding of an ultimate return to the Court.[61]

The tragic crime in Dallas brought one of the country's master politicians to the Presidency in the person of Lyndon Baines Johnson. Superb legislative leader, arm-twister, and I.O.U.-collector, he stepped into office and maneuvered some of the most far-reaching domestic legislation since the days of the New Deal. The nation had barely begun to recover from the wrench and trauma of President Kennedy's funeral when the tempestuous, mercurial man began to wheel and deal the languishing Kennedy program into enactment, adding a full measure of his own. In his first speech to Congress as President, he propelled legislators as well as citizens into action on the civil rights front: "We have talked for 100 years or more. It is now time to write it in the books of law."

And so Congress did by passing the landmark Civil Rights Act of 1964, the most significant and certainly the most substantial statute on the subject in almost a century. And, encouraged by his smashing defeat of Senator Barry Goldwater in the Presidential election of 1964—his 61.1 per cent of the popular vote exceeding even that of F.D.R. in 1936—L.B.J. went on to post an impressive roster of legislative accomplishments. Among these were Medicare; improved social security benefits; higher minimum wages; environmental amelioration; the Voting Rights Act of 1965; the first massive federal aid to primary and secondary education; major housing programs. His motto of "come now, and let us reason together" succeeded everywhere along the line.

Yet Lyndon Johnson's Waterloo was foreign policy, Vietnam in particular. He was impatient with the intricacies of foreign policy diplomacy; his naïve belief that his internal modus operandi could be applied externally as well; his short temper and lack of patience; his emotional reactions to what he sensed were the foreign diplomats' sneering view of his manners and bearing; his craving for adulation; his ill-applied concept of national honor and sincere, yet almost puerile patriotism; and his inability to lose allowed him to be pulled deeper and deeper into the quagmire of Vietnam. By the beginning of 1968, with more than half a million American forces committed to Vietnam; with internecine warfare at home; with the campuses aflame; with Senator Eugene McCarthy ringing up astonishing numbers of votes in primary elections, the heartsick President went on the air to announce that he would not run again that fall. Instead, he announced, he would devote every waking moment to the pursuit of peace. Yet his subsequent efforts were in vain—largely because he was basically incapable of shifting gears sufficiently; and L.B.J. went back to Texas and his beloved ranch.

The final verdict on Lyndon Johnson must await more passage of time: how to weigh accomplished brilliance at home with abject failure abroad will prove to be no easy task. He had the perhaps macabre satisfaction of seeing his successor wrestle just as unsuccessfully with Vietnam until, on the day before Mr. Johnson died late in January 1973, Richard M. Nixon's emissaries concluded a shaky settlement of the terrible war.

Lyndon Johnson made four nominations to the Court but he succeeded with only two. The first (Abe Fortas as Associate Justice in 1965) came as a result of coaxing Goldberg off the bench and into the United Nations; the second (Thurgood Marshall in 1967) was the first appointment of a black to the Court; the third (Fortas's projected promotion in 1968 to Chief Justice to replace Earl Warren) failed ignominiously; and as a result the fourth (Homer Thornberry's projected replacement of Fortas as Associate Justice) never materialized. With the exception of the Marshall appointment, which was as noble and timely as it was strategic, the Johnson nominations were sheer cronyism. Yet the nominees were not without qualifications. Judge Thornberry, while not outstanding, was a capable and experienced public servant; and not even Fortas's most advanced detractors would deny his uncanny ability, indeed brilliance. It is a pity that by ill-conceived, downright stupid, off-the-bench actions he found it necessary to resign after a few short years as Associate Justice.

Ironically, Abe Fortas had not at all sought a seat on the Court. In fact, he had demurred repeatedly, addressing the following letter to the President on July 19, 1965: [62]

> For The President:
> Again, my dear friend, I am obligated and honored by your confidence and generosity—to an extent which is beyond my power adequately to acknowledge.
> But after painful searching, I've decided to decline—with a heart full of gratitude. Carol thinks I should accept this greatest honor that a lawyer could receive—this highest appointive post in the nation. But I want a few more years of activity. I want a few more years to try to be of service to you and the Johnson family. And I want and feel that in justice I should take a few more years to stabilize this law firm in the interests of the young men who have enlisted here.
> This has been a hard decision—but not nearly as hard as an-

other which had the virtue of continuing association with your trials and tribulations and greatness.

I shall always be grateful.

Abe

It took all of the President's persuasive powers during an entire week to get the balky Fortas to agree. In fact, Fortas never actually said "yes": the President, having invited him to his White House office on July 28, simply informed him that he was about to go over to the theater in the East Wing "to announce his appointment to the Supreme Court," and that he could either stay in the office or accompany him.[63] Fortas opted for the latter course. But to the assembled reporters he appeared only slightly less disenchanted than had been the grim-faced Goldberg who, with his tearful wife, Dorothy, and their son, Robert, by his side, had reluctantly accepted the post of Ambassador to the United Nations, following Adlai E. Stevenson's sudden death: "I shall not, Mr. President, conceal the pain with which I leave the Court after three years of service. It has been the richest and most satisfying period of my career." [64]

President Johnson's regard for Abe Fortas was matched only by his regard for the Court as an institution itself. His choice may well have had its genesis seventeen years earlier: at the time, U.S. Representative Lyndon B. Johnson (D.-Tex.) was engaged in a bruising primary battle for the Texas Democratic Senatorial nomination with ex-Governor Coke Stevenson. Neither candidate had received an absolute majority in the initial race; thus they faced a run-off. Almost one million votes were cast in the runoff with Johnson emerging as victor by the hairbreadth margin of eighty-seven votes. Amid charges of gross irregularities, an acrimonious legal battle ensued in which a federal district court issued a restraining order confirmed by the United States Court of Appeals for the Fifth Circuit, against printing Johnson's name on the general election ballot in November. The frantic Johnson lawyers rushed to the nation's capital, where a thirty-eight-year-old attorney, an L.B.J. acquaintance named Abe Fortas, filed an urgent appeal to the Supreme Court. The member of the Court in charge of the Fifth Circuit was Mr. Justice Hugo L. Black, who ordered a stay of the lower court's restraining order, thus enabling Johnson to get his name on that crucial ballot. He easily won the November election, and he never forgot Fortas's service. The two men became the closest of friends, with Johnson often leaning heavily for advice and counsel on Fortas, for whom he felt a personal affection and respect bordering on adulation. Indeed, it was the President's unwillingness to forego those services even after he had sent Fortas to the Court that proved to be one of the key weapons in the hands of the opponents to the latter's proposed elevation to the Chief Justiceship. For admittedly, Mr. Justice Fortas continued to serve the Chief Executive by participating in important military and diplomatic strategy conferences; by rendering advice on such delicate issues as racial controversies and street rioting; and by generally answering presidential calls for assistance. That sundry other members of the high bench throughout the Court's history had provided similar services to their President does not gainsay the compromising of separation of powers attending such practices. Yet, confident and proud, the two long-time associates could see no wrong in their continuing relationship.

Fortas, whose nomination the Senate quickly confirmed in early August—with only Republican Senators Carl T. Curtis (Nebraska), Strom Thurmond (South Carolina), and John J. Williams (Delaware) voicing opposition—brought with him a remarkable record of achievement. A native of Memphis, son of a Jewish cabinet-maker who had moved to Tennessee from England, Fortas, like many of his colleagues on the bench, had gone to Yale Law School. A superb student, and the editor of the *Yale Law Journal,* he was fascinated by the New Deal. He soon joined it, initially under Chairman William O. Douglas of the Securities and Exchange Commission, eventually gravitating to such governmental units then close to the policy center of the Roosevelt era as the Department of the Interior and the Public Works Administration (PWA). Nine years later, when he was but thirty-two, he became Under-Secretary of the Interior under the redoubtable Harold L.

Ickes. He stayed in that post until 1946 when he joined two other well-known, successful New Deal figures, Thurman Arnold and Paul A. Porter, in establishing what became one of Washington's most prestigious and lucrative law firms (Arnold, Fortas, and Porter). But it was also a public-spirited firm that became famous— or infamous—as the one firm willing to lend its talents, often gratis, to the many victims of the McCarthy era. Later the firm continued its aid to the underdogs of society: Abe Fortas was the attorney whom the Supreme Court assigned to Clarence Earl Gideon in his successful battle to win the right of counsel for indigents in non-capital as well as capital criminal cases.[65]

In his less than four years on the Court Fortas showed himself to be a libertarian when it came to fundamental human rights. In that sense he filled Goldberg's shoes, although Goldberg tended to side with those who favored government-regulatory powers when it came to interpreting certain aspects of antitrust legislation. But Fortas's scholarly and structured style, his penchant for effective phrase-making, and his additional year on the bench have prompted the Court experts to give him a "near great" rating, an entire category higher than Goldberg. In view of his brief service the rating is probably rather generous. Yet it is not surprising given such trail-blazing opinions as that in the *Gault* case (1967), for example, which wrought a revolution in constitutional law by extending most of the Bill of Rights safeguards to juvenile offenders.[66] In that opinion Fortas's gift for phrase-making becomes especially clear; words such as: "Under our Constitution, the condition of being a boy does not justify a kangaroo court" [67] will long serve to associate decision and author. Nor is it surprising, given his uncanny ability to reach the heart of a matter as he did in writing a stinging dissent in *The New York Textbook Case of 1968* (in which the Court upheld 6:3 the state's requirement to lend textbooks to students in private and parochial schools):

> Apart from the differences between textbooks and bus rides, the present statute does not call for extending to children attending sectarian schools the same service or facility extended to children in public schools. This statute calls for furnishing special, sepa-

rate, and particular books, especially, separately, and particularly chosen by religious sects or their representatives for use in their sectarian schools. This is the infirmity. . . .[68]

But Fortas's promising career was to be cut short by a combination of political power plays and personal greed. When Mr. Chief Justice Warren wrote the President on June 13, 1968, announcing his intention to retire "effective at your leisure," Johnson—with the enthusiastic concurrence of Warren—two weeks later made Warren's decision public and at the same time nominated Fortas to succeed him. It was, of course, a logical choice. It was also just a few months before the Presidential elections of that year—one in which the Republican party had every reason to sense victory. Perhaps, with the aid of such influential G.O.P. stalwarts as Minority Leader Everett McKinley Dirksen, Fortas could have been confirmed. But L.B.J.'s unwise move of simultaneously nominating old crony William Homer Thornberry for the resultant vacancy was simply too much for a good many objective and fair-minded Senators, such as William B. Spong, Jr. (D.-Va.). Thornberry was a one-time mayor of Austin; for seven terms the holder of L.B.J.'s former seat in the House, and a Johnson-appointed federal district and appellate judge preceding his nomination to the Supreme Court. The choice was obviously dictated by personal and political friendship. Judge Thornberry—one of those who would support the Nixon nomination of G. Harrold Carswell two years later—was a decent public servant of moderate ability, but hardly of the caliber that would have prompted a basically hostile Senate to overlook political factors.

Thus, cronyism; the timing of the nominations; the political climate; accumulated hostility to the Warren Court; Fortas's posture on some of the more controversial issues in which he participated (and some in which he did not); charges of judicial impropriety by his continuing active counseling of the President; and the revelation that he had accepted a huge lecture fee ($15,000) to conduct a series of university seminars during the summer of 1968 combined ultimately to doom the proposed Fortas promotion, and with it the Thornberry nomination. While the Senate Judiciary

Committee did report Fortas's designation favorably, 11:6, it ran into a filibuster on the Senate floor, and a motion to terminate the latter by closure failed by a wide margin. Shortly thereafter Fortas asked Johnson to withdraw his nomination; the President complied, disdaining any other attempted appointment; Thornberry's nomination was thus moot; and Earl Warren remained at the helm for another year.

It was not until May 4, 1969, that the final chapter in the Fortas tragedy began to be written with *Life* magazine's revelations that in 1966 the Justice had accepted, although several months later returned, a $20,000 fee from the family foundation of Louis E. Wolfson, the multi-millionaire industrialist who had since been imprisoned for stock manipulations. Initially based on an arrangement that was intended to be a life-long association in an advisory capacity with the foundation, the canceled agreement had provided for an annual stipend of $20,000 which would devolve upon Mrs. Fortas in the event of the Justice's demise. On May 15, 1969, under heavy fire gleefully and subtly augmented by Attorney General Mitchell and the President himself,[69] the career of one of the most gifted individuals ever to sit on the Supreme Court ended. Abe Fortas resigned in a two-sentence letter to Nixon, to which the President consented in a one-sentence reply. In a long letter to Mr. Chief Justice Warren—a copy of which he sent to Nixon with Warren's consent—the devastated Fortas recounted in close detail the history of his involvement with Wolfson and avowed his complete innocence of any wrongdoing.

Mr. Justice Tom Clark's retirement at the end of the Court's 1966–67 term afforded President Johnson his last opportunity to fill a vacancy—and the chance to realize one of his repeatedly voiced dual goals: to send a non-white and non-male to the high bench. His choice was as easy as it was obvious: his Solicitor General Thurgood Marshall, previously a judge on the U.S. Court of Appeals for the Second Circuit, and before that Counsel to the Legal Defense and Educational Fund of the National Association for the Advancement of Colored People. "MARSHALL NAMED FOR HIGH COURT, ITS FIRST NEGRO," read the front page headline in the *New York Times*. The subtitle read: "Johnson Calls Nominee 'Best Qualified,' and Rights Leaders are Jubilant—Southerners Silent on Confirmation." [70] Following his dramatic announcement in the White House Rose Garden, with the nominee by his side, the President told reporters that he had been subjected to "very little pressure of any kind" on the fifty-eight-year-old Marshall's nomination, declaring that it was one clearly earned by the nominee's "distinguished record" in the law, and added: "He is best qualified by training and by very valuable service to the country. I believe it is the right thing to do, the right time to do it, the right man and the right place." [71] Only one other individual had in fact closely participated in the President's selection: his new Attorney General, Ramsey Clark, the son of the retiring Justice, Tom C. Clark.

Marshall, the great-grandson of a slave, the son of a Pullman car steward, thus broke the racial barrier. If anyone was a logical and deserving choice to do so it was this long-time champion of equality of opportunity. His parents had believed to the utmost in the value of education—his Mother sold her engagement ring to pay for at least part of his college expenses at Lincoln University in Oxford, Pennsylvania. From there he went to Howard University Law School, ranking at the top of the Class of 1933. Soon entering the field of civil rights, he won his first bittersweet victory in 1935 when his legal acumen and strategy compelled the University of Maryland (which had earlier denied him admission to its Law School) to accept Donald Murray as its first Negro law student; [72] indeed he was the first of his race to enter any state law school below the Mason-Dixon Line. Marshall joined the N.A.A.C.P.'s legal department in 1936 and was named its chief counsel two years later. In 1961 President Kennedy appointed him to the Court of Appeals, and late in 1965 President Johnson brought him back to active legal work by naming him Solicitor General (the third-highest post in the Department of Justice).

Thurgood Marshall's career as counsel for the N.A.A.C.P. mirrors the story of the upward climb of the fortunes of America's black men and women. Handling hundreds of cases, he tried thirty-two before the Supreme Court, winning all but three of them. His most notable victory was the Court's 1954 decision on segregation in the public schools.

Predictably, the Marshall nomination ran into considerable and protracted opposition, led by Democratic Senators from the Deep South. They had recognized the inevitability of a black appointment for some time, but they were not about to accept it without a battle, concentrating their attacks on his well-known liberal philosophy and what some regarded as defective legal knowledge. Thus Senator Strom Thurmond of South Carolina at one point read more than sixty questions, studded with quotes from and about political figures of the 1860s, to the nominee during lengthy hearings before the Judiciary Committee. The vote on confirmation was delayed for two and a half months until August 31. When it came, it was by the decisive margin of 69:11. Of those Senators who were present and voting in opposition to Marshall, all except one—Robert C. Byrd (D.-W.Va.)—were from the Deep South. And all but one—Strom Thurmond—were Democrats (Thurmond being a Democrat-turned-Republican).[73] A sign of the changing times was that among those casting affirmative votes were six Southern Senators: Democrats William J. Fulbright of Arkansas, Albert Gore of Tennessee, William B. Spong, Jr., of Virginia, and Ralph Yarborough of Texas; and Republicans Howard H. Baker, Jr., of Tennessee and John G. Tower of Texas. On October 2, 1967, Lyndon Johnson paid an unannounced visit to the Supreme Court where he witnessed the swearing in of the broadly beaming Mr. Justice Thurgood Marshall.

The new appointee readily sided with Douglas, Warren, Brennan, Fortas, and somewhat less frequently, Black, during the remaining two years of the Warren Court. When the latter became the Burger Court, Marshall became an even more identifiable ally of the remaining libertarian activists on the Court. Now in his seventh year on the Court, his career there has been somewhat spotty, reaching high points in the areas of his greatest concern—equal protection of the laws, due process, and First Amendment cases —and betraying a rather indifferent, even bored, attitude toward some of the more technical problems in areas other than those of civil rights and liberties. Consequently, the Court's observers have quite properly given him an "average" rating. Yet he will be remembered if only because he broke the last remaining color barrier in high public service—save for the Presidency itself.

It is tempting to essay a preliminary appraisal of President Nixon and his appointees. Yet the former's record has not run its course, and that of the latter is far too recent to permit fair judgment.

—10—
Epilogue

It may now be well to reflect briefly on some of the myths and truths that so often characterize public attitudes toward the Justices of the Supreme Court and that remarkable institution itself.

The Court does not operate in a vacuum, nor is it composed of Olympians. It functions as a legal, governmental, *and* political institution under a basic document that stands in constant need of interpretation against the backdrop of what Holmes referred to as the "felt necessities of the times."

Our Founding Fathers created a magnificent Constitution. But they could hardly foresee some of the contemporary problems that have found their way to the Court for resolution. Indeed, while for most of our history we have made laws in order to help solve public issues, in recent years the byword has been "let's go to court." It is a regrettable development but one that is here to stay.

The nine Supreme Court Justices who interpret the Constitution are steeped and trained in the law. But they respond to human situations; they are, in Mr. Justice Frankfurter's words, "Men . . . not disembodied spirits, they respond to human emotions. . . ." "The great tides and currents which engulf the rest of mankind," in Mr. Justice Cardozo's beautiful and telling words, "do not turn aside in their course and pass the judges idly by."

Yet, notwithstanding the human factor, the Court operates in a setting that forces responsibility upon it. Judges are bound within walls, lines, and limits that are often unseen by the layman—walls, lines, and limits built from the heritage of the law; the impact of the cases as they have come down through the years; the regard for precedent; the crucial practice of judicial restraint; the deference to the legislative process; in brief, the tradition of the law.

Moreover, the justices are well aware of two important facts of life: ultimately they do not have the power to enforce their decisions, for the purse is in the hands of the legislature and the sword in that of the executive; and, the Court may be reversed by legislative action or by constitutional amendment.

We should recognize that much of our reaction to the Court's ruling is highly subjective. A "good" decision is one that pleases us; a "poor" one is one that does not. All too often our response depends upon "whose ox is gored." Nor is that bit of wisdom confined to laymen. It includes political leaders, such as President Nixon, whose frequent call for a "strict constructionist" on the bench is a thinly disguised synonym for Justices who agree with his philosophy of government and politics.

There is, of course, nothing wrong in the President's attempt to staff the Court with jurists who read the Constitution his way. All Presidents have tried to pack the Court, to mold it in their images. Nothing is wrong with this, provided, however, that the nominees are professionally, intellectually, and morally qualified to serve. But sloganeering and labeling, be it "strict constructionist" or "liberal" or "conservative," are as unhelpful in an understanding of the nature and function of the judicial process as they are misleading.

Is a Justice who upholds the Bill of Rights a liberal or a conservative? It depends upon one's point of view. Were the three of the four strict constructionists whom President Nixon appointed to the Court under that label "strict" or "loose" constructionists when they joined in the majority decision to throw out abortion control statutes in forty-five states early in 1973? The point is that there simply is no easy answer—and that one of the most difficult tasks in analyzing the judicial process is to be at once objective and consistent.

The Supreme Court of the United States is indeed engaged in the political process. But, in Mr. Justice Frankfurter's admonition, it is "the Nation's ultimate judicial tribunal, not a super-legal aid bureau." Neither is the Court, in the second Mr. Justice Harlan's words, "a panacea for every blot upon the public welfare, nor should this Court ordained as a judicial body, be thought of as a general haven for reform movements." In other words, the Constitution of the United States was simply not designed to provide judicial remedies for every social or political ill.

The Supreme Court is much better at saying "yes" or "no" to the government than in prescribing policy; indeed, it should resolutely shun prescriptive policy-making. It has quite enough to do in constitutional and statutory interpretation and application. Paraphrasing Professor Paul Freund, the question is not whether the Court can do everything, but whether it can do something in its proper sphere.

Of course, all judging involves decision-making, and the Court can escape neither controversy nor criticism, nor should it. In Mr. Justice Holmes's oft-quoted words: "We are very quiet up there, but it is the quiet of a storm center, as we all know." As an institution at once legal, political, and human, it possesses both the assets and liabilities that attend these descriptive characteristics.

Yet when all is said and done, the Court is the "living voice of the Constitution," as Lord Bryce once phrased it. As such it is both arbiter and educator and, in essence, represents the sole solution short of anarchy under the American system of government as we know it. Within the limits of procedure and deference to the presumption of the constitutionality of legislation, the Court—our "sober second thought"—is the natural forum in American society for the individual and small groups, what Madison, the father of the Bill of Rights, fervently hoped it would always be. The Court is infinitely more qualified to protect minority rights than the far more easily pressured, more impulsive, and more emotion-charged Legislative and Executive branches. All too readily do these two yield to the politically expedient and the popular, for they are close indeed to what Judge Learned Hand once called "the pressure of public panic, and public greed."

A remarkable common constitutional sense has served the Supreme Court of the United States well in its striving to maintain the blend of continuity and change which is the sine qua non for desirable stability in the basic governmental processes of a democracy. In that role it will live in history.

Notes

CHAPTER 2

1. (New York: Alfred A. Knopf, 1941), p. 3. (H. L. Mencken once quipped that a judge is a law student who marks his own exams.)

2. He was Circuit Court Judge Marion Walter, who had been prominently identified with the discredited Pendergast machine.

3. By late 1973, variants of the Missouri Plan existed in the following states. Michigan, Minnesota, Ohio, Wisconsin, Wyoming, Arizona, Idaho, Montana, Nevada, North Dakota, South Dakota, Washington, Tennessee, and Oregon.

4. Herbert Kaufman, *Politics and Policies in State and Local Governments* (Englewood Cliffs, N.J.: Prentice-Hall, 1963), p. 60.

5. *Congressional Record,* Vol. 97 (Part 10), 82d Cong., 1st sess. (October 9, 1951), pp. 12838, 12840.

6. As quoted by Alpheus Thomas Mason, *William Howard Taft: Chief Justice* (New York: Simon and Schuster, 1965), p. 173.

7. Speech to the Annual Convention of the American Bar Association, Dallas, Texas, August 10, 1969.

8. September 29, 1965. For a fuller treatment of the Morrissey case, see Harold W. Chase, *Federal Judges: The Appointing Process* (Minneapolis: University of Minnesota Press, 1972), pp. 173–77.

9. Report of the Standing Committee on Federal Judiciary, 88 *American Bar Association Reports* (1963), p. 195.

10. Reprinted in the *New York Times,* October 22, 1971, p. 24c.

11. Interview with Robert L. Trescher, Esquire, December 9, 1971.

12. *United Mine Workers* v. *Red Jacket Consolidated Coal and Coke Co.,* 18 F. 839 (1927).

13. *Hitchman Coal and Coke Co.* v. *Mitchell,* 245 U.S. 229 (1917).

14. *Hearings before the Subcommittee of the Committee of the Judiciary, U.S. Senate, on the Confirmation of John J. Parker to Be an Associate Justice of the Supreme Court of the United States,* 71st Cong., 2d sess., 1930, p. 74.

15. 165 F.2d 387. (It sustained 72 F.Supp. 516.)

16. 354 U.S. 449.

17. An interesting and widely reported poll of sixty-five experienced Court observers and experts—of whom I was asked to be one—was conducted just prior to the accession of Mr. Chief Justice Burger in 1969. The then ninety-six Justices who sat on the Supreme Court were ranked in the following categories: "great" (12); "near great" (15); "average" (55); "below average" (6); and "failures" (8). The poll, which was published in abbreviated form in the October 15, 1971 issue of *Life Magazine* (pp. 52ff.) and in a fuller version in 58 *American Bar Association Journal* (November 1972), pp. 1183–89, is reproduced in summary form as Appendix A, *infra.*

18. After barely fifteen months on the high bench, Byrnes resigned to become F.D.R.'s "Assistant President for Domestic Affairs."

CHAPTER 3

1. Felix Frankfurter, "The Supreme Court in the Mirror of Justices," 105 *University of Pennsylvania Law Review* (1957), p. 781.

2. As quoted in the *New York Times Magazine,* November 28, 1954, p. 14.

3. Frankfurter, n. 1, *op. cit.,* p. 793.

4. See press conferences of May 22, 1969; March 22, 1970; and December 8, 1971—all referring at least partly to the point.

5. *New York Times,* June 14, 1967, p. 1.

6. *Ibid.,* May 17, 1969, p. 1.

7. Henry Cabot Lodge, *Selections from the Correspondence of Theodore Roosevelt and Henry Cabot Lodge, 1884–1918* (New York: Charles Scribner's Sons, 1925), Vol. II, pp. 228, 230, 231.

8. *Ibid.,* p. 229.

9. *The Supreme Court in United States History,* rev. ed. (Boston: Little, Brown, and Company, 1926), Vol. II, p. 22.

10. 193 U.S. 197 (1904).

11. As quoted by James E. Clayton, *The Making of Justice: The Supreme Court in Action* (New York: E. P. Dutton & Co., 1964), p. 47.

12. As quoted by Arthur Krock, *New York Times,* October 19, 1971, p. 43L.

13. Lecture at Columbia University, New York, April 28, 1959.

14. As quoted in *Time Magazine,* May 23, 1969, p. 24.

15. Comment to Anthony Lewis, "A Talk with Warren On Crime, the Court, the Country," *New York Times Magazine,* October 19, 1969, pp. 128–29.

CHAPTER 4

1. See the polls conducted for *Life* Magazine in 1948 and 1962 by fifty-five and seventy-five, respectively, experienced historian-observers of the Presidency under the chairmanship of Professor Arthur M. Schlesinger, Sr. The widely published and reproduced poll is summarized as Appendix B, *infra*. (For a full account, see the *New York Times Magazine*, July 29, 1962, pp. 12ff.)

2. Fred L. Israel, "John Blair," in Leon Friedman and Fred L. Israel (eds.), *The Justices of the United States Supreme Court, 1789–1969* (New York: Chelsea House, 1969), p. 111.

3. Richard Berry, *Mr. Rutledge of South Carolina* (New York: Duell, Sloan and Pearce, 1942), p. 353.

4. Gertrude S. Wood, *William Paterson of New Jersey, 1745–1806* (Fair Lawn, N.J.: Fair Lawn Press, 1833), p. 101.

5. As quoted in Samuel Eliot Morison, Henry Steele Commager, and William E. Leuchtenburg, *The Growth of the American Republic*, 6th ed. (New York: Oxford University Press, 1969), Vol. I, p. 346.

6. Fred L. Israel, "James Iredell," in Friedman and Israel (eds.), *op. cit.*, p. 128.

7. See my *The Judicial Process: An Introductory Analysis of the Courts of the United States, England, and France*, 2d ed. (New York: Oxford University Press, 1968), p. 344.

8. *Ibid.*, p. 310.

9. As quoted by Charles Warren, *The Supreme Court in United States History*, rev. ed. (Boston: Little, Brown, and Company, 1926), Vol. I, p. 178.

10. Robert J. Steamer, *The Supreme Court in Crisis: A History of Conflict* (Amherst: The University of Massachusetts Press, 1971), p. 35.

11. *McCulloch* v. *Maryland*, 4 Wheaton 316 (1819), at 407.

12. *Osborn* v. *United States Bank*, 9 Wheaton 738 (1824), at 866.

13. 1 Cranch 137.

14. 4 Wheaton 316.

15. 4 Wheaton 518.

16. 9 Wheaton 1.

17. Benjamin N. Cardozo, *The Nature of the Judicial Process* (New Haven: Yale University Press, 1921), pp. 169–70.

18. Fred Israel, "Thomas Todd," in Friedman and Israel (eds.), *op. cit.*, p. 409.

19. Letter to Thomas Ritchie, December 25, 1820, quoted in Andrew A. Lipscomb and Albert E. Bergh (eds.), Thomas Jefferson, *Writings* (Washington, D.C.: The Thomas Jefferson Memorial Association, 1903), Vol. XV, pp. 297–98.

20. R. Kent Newmyer, "A Note on the Whig Politics of Justice Joseph Story," 48 *The Mississippi Valley Historical Review* (December 1961), p. 482.

21. 9 Wheaton 1.

CHAPTER 5

1. 6 Peters 515.

2. Quoted widely by a host of authors and commentators, e.g., Charles Warren in his *The Supreme Court in United States History*, rev. ed. (Boston: Little, Brown, and Company, 1926), Vol. I, p. 759. (See also his note 1, Chapter 1.)

3. *Register of Debates in Congress*, 22d Cong., 1st sess., 1832, Vol. VIII, Part 3, Appendix, p. 76. (Italics added.)

4. *Dred Scott* v. *Sandford*, 19 Howard 393.

5. In an essay on "politically motivated judges," Alexander M. Bickel termed McLean the "most notoriously so." (*Politics and the Warren Court*, New York: Harper & Row, 1965, p. 135.)

6. In 1852 he had refused the Native American party's nomination, which would have been a fifth!

7. E.g., *United States* v. *Gratiot*, 14 Peters 526 (1840); *Holmes* v. *Jennison*, 14 Peters 540 (1840); *Prigg* v. *Pennsylvania*, 16 Peters 539 (1842); the *Passenger Cases*, 7 Howard 283 (1849); and *Cooley* v. *Board of Wardens of the Port of Philadelphia*, 12 Howard 299 (1851).

8. Samuel Taylor, *Roger Brooke Taney* (Baltimore: John Murphy and Co., 1872), p. 223.

9. As quoted by Warren, *op. cit.*, vol. II, p. 10. (Italics added.)

10. Alexander M. Bickel, *The Least Dangerous Branch: The Supreme Court at the Bar of Politics* (Indianapolis: The Bobbs-Merrill Co., 1963), p. 45.

11. *Dred Scott* v. *Sandford*, loc. cit., at 454–55.

12. Vol. I (1915), pp. 192–94. (Italics in original.)

13. *Cooley* v. *Board of Wardens of the Port of Philadelphia*, op. cit., and other illustrations alluded to in note 7, *supra*.

14. See the account by Roy Franklin Nichols, *Franklin Pierce: Young Hickory of the Granite Hills* (Philadelphia: University of Pennsylvania Press, 1931), pp. 253, 276, 277.

15. Philip Shriver Klein, *President James Buchanan* (University Park, Pa.: The Pennsylvania State University Press, 1962), pp. 401–2.

16. 17 Fed. Cases 144, No. 9487 (CCD Md.).

17. *The Supreme Court in the American System of Government* (Cambridge, Mass.: Harvard University Press, 1955), p. 76.

18. 16 Wallace 36.

19. 4 Wallace 2 (1866).

20. 2 Black 635 (1863).

21. Carl Sandburg, *Abraham Lincoln: The War Years* (New York: Harcourt, Brace and Co., 1939, Vol. III, and David M. Silver, *Lincoln's Supreme Court* (Urbana, Ill.: University of Illinois Press, 1956), *passim*.

22. *Hepburn* v. *Griswold* (*The First Legal Tender Case*), 8 Wallace 603 (1870).

23. 12 Wallace 457 (1871).

24. (New York: Pocket Books, 1957), especially Chapter VI on Senator Ross, "I Looked Down Into My Open Grave," pp. 107–28.

25. E.g., Ex parte *Milligan,* 4 Wallace 2 (1866); *Cummings* v. *Missouri,* 4 Wallace 277 (1867); and Ex parte *Garland,* 4 Wallace 333 (1867).

26. E.g., *Mississippi* v. *Johnson,* 4 Wallace 475 (1867); *Georgia* v. *Stanton,* 6 Wallace 50 (1867); Ex parte *McCardle,* 7 Wallace 506 (1869); and *Texas* v. *White,* 7 Wallace 700 (1869).

CHAPTER 6

1. When the counting of the disputed votes had started, Tilden needed but one of the twenty votes, Hayes all of them to win. The Congressionally established fifteen-member commission was composed of five Democratic and five Republican legislators, and five Supreme Court Justices: Democrats Clifford and Field, Republicans Miller and Strong, and moderate "neutral" Republican Mr. Justice David Davis, who had been selected by his judicial colleagues. But Davis, afflicted with an arguable case of cold political feet, allowed himself to be elected to the U.S. Senate by the Illinois legislature, decisively by Democratic votes. Then, at Davis's own request and with the approval of both political parties he was replaced on the commission by Bradley. The latter came through nobly for his party and its candidate.

2. *United States* v. *Reese,* 92 U.S. 214 (1876), and *United States* v. *Cruikshank,* 92 U.S. 542 (1876).

3. *United States* v. *Harris,* 106 U.S. 629 (1883), and the *Civil Rights Cases,* 109 U.S. 3 (1883), respectively.

4. As quoted by Howard Jay Graham, "The Waite Court and the Fourteenth Amendment," 17 *Vanderbilt Law Review* (March 1964), p. 525.

5. 16 Wallace 36 (1873).

6. *United States* v. *Cruikshank,* 92 U.S. 542 (1876), at 554.

7. 94 U.S. 113.

8. E.g., his dissenting opinions in such key cases at *Hurtado* v. *California,* 110 U.S. 516 (1884); *Plessy* v. *Ferguson,* 163 U.S. 537 (1896); *Giles* v. *Kentucky,* 189 U.S. 475 (1903); and *Berea College* v. *Kentucky,* 211 U.S. 45 (1908).

9. Fred Rodell, *Nine Men* (New York: Random House, 1955), p. 143.

10. 163 U.S. 537, at 559.

11. March 13 and 15, 1881.

12. Wilson allegedly suggested to the old-guard Republican Union League Club of Philadelphia that it might be well to find a place for "Old Grover's" portrait in its elegant gallery reserved for the likenesses of Republican Presidents.

13. E.g., White's votes in the two *Income Tax Cases* of 1895 (157 U.S. 429 and 158 U.S. 601, both recorded as *Pollock* v. *Farmers' Loan and Trust Co.).*

14. Allan Nevins, *Grover Cleveland: A Study in Courage* (New York: Dodd, Mead & Company, 1932), p. 415.

15. 198 U.S. 45.

16. 10 *Railway and Corporation Law Journal* (October 10, 1891), p. 281.

17. *Lochner* v. *New York,* 198 U.S. 45.

18. *Holden* v. *Hardy,* 169 U.S. 366.

19. 163 U.S. 537.

20. Willard L. King, *Melville Weston Fuller: Chief Justice of the United States, 1888–1910* (New York: The Macmillan Co., 1950), p. 181.

21. *Pollock* v. *Farmers' Loan and Trust Co.,* 158 U.S. 601 (1895).

CHAPTER 7

1.   *Theodore Roosevelt: An Autobiography* (New York: The Macmillan Co., 1913), p. 406.

2.   *Selections from the Correspondence of Theodore Roosevelt and Henry Cabot Lodge, 1884–1918,* edited by H. C. Lodge and C. F. Redmond (New York: Charles Scribner's Sons, 1925), Vol. II, p. 519.

3.   "Annual Message to Congress," *Congressional Record,* 60th Cong., 2d sess., Vol. 43, Pt. 1, December 8, 1908, p. 21.

4.   *Selections, op. cit.,* pp. 228–29.

5.   Theodore Roosevelt, *Letters,* edited by Elting E. Morison (Cambridge, Mass.: Harvard University Press, 1952), Vol. V, p. 396.

6.   *Northern Securities Co.* v. *United States,* 193 U.S. 197.

7.   176 Mass. 492, at 505.

8.   As told by Francis Biddle, *Justice Holmes, Natural Law, and the Supreme Court* (New York: The Macmillan Co., 1961), p. 9.

9.   Wallace Mendelson, *Capitalism, Democracy, and the Supreme Court* (New York: Appleton-Century-Crofts, 1960), p. 75.

10. As quoted by Charles P. Curtis in *Lions Under the Throne* (Boston: Houghton Mifflin Co., 1947), p. 281.

11. *Lochner* v. *New York,* 198 U.S. 45, at 74.

12. *Hammer* v. *Dagenhart,* 247 U.S. 251, at 280.

13. *Abrams* v. *United States,* 250 U.S. 616, at 630.

14. *Gitlow* v. *New York,* 268 U.S. 652, at 673.

15. *Olmstead* v. *United States,* 277 U.S. 438, at 469–70.

16. *Hammer* v. *Dagenhart,* 198 U.S. 45, at 74.

17. Paul T. Heffron, "Theodore Roosevelt and the Appointment of Mr. Justice Moody," 18 *Vanderbilt Law Review* (March 1965), p. 545.

18. 211 U.S. 78. The overruling came in 1964, in *Malloy* v. *Hogan,* 378 U.S. 1, by a vote of 5:4.

19. (New York: Columbia University Press, 1916), p. 144.

20. Alpheus Thomas Mason, *William Howard Taft: Chief Justice* (New York: Simon and Schuster, 1965), p. 15.

21. As quoted by Henry F. Pringle in *The Life and Times of William Howard Taft* (New York: Farrar & Rinehart, 1939), p. 531.

22. As quoted in Merlon J. Pusey, *Charles Evans Hughes* (New York: The Macmillan Co., 1951), Vol. I, p. 271.

23. *Ibid.*, p. 272. (Italics added.)

24. *De Jonge* v. *Oregon,* 299 U.S. 353 (1937), opinion for the Court, at 365.

25. Mark De Wolfe Howe (ed.), *Holmes-Pollock Letters* (Cambridge, Mass.: Harvard University Press, 1941), Vol. I, p. 170.

26. As quoted in Pringle, *op. cit.,* p. 534.

27. December 10, 1912, p. 1.

28. Pringle, *op. cit.,* p. 535.

29. As quoted in Mason, *op. cit.,* p. 39.

30. The six decisions were, respectively: *Wilson* v. *New,* 243 U.S. 332 (1917); *Buttfield* v. *Stranahan,* 192 U.S. 470 (1904); *Northern Securitites Co.* v. *United States,* 193 U.S. 197 (1904); *Pollock* v. *Farmers' Loan & Trust Co.,* 158 U.S. 601 (1895); *United States* v. *American Tobacco Co.,* 22 U.S. 106 (1911); and *Hammer* v. *Dagenhart,* 247 U.S. 251 (1918).

31. *McCabe* v. *Atcheson, Topeka, & Santa Fé Railroad,* 186 F. 966.

32. As quoted in both Mason, *op. cit.,* p. 213, and Pringle, *op. cit.,* p. 971.

33. As quoted by Louis W. Koenig, *The Chief Executive,* rev. ed. (New York: Harcourt, Brace & World, 1968), p. 302.

34. Josephus Daniels, *The Wilson Era, Years of Peace: 1910–1916* (Chapel Hill: University of North Carolina Press, 1944), p. 115.

35. As quoted in Mason, *op. cit.,* pp. 216–17.

36. *Ibid.*, p. 217.

37. *Ibid.*, p. 167.

38. As quoted in Pringle, *op. cit.,* p. 971.

39. *Coppage* v. *Kansas,* 236 U.S. 1 (1915).

40. E.g., wiretapping, in *Olmstead* v. *United States,* 277 U.S. 438 (1928).

41. 208 U.S. 412.

42. As quoted by Mason, *op. cit.,* p. 72. (Italics in original.)

43. E.g., *Abrams* v. *United States,* 250 U.S. 616 (1919) and *Gitlow* v. *New York,* 268 U.S. 652 (1925).

44. *Whitney* v. *California,* 274 U.S. 357 (1927), at 377.

45. Hoyt L. Warner, *The Life of Mr. Justice Clarke* (Cleveland: Western Reserve University Press, 1959), p. 116.

46. *Bailey* v. *Drexel Furniture Co.,* 259 U.S. 20 (1922).

47. As quoted in Arthur M. Schlesinger, Jr., *The Age of Roosevelt: The Crisis of the Old Order, 1919–1933* (Boston: Houghton Mifflin Co., 1957), pp. 50–51.

48. *Ibid.*, p. 51.

49. *Ibid.*, p. 50, quoting from one of Alice Longworth's (Teddy Roosevelt's daughter) cruelly frank epigrams.

50. *Adkins* v. *Children's Hospital,* 261 U.S. 525 (1923).

51. Alpheus Thomas Mason, "William Howard Taft," in Leon Friedman and Fred L. Israel (eds.), *The Justices of the United States Supreme*

Court, 1789–1969 (New York: Chelsea House, 1969), Vol. III, p. 2113.

52. Mason, *op. cit.*, p. 167.

53. Pringle, *op. cit.*, p. 972.

54. Mason, *op. cit.*, pp. 77–78.

55. Fred Rodell, *Nine Men* (New York: Random House, 1955), p. 189.

56. It was drafted for the Senate Judiciary Committee largely by Justices Van Devanter, McReynolds, and Day, with the active assistance of Mr. Justice Sutherland and Mr. Chief Justice Taft himself.

57. Joel Francis Paschal, *Mr. Justice Sutherland: A Man Against the State* (Princeton: Princeton University Press, 1951), p. 113.

58. *Ibid.* The biography's subtitle.

59. 287 U.S. 45.

60. E.g., *Panama Refining Co.* v. *Ryan,* 293 U.S. 388 (1935); *Schechter Poultry Corp.* v. *United States,* 295 U.S. 495 (1935); *United States* v. *Butler,* 297 U.S. 1 (1936); *Carter* v. *Carter Coal Co.,* 298 U.S. 238 (1936).

61. 299 U.S. 304 (1936).

62. For an informative account of the Butler nomination and appointment, see David J. Danelski, *A Supreme Court Justice Is Appointed* (New York: Random House, 1964), esp. Chaps. 6–8.

63. *Olmstead* v. *United States,* 277 U.S. 438.

64. E.g., *United States* v. *Schwimmer,* 279 U.S. 644.

65. *Gitlow* v. *New York,* 268 U.S. 652.

66. *Ibid.,* at 666.

67. As quoted in Pringle, *op. cit.,* p. 1043.

68. As quoted by Mason, *Harlan Fiske Stone,* p. 184.

69. *Ibid.,* pp. 182–85.

70. 297 U.S. 1. The famous quote is at p. 94.

71. The well-known account of his last moments is taken from Mason's biography of him, pp. 804–6. The citation is from one of three opinions he was about to read during the Court's session on that Opinion Monday (*Girouard* v. *United States,* 328 U.S. 61, at 79).

72. *United States* v. *Carolene Products,* 304 U.S. 144, at 152–53.

73. He went abroad for Truman in connection with war relief work; and he rendered valuable service as head of the Hoover Commissions between 1949 and 1955, which made important recommendations on the reorganization of the Executive Branch of the federal government.

74. As quoted by Mason, *William Howard Taft,* p. 234.

75. Although he hedges somewhat, that seems to be Mason's conclusion too. See his volumes on Taft, *op. cit.,* pp. 297–99, and, especially, that on Stone, pp. 277–83.

76. E.g., his opinion for the 5:4 Court in 1934 upholding New York State's milk-price-control law (*Nebbia* v. *New York,* 291 U.S. 502) and his joining of the 5:4 opinion for the Court by Mr. Chief Justice Hughes; again in 1934, in upholding Minnesota's statute against real

estate foreclosures (*Home Building & Loan Association* v. *Blaisdell,* 290 U.S. 398).

77. (New Haven: Yale University Press, 1921.)

78. Mason, *Harlan Fiske Stone,* p. 336.

79. Claudius O. Johnson, *Borah of Idaho* (New York: Longmans, Green & Co., 1936), p. 452.

80. Herbert Hoover, *The Memoirs of Herbert Hoover: The Cabinet and the President, 1920–1933* (New York: The Macmillan Co., 1952), Vol. II, p. 269.

81. Mason, *Harlan Fiske Stone,* p. 337.

82. February 15, 1932, p. 1. For a memorial resolution, styling Hoover's act in appointing Cardozo as "the finest act of his career as President," see Mason, *Stone, op. cit.,* March 2, 1932, p. 13. The author of the resolution was Senator Clarence R. Dill (D.-Wash.).

83. *Steward Machine Co.* v. *Davis,* 301 U.S. 548, and *Helvering* v. *Davis,* 301 U.S. 619.

84. 302 U.S. 319 (1937).

85. *Ibid.,* at 325–27.

86. As re-quoted in *The New Yorker,* "The Talk of the Town," April 4, 1970, p. 33.

87. *Dictionary of American Biography,* Vol. 22, Supp. 2, p. 95.

CHAPTER 8

1. See, among others, the accounts by Leonard Baker, *Back to Back: The Duel Betweeen F.D.R. and the Supreme Court* (New York: The Macmillan Co., 1967), and Joseph Alsop and Turner Catledge, *The 168 Days* (Garden City, N.Y.: Doubleday, Doran, 1938).

2. 300 U.S. 379.

3. *N.L.R.B.* v. *Jones & Laughlin Steel Corporation,* 301 U.S. 1.

4. *Helvering* v. *Davis,* 301 U.S. 619, and *Steward Machine Co.* v. *Davis,* 301 U.S. 548, respectively.

5. *Jim Farley's Story* (New York: McGraw-Hill Book Co., 1948), p. 86.

6. As quoted by Virginia Van der Veer Hamilton, *Hugo Black: The Alabama Years* (Baton Rouge: Louisiana State University Press, 1972), p. 275.

7. As *The Washington Post,* for one, put it on August 13, 1937. (Editorial.)

8. Sixty Democrats and three Republicans—Robert La Follette (Wisconsin), Arthur Capper (Kansas), and Lynn J. Frazier (North Dakota)— voted "aye"; ten Republicans and six Democrats "nay."

9. John P. Frank, *Mr. Justice Black: The Man and His Opinions* (New York: Alfred A. Knopf, 1949), p. 105.

10. The *New York Times,* October 2, 1937, p. 1.

11. As quoted by Frank, *op. cit.,* p. 102.

12. See his poignant valedictory publication, *A Constitutional Faith* (New York: Alfred A. Knopf, 1968).

13. *Adamson* v. *California,* 332 U.S. 46.

14. *Palko* v. *Connecticut,* 302 U.S. 319.

15. For a detailed description, see my *Freedom and the Court: Civil Rights and Liberties in the United States,* 2d ed. (New York: Oxford University Press, 1972), Chap. III: "The Bill of Rights and Its Applicability to the States," pp. 29–88.

16. 372 U.S. 335.

17. *Betts* v. *Brady,* 316 U.S. 455 (1942).

18. *Chambers* v. *Florida,* 309 U.S. 227 (1940), at 241.

19. John P. Frank, "Hugo L. Black: He Has Joined the Giants," 58 *American Bar Association Journal* (January 1972), p. 25.

20. 328 U.S. 373.

21. 321 U.S. 649.

21. 321 U.S. 649.

22. See the fascinating account by Alpheus Thomas Mason, *Harlan Fiske Stone: Pillar of the Law* (New York: Viking Press, 1956), pp. 614–15. See also my *The Judicial Process: An Introductory Analysis of the Courts of the United States, England, and France,* 2d ed. (New York: Oxford University Press, 1968), pp. 208–10.

23. See Liva Baker, *Felix Frankfurter* (New York: Coward-McCann, 1969), pp. 201–6.

24. As quoted by Eugene C. Gerhart, *America's Advocate: Robert H. Jackson* (Indianapolis: The Bobbs-Merrill Co., 1958), p. 165.

25. As quoted by Harold L. Ickes, *The Secret Diaries of Harold L. Ickes* (New York: Simon and Schuster, 1954), Vol. II, p. 539.

26. *Felix Frankfurter Reminisces.* Recorded in Talks with Harlan B. Phillips. (Garden City, N.Y.: Doubleday & Co., 1962), pp. 328–29, 334–35.

27. Fred Rodell, *Nine Men* (New York: Random House, 1955), p. 271.

28. As quoted by Rodell, *ibid.,* p. 271.

29. 342 U.S. 165.

30. *Louisiana* ex rel. *Francis* v. *Resweber,* 329 U.S. 459 (1947).

31. As quoted by Marvin Braiterman, "Frankfurter and the Paradox of Restraint," *Midstream* (November 1970), p. 21.

32. *Minersville School District* v. *Gobitis,* 310 U.S. 586 (1940).

33. *West Virginia State Board of Education* v. *Barnette,* 319 U.S. 624 (1943).

34. *Ibid.,* at 646.

35. 369 U.S. 186.

36. *Ibid.,* at 270.

37. February 24, 1965, p. 40.

38. John P. Frank, "William O. Douglas," in Leon Friedman and Fred L. Israel (eds.), *The Justices of the United States Supreme Court, 1789–1969* (New York: Chelsea House, 1969), Vol. IV, p. 2453.

39. *Ibid.,* p. 2454.

40. *Griswold* v. *Connecticut,* 381 U.S. 479, at 481.

41. As quoted in the *New York Times Magazine*, May 26, 1969, p. 26.

42. J. Woodford Howard, *Mr. Justice Murphy* (Princeton: Princeton University Press, 1968), pp. 215–16.

43. As quoted by Gerhart, *op. cit.*, p. 167.

44. 323 U.S. 214.

45. *Ibid.*, beginning at p. 233.

46. In re *Yamashita*, 327 U.S. 1.

47. *Ibid.*, at 29.

48. 332 U.S. 46. Murphy's dissent begins at p. 124.

49. *Ibid.*, at 75.

50. James E. Byrnes, *All in One Lifetime* (New York: Harper and Bros., 1958), p. 130.

51. *The Nine Young Men* (New York: Harper and Bros., 1947), p. 243.

52. *Edwards* v. *California*, 314 U.S. 160 (1941).

53. Merlo J. Pusey, *Charles Evans Hughes* (New York: The Macmillan Co., 1951), Vol. II, pp. 787–88.

54. As quoted by Mason, *Stone*, pp. 566–67.

55. *Ibid.*, p. 573.

56. As quoted by Gerhart, *op. cit.*, p. 191.

57. E.g., *West Virginia State Board of Education* v. *Barnette*, 319 U.S. 624 (1943); *Korematsu* v. *United States*, 323 U.S. 214 (1944); and *Thomas* v. *Collins*, 323 U.S. 516 (1945).

58. E.g., *Kunz* v. *New York*, 340 U.S. 290 (1951); *Dennis* v. *United States*, 341 U.S. 494 (1951); and *Adler* v. *Board of Education*, 342 U.S. 485 (1952).

59. *West Virginia State Board of Education* v. *Barnette*, 319 U.S. 624 (1943), at 638, 642.

60. *Brown* v. *Board of Education of Topeka*, 347 U.S. 483, and *Bolling* v. *Sharpe*, 347 U.S. 497.

61. Gerhart, *op. cit.*

62. 332 U.S. 46, at 124. (Italics added.)

63. 327 U.S. 1 (1946), at 43.

64. 330 U.S. 1 (1947), at 59.

65. Harry S Truman, *Memoirs: Year of Decisions* (Garden City, N.Y.: Doubleday & Co., 1955), pp. 5, 44.

66. *Youngstown Sheet & Tube Co.* v. *Sawyer*, 343 U.S. 579 (1952).

67. E.g., *Louisiana* ex rel. *Francis* v. *Resweber*, 329 U.S. 459 (1951); *Garner* v. *Board of Public Works of Los Angeles*, 341 U.S. 716 (1951); and *Joint Anti-Fascist Refugee Committee* v. *McGrath*, 341 U.S. 123 (1951).

68. E.g., *Everson* v. *Board of Education*, 330 U.S. 1 (1947).

69. See the account by Frank in *Mr. Justice Black*, Chap. 7, "The Chief Justiceship," pp. 123–31.

70. See C. Herman Pritchett, *The Roosevelt Court* (Chicago: Quadrangle Books, 1948), p. 26.

71. President Truman so asserted in his press conference of September

15, 1951. See the *New York Times,* September 16, 1951, p. 15. There exists controversy regarding Hughes's recommendation. Some observers, for example, his principal biographer, Merlo J. Pusey, hold that Hughes's first choice was really Jackson—a claim not necessarily incompatible with the Truman assertions, however.

72.   Richard Kirkendall, "Harold Burton," in *Justices,* Vol. IV, p. 2641.

73.   *Youngstown Sheet & Tube Co.* v. Sawyer, 343 U.S. 579.

74.   *Dennis* v. *United States,* 341 U.S. 494.

75.   *Sweatt* v. *Painter,* 339 U.S. 629, and *McLaurin* v. *Oklahoma State Regents,* 339 U.S. 637.

76.   *Shelley* v. *Kraemer,* 334 U.S. 1 and *Hurd* v. *Hodge,* 334 U.S. 24.

77.   CXXI (August 15, 1949), p. 11.

78.   *Youngstown Sheet & Tube Co.* v. *Sawyer,* 343 U.S. 579.

79.   *Wieman* v. *Updegraff,* 344 U.S. 183.

80.   *Burstyn* v. *Wilson,* 343 U.S. 195.

81.   363 U.S. 643 (1961).

82.   *New York Times,* Obituary, April 10, 1965, p. 29.

83.   *Brown* v. *Board of Education* v. *Topeka,* 347 U.S. 483, and *Bolling* v. *Sharpe,* 347 U.S. 497.

CHAPTER 9

1.   Harry S Truman, *Memoirs: Years of Trial and Hope* (Garden City, N.Y.: Doubleday & Co., 1956), pp. 384–85.

2.   Dwight D. Eisenhower, *The White House Years: Mandate for Change, 1953–1956* (Garden City, N.Y.: Doubleday & Co., 1963), pp. 226–27.

3.   *Ibid.,* pp. 227–28.

4.   *Ibid.,* p. 230.

5.   *Ibid.,* p. 227.

6.   *Ibid.,* p. 226.

7.   *Ibid.,* p. 227.

8.   *Ibid.,* p. 228.

9.   *Ibid.*

10.   347 U.S. 483.

11.   *Ibid.* (*Bolling* v. *Sharpe,* 347 U.S. 497, applied the *Brown* ruling to the District of Columbia on the same day.)

12.   J. P. Frank, *Marble Palace: The Supreme Court in American Life* (New York: Alfred A. Knopf, 1958), p. 86.

13.   354 U.S. 178. The sole dissenter was Clark.

14.   377 U.S. 533, at 562.

15.   384 U.S. 436.

16.   395 U.S. 486.

17.   370 U.S. 421.

18.   376 U.S. 254.

19.   *New York Times,* October 21, 1969, p. 28.

20. 347 U.S. 483. The data concerning Jackson's health are from Eugene C. Gerhart, *America's Advocate: Robert H. Jackson* (Indianapolis: The Bobbs-Merrill Co., 1958), pp. 467–68.

21. 354 U.S. 298 (1957).

22. 377 U.S. 533, at 624–25. (Italics added.)

23. 163 U.S. 537.

24. As quoted by Anthony Lewis in the *New York Times,* November 4, 1972, p. 33.

25. Eisenhower, *op. cit.,* p. 230.

26. *The New York Times* v. *Sullivan,* 376 U.S. 254.

27. E.g., *Roth* v. *United States* and *Alberts* v. *California,* 354 U.S. 476 (1957); *Freedman* v. *Maryland,* 380 U.S. 51 (1965); *Ginzburg* v. *United States,* 383 U.S. 463 (1966); and *Ginsberg* v. *New York,* 390 U.S. 629 (1968).

28. The 1973 decisions, rendered that June by Mr. Chief Justice Burger for a narrowly divided 5:4 Court, were *Miller* v. *California,* 93 S.Ct. 2607 and *Paris Adult Theatre* v. *Slaton,* 93 S.Ct. 446.

29. 369 U.S. 186. Mr. Chief Justice Warren pronounced the *Baker* decision the most important of his time, outranking even the 1954 *Desegregation Cases.* Mr. Justice Douglas agreed. (October 30, 1973, interview.)

30. *Jencks* v. *United States,* 353 U.S. 657 (1957), at 660, majority opinion.

31. Whittaker's godson, John H. Bracken, Jr., told me in a telephone interview on January 16, 1970, that, according to his godfather's assertion, Arthur Eisenhower was the key figure in the nomination.

32. *Congressional Record,* 86th Cong., 1st sess., May 5, 1959, p. 6693.

33. *New York Times,* May 6, 1959, p. 32.

34. *Ibid.*

35. *Ibid.*

36. Democratic Senators George Smathers of Florida, Estes Kefauver and Albert Gore of Tennessee, and Lyndon B. Johnson and Ralph Yarborough of Texas joined the entire Republican delegation in the Senate in supporting the nomination.

37. 378 U.S. 184, at 197, concurring opinion.

38. *Kingsley International Pictures Corporation* v. *Regents,* 360 U.S. 684 (1959), at 686.

39. 378 U.S. 478 (1964).

40. 384 U.S. 436 (1966).

41. E.g., Anthony Lewis, then the *New York Times*'s Court expert, in an article in the *Times,* April 2, 1962, p. 17.

42. James E. Clayton of the *Washington Star,* in his *The Making of Justice: The Supreme Court in Action* (New York: E. P. Dutton & Co., 1964), p. 52.

43. Saturday, March 31, 1962, p. 1.

44. 378 U.S. 478 (1964).

45. 384 U.S. 436 (1966).

46. E.g., *Street* v. *New York* 394 U.S. 576 (1969).
47. He gave notice of that posture as early as *Ginzburg* v. *United States,* 383 U.S. 463 (1966). In the June 1973 cases (see n. 28, above) he thus sided with the Chief Justice and Associate Justices Blackman, Powell, and Rehnquist. The four dissenters were Douglas, Brennan, Stewart, and Marshall.
48. E.g., *Reitman* v. *Mulkey,* 387 U.S. 369 (1967).
49. *Roe* v. *Wade* and *Doe* v. *Bolton,* 410 U.S. 113 410 U.S. 179.
50. *Furman* v. *Georgia,* 408 U.S. 238.
51. *The New York Times* v. *United States* and *United States* v. *The Washington Post,* 403 U.S. 713.
52. *San Antonio School District* v. *Rodriguez,* 411 U.S. 980.
53. *Bradley* v. *School Board of the City of Richmond,* 411 U.S. 913.
54. *Time,* September 7, 1962, p. 15.
55. As quoted in the *New York Times,* August 30, 1962, p. 14c.
56. *Snider* v. *Cunningham* and *Rudolph* v. *Alabama,* 375 U.S. 889 (1963).
57. *Griswold* v. *Connecticut,* 381 U.S. 479 (1965), at 488, concurring opinion.
58. *Aptheker* v. *Secretary of State,* 378 U.S. 500 (1964).
59. 378 U.S. 478.
60. Lyndon B. Johnson, *The Vantage Point: Perspectives of the Presidency, 1963–1969* (New York: Holt, Rinehart and Winston, 1971), p. 543.
61. As told to me by Arthur J. Goldberg, Georgetown, Washington, D.C., May 24, 1969.
62. Johnson, *op. cit.,* pp. 544–45.
63. *Ibid.*
64. Televised Presidential News Conference, July 20, 1965.
65. The story is well told by Anthony Lewis in his fine *Gideon's Trumpet* (New York: Alfred A. Knopf, 1964; Vintage Books, 1966).
66. *In re Gault,* 387 U.S. 1.
67. *Ibid.,* at 28.
68. *Board of Education* v. *Allen,* 392 U.S. 236, at 271. The other two dissenters were Justices Black and Douglas.
69. Their roles are discussed in Robert Shogan's *A Question of Judgment: The Fortas Case and the Struggle for the Supreme Court* (Indianapolis: The Bobbs-Merrill Co., 1972).
70. June 14, 1967, p. 1.
71. *Ibid.*
72. *Pearson* v. *Murray,* 169 Md. 478 (1936).
73. The other nine were: Eastland (Miss.), Ellender and Long (La.), Ervin (N.C.), Hill and Sparkman (Ala.), Holland (Fla.), Hollins (S.C.), and Talmadge (Ga.). Absent but paired against the nomination were McClelland (Ark.), Russell (Ga.), Smathers (Fla.), and Stennis (Miss.). Byrd (Va.) and Jordan (N.C.) were absent but unrecorded.

Appendix A
Rating Supreme Court Justices

In June 1970 sixty-five law school Deans, Professors of law, history, and political science (including myself) were asked by law professors Roy M. Mersky (University of Texas) and Albert P. Blaustein (Rutgers University) to evaluate the performance of the ninety-six Justices who had served on the Supreme Court from 1789 until 1969, just prior to the appointment of Mr. Chief Justice Burger. We were requested to use a survey model that would employ the categories of "great," "near great," "average," "below average," and "failure." Our only other specific instruction was to "select the nine outstanding Justices of both centuries"—a stipulation that ultimately resulted in the selection of twelve "great" Justices (See note 17, Chapter 2, *supra*.)

The following categories are arranged *chronologically* (See Appendix C and Chapter 3 for convenient tabular data on all Justices, indicating a variety of background information.)

"GREAT" (12)

J. Marshall	Brandeis
Story	Stone
Taney	Cardozo
Harlan I	Black
Holmes	Frankfurter
Hughes	Warren

"NEAR GREAT" (15)

W. Johnson	Sutherland
Curtis	Douglas
Miller	R. H. Jackson
Field	W. B. Rutledge
Bradley	Harlan II
Waite	Brennan
White	Fortas
Taft	

"AVERAGE" (55)

Jay	McKinley	Shiras
J. Rutledge	Daniel	Peckham
Cushing	Nelson	McKenna

"AVERAGE" (55) (*Continued*)

Wilson
Blair
Iredell
Paterson
S. Chase
Ellsworth
Washington
Livingston
Todd
Duval
Thompson
McLean
Baldwin
Wayne
Catron
Brown

Woodbury
Grier
Campbell
Clifford
Swayne
Davis
S. P. Chase
Strong
Hunt
Matthews
Gray
Blatchford
L. Q. C. Lamar
Fuller
Brewer

Day
Moody
Lurton
J. R. Lamar
Pitney
J. H. Clarke
Sanford
Roberts
Reed
Murphy
T. C. Clark
Stewart
White
Goldberg
T. Marshall

"BELOW AVERAGE" (6)

T. Johnson
Moore
Trimble
Barbour
Woods
H. E. Jackson

"FAILURES" (8)

Van Devanter
McReynolds
Butler
Byrnes
Burton
Vinson
Minton
Whittaker

Appendix B
Rating Presidents

The ranked order in which the seventy-five historians categorized our Presidents (see note 1, Chapter 4, *supra*) follows below. The rankings, established in 1962, omit Henry Harrison and James A. Garfield because of their short tenure. They also obviously omit John F. Kennedy, Lyndon B. Johnson, and Richard M. Nixon, who went to the Presidency after the poll was taken.

"GREAT" (5)

(1) Lincoln, (2) Washington, (3) F. D. Roosevelt, (4) Wilson, (5) Jefferson.

"NEAR GREAT" (6)

(6) Jackson, (7) T. Roosevelt, (8) Polk, (9) Truman, (10) J. Adams, (11) Cleveland.

"AVERAGE" (12)

(12) Madison, (13) J. Q. Adams, (14) Hayes, (15) McKinley, (16) Taft, (17) Van Buren, (18) Monroe, (19) Hoover, (20) B. Harrison, (21) Arthur, (22) Eisenhower, (23) A. Johnson.

"BELOW AVERAGE" (6)

(24) Taylor, (25) Tyler, (26) Fillmore, (27) Coolidge, (28) Pierce, (29) Buchanan.

"FAILURES" (2)

(30) Grant, (31) Harding.

TABLE OF SUCCESSION OF THE JUSTICES OF THE SUPREME COURT OF THE UNITED STATES
Showing Years of Active Service on the Court

Year	Judiciary Act of 1789 provided for a Chief Justice and 5 Associate Justices					
1789 1790	John Jay 1789-1795	John Rutledge 1789-1791	William Cushing 1789-1810	James Iredell 1790-1799	James Wilson 1789-1798	John Blair 1789-1796
1800	John Rutledge 1795 / Oliver Ellsworth 1796-1799 / John Marshall 1801-1835	Thomas Johnson 1791-1793 / William Paterson 1793-1806		Alfred Moore 1799-1804 / William Johnson 1804-1834	Bushrod Washington 1798-1829	Samuel Chase 1796-1811
1810		Henry B. Livingston 1806-1823	Joseph Story 1811-1845			Gabriel Duval 1811-1836
1820		Smith Thompson 1823-1843				
1830	Roger B. Taney 1836-1864			James M. Wayne 1835-1867	Henry Baldwin 1830-1844	Philip P. Barbour 1836-1841
1840		Samuel Nelson 1845-1872	Levi Woodbury 1846-1851		Robert C. Grier 1846-1870	Peter V. Daniel 1841-1860
1850			Benjamin R. Curtis 1851-1857 / Nathan Clifford 1858-1881			
1860	Salmon P. Chase 1864-1873					Samuel F. Miller 1862-1890
1870	Morrison R. Waite 1874-1888	Ward Hunt 1872-1882			William Strong 1870-1880	
1880	Melville W. Fuller 1888-1910	Samuel Blatchford 1882-1893	Horace Gray 1881-1902		William B. Woods 1880-1887 / Lucius Q. C. Lamar 1888-1893	Henry B. Brown 1890-1906
1890		Edward D. White J 1894 CJ 1910-1921			Howell E. Jackson 1893-1895 / Rufus W. Peckham 1895-1909	
1900			Oliver Wendell Holmes 1902-1932			William H. Moody 1906-1910
1910	Edward D. White J 1894 CJ 1910-1921	Willis Van Devanter 1910-1937			Horace H. Lurton 1909-1914 / James C. McReynolds 1914-1941	Joseph R. Lamar 1910-1916 / Louis D. Brandeis 1916-1939
1920	William H. Taft 1921-1930		Benjamin N. Cardozo 1932-1938 / Felix Frankfurter 1939-1962			
1930	Charles E. Hughes 1930-1941					
1940	Harlan F. Stone J 1925 CJ 1941-1946 / Fred M. Vinson 1946-1953	Hugo L. Black 1937-1971			James F. Byrnes 1941-1942 / Wiley Rutledge 1943-1949 / Sherman Minton 1949-1956	William O. Douglas 1939
1950	Earl Warren 1953-1969				William J. Brennan 1956	
1960	Warren E. Burger 1969		Arthur J. Goldberg 1962-1965 / Abe Fortas 1965-1969			
1970		Lewis F. Powell, Jr. 1972	Harry A. Blackmun 1970			
1980						

Act of July 23, 1866, provided for reduction of the Court to 7 members as vacancies should occur.

TABLE OF SUCCESSION OF THE JUSTICES OF THE SUPREME COURT OF THE UNITED STATES

Vertical column annotations (Acts of Congress):

- Act of February 24, 1807, provided for increase of the Court to 7 members.
- Act of March 3, 1837, provided for increase of the Court to 9 members.
- Act of March 3, 1863, provided for increase of the Court to 10 members.
- Act of March 3, 1866, provided for reduction of the Court to 7 members as vacancies should occur. (Actually the Court fell to 8.)
- Act of April 10, 1869, provided for increase of the Court to 9 members.
- Act of July 23, 1866, provided for reduction of the Court to 7 members as vacancies should occur.
- Act of July 23, 1866, provided for reduction of the Court to 7 members (fell to 8.)

Seat 1	Seat 2	Seat 3	Seat 4	Seat 5	Year
					1789 / 1790
					1800
Thomas Todd 1807-1826					1810
					1820
Robert Trimble 1826-1828					
John McLean 1829-1861					1830
	John Catron 1837-1865	John McKinley 1837-1852			1840
					1850
		John A. Campbell 1853-1861			
Noah H. Swayne 1862-1881		David Davis 1862-1877	Stephen J. Field 1863-1897		1860
				Joseph P. Bradley 1870-1892	1870
		John M. Harlan 1877-1911			1880
Stanley Matthews 1881-1889					
David J. Brewer 1889-1910				George Shiras, Jr. 1892-1903	1890
			Joseph McKenna 1898-1925		
				William R. Day 1903-1922	1900
Charles E. Hughes 1910-1916					1910
John H. Clarke 1916-1922		Mahlon Pitney 1912-1922			
George Sutherland 1922-1938		Edward T. Sanford 1923-1930	Harlan F. Stone J 1925 CJ 1941-1946	Pierce Butler 1922-1939	1920
		Owen J. Roberts 1930-1945			1930
Stanley F. Reed 1938-1957					
			Robert H. Jackson 1941-1954	Frank Murphy 1940-1949	1940
		Harold H. Burton 1945-1958		Tom C. Clark 1949-1967	1950
Charles E. Whittaker 1957-1962		Potter Stewart 1959	John M. Harlan 1955-1971		
Byron R. White 1962					1960
				Thurgood Marshall 1967	
		Wm. H. Rehnquist 1972			1970
					1980

A Bibliographical Note

The sources and related readings for a book of this type are numerous, eclectic, and sometimes elusive. Primary information, which consists largely of personal and official papers of the principals, can be especially elusive. Many of these documents are not available because many of the Justices have provided for the deliberate destruction or sealing off from publication of sundry notes and papers. Presidents, too, have been reticent to "go public." Public repositories, however, such as the Library of Congress and the National Archives, the *Congressional Record,* the Reports of the Committee on the Judiciary of the U.S. Senate, and Presidential Libraries provide much valuable data.

Secondary sources pertaining to Justices, Presidents, and other public and private personages apposite to the subject are indeed vast. Autobiographies and biographies of the individuals discussed or mentioned in this book are not only readily obtained but are often separately catalogued in special bibliographical publications, some of which are annotated. Helpful reference sources are numerous; only a few are listed here. Louis W. Koenig's *The Chief Executive* (New York: Harcourt, Brace and World, Inc., 1968) lists general and specialized works on the Presidency as well as biographies, papers, and memoirs of Presidents (pp. 446–52). Thomas A. Bailey, *Presidential Greatness, The Image and the Man from George Washington to the Present* (New York: Appleton-Century-Crofts, 1966) has an excellent annotated bibliography (Appendixes C and D) as well as a serviceable selected biographical Appendix covering all Presidents through L. B. Johnson. A first-rate compendium of the bulk of Presidential writings is Arthur B. Tourtellot, *The Presidents on the Presidency* (Garden City, N.Y.: Doubleday & Co., 1964), pp. 471–85. My *The Judicial Process: An Introductory Analysis of the Courts of the United States, England, and France,* 2d ed. (New York: Oxford University Press, 1968) has several bibliographies, one of which lists some 200 biographies, autobiographies, and related works of the Justices (pp. 414–20). Two other lengthy ones deal with the whole spectrum of the judicial process (pp. 381–414 and 429–72). An earlier work by Dorothy C. Thompson, *The Supreme Court of the United States: A Bibliography* (Berkeley: University of California Press, 1959), is devoted wholly to bibliographical data, although not on an exhaustive scale. The ambitious, four-volume, 3373-page collection of essays written by thirty-eight scholars and edited by Leon Friedman and Fred L. Israel, *The Justices of the United States Supreme Court, 1789–1969: Their Lives and Major Opinions* (New York: Chelsea House, in association with R. R. Bowker Co., 1970), contains a multitude of references to writings about Supreme Court Justices.

Although very markedly uneven in the quality of its essays, the last-mentioned work is also a good up-to-date source of certain aspects of the appointment process and contains a major statistical compendium, "On the Supreme Court: The Statistics," by Albert P. Blaustein and Roy M. Mersky. Daniel S. McHargue's unpublished doctoral dissertation, "Factors Influencing the Selection and Appointment of Members of the United States Supreme Court, 1789–1932" (University of California, Los Angles, 1949), was probably the first systematic attempt to explain Presidential motivations in selecting Justices, and it influenced me in commencing my research on the matter in the 1950s. John P. Frank, in three important articles in the 1941 *Wisconsin Law Review* (beginning at pages 172, 343, and 461, respectively), collectively entitled "The Appointment of Supreme Court Justices," made a similarly valuable contribution by treating the appointment of Justices from John A. Campbell (Pierce) through William O. Douglas (F.D.R.).

Important works on court staffing are Harold W. Chase's fine new book, *Federal Judges: The Appointing Process* (Minneapolis: University of Minnesota Press, 1972), which confines itself to the lower federal judiciary; Evan Haynes's comparative, though dated, *Selection and Tenure of Judges* (Newark, N.J.: National Conference of Judicial Councils, 1944), dealing with all levels of judicial selection; Joseph P. Harris's seminal *The Advice and Consent of the Senate* (Berkeley: University of California Press, 1953); Joel B. Grossman's controversial study of the Committee on Judiciary of the American Bar Association, *Lawyers & Judges: the ABA and the Process of Judicial Selection* (New York: John Wiley and Sons, 1965); John R. Schmidhauser's pioneering *The Supreme Court: Its Politics, Personalities, and Procedures* (New York: Holt, Rinehart and Winston, 1960); and Robert Scigliano's *The Supreme Court and the Presidency* (New York: The Free Press, 1971), which includes a perceptive discussion of appointments and performances in the light of Presidential expectations (Chapters 5 and 6).

Although there are a good many histories of the Supreme Court, most of them either confine themselves to specific eras, specific personnel, and specific Courts; or are dated; or do not emphasize the appointment process. A few histories however, have either concerned themselves with the appointment process or are so significant that they ought to be listed in any bibliographical note on the Supreme Court. These include the still widely used two-volume work by Charles Warren, revised in 1926 and reprinted several times since, *The Supreme Court in United States History* (Boston: Little, Brown, and Company, 1926), which has served generations of students as a source of the Court's work and its personnel, although its strength is broadly confined to the period preceding the turn of the century. Once the multivolumed *Oliver Wendell Holmes Devise History of the Supreme Court of the United States*—a still incomplete major history of the Court financed by a special bequest of $263,000 to the United States by Mr. Justice Holmes—has appeared (to date only two volumes have been published), the Warren work will be replaced. The briefest and most objective recent history is Robert G. McCloskey's elegantly written *The American Supreme Court* (Chicago: The University of Chicago Press, 1960), which also contains a fine bibliographical essay (pp. 236–52). Robert J. Steamer's fairly compact study with considerable emphasis on personnel, *The Supreme Court in Crisis: A History of Conflict* (Amherst: The University of Massachusetts Press, 1971), comes down to the days of the Burger Court. A lively, popular treatment is John P. Frank's *Marble Palace: The Supreme Court in American Life* (New York: Alfred A. Knopf, 1958), and a colorful, highly subjective, and partisan account is Fred Rodell's *Nine Men: A Political History of the Supreme Court of the United States from 1790 to 1955* (New York: Alfred A. Knopf, 1955, Vintage Books, 1964). Digging into some of the following older histories may prove to be enlightening as well as intriguing: Ernest Sutherland Bates, *The Story of the Supreme Court* (New York: The Bobbs-Merrill Co., 1938); Tom W. Campbell, *Four-Score Forgotten Men* (Little Rock, Ark.: Pioneer Publishing Co., 1950); Hampton L. Carson, *The Supreme Court of the United States: Its History* (Philadelphia: John Y. Huber Co., 1891); Cortez A. M. Ewing, *The Judges of the Supreme Court, 1789–1937* (Minneapolis: The University of Minnesota Press, 1938); and James Barbar, *The Honorable Eighty-Eight* (New York: Vantage Press, 1957).

And, of course, a great deal of reference material is included among the citations following the several chapters of my book itself. The judicial biographies especially are gold mines, as exemplified in recent years by such authors as Alpheus Thomas Mason (Brandeis, Stone, and Taft), Williard L. King (Davis and Fuller), Carl Brent Swisher (Taney and Field), Samuel J. Konefsky (Holmes and Brandeis), Charles P. Magrath (Waite), Wallace Mendelson and Liva Baker (Frankfurter), Joel F. Paschal (Sutherland), Merlo J. Pusey (Hughes), J. Woodford Howard, Jr. (Murphy), John P. Frank (Daniel and Black). They and earlier biographers—notable among them Albert J. Beveridge with his monumental 1916 four-volume work on John Marshall—have given us often fascinating information and insight about members of the Court. We are indebted to them, indeed.

Index

I. NAME INDEX

II. COURT CASES INDEX